Melville's "Benito Cereno"

Melville's "Benito Cereno"
An Interpretation
with Annotated Text
and Concordance

William D. Richardson

Carolina Academic Press
Durham, North Carolina

© William Donald Richardson 1987
All rights reserved

International Standard Book Number: 0-89089-274-1
Library of Congress Catalog Number: 86-70369
Printed in the United States of America

Carolina Academic Press
Post Office Box 8795
Durham, North Carolina 27707

This book is dedicated to my father,
DONALD E. RICHARDSON

Contents

Preface

Unlike those who study the works of justly renowned philosophers such as Plato or Machiavelli, a commentator—particularly if he is a political scientist—who examines a work of literature feels compelled to offer some justification for his choice of subjects. The need for justification is especially acute when he contends, as I do, that an author such as Herman Melville, while no philosopher, understood certain fundamental political truths and circumspectly sought to teach them to others.[1] Melville's poetic art enabled him to delight his readers, and it is this ability to delight that is capable of "charming" most readers at the same time that it intrigues some long enough for them to be set upon the arduous task of unravelling his teachings.

In the case of "Benito Cereno," I have distinguished between the "delighting" and "teaching" aspects of Melville's art by contending that the former is the "citizen perspective" and the latter the "statesman perspective."[2] The citizen or surface view of the tale is essentially a salutary myth, for it presents the intended audience of American readers with a stalwart, democratic hero in the guise of good Captain Amasa Delano, who calmly and efficiently vanquishes the rebellious black slaves and saves the day for the ineffectual aristocrat, Benito Cereno. The citizen-reader finishes the tale with a feeling of satisfaction, for his prejudices about whites, blacks, democrats, and aristocrats have probably been "delightfully" unchallenged. In a sense, the reader has selectively seen what he wanted to see in this tale. The art which has made this selectivity possible has, at the very least, done the citizen-reader no harm. Seen at this level, Melville is a good citizen-poet presenting an entertaining story which does not subvert the common opinions that make America a unique political community.

At the deeper level of the statesman perspective, however, one discovers that the opinions which are seemingly advanced on the surface are seriously challenged by certain fundamental political problems Melville is addressing. By "fundamental political problems," I do not mean the too prevalent contemporary preoccupation with political socialization, the transmission of culture, methods of human communication, or similar matters. I am using "political" in its broadest sense here—that sense which, above all, is concerned with human nature and the limits of politics. Some of the fundamental political problems confronted in "Benito Cereno" involve the tensions between such things as conventional and natural inequality, the preservation of existing political orders and revolution, the demands of a secular state and those of a state captivated by religion, democracy and aristocracy, the requirements of justice and those of the law, and, finally, the dictates of reason and those of unreasoning forces such as prejudice—particularly racial prejudice.

To see Melville's treatment of these political problems requires the most careful attention to the text, especially to the interplay between the characters' speeches, the narrator's descriptions, and the dramatic action. It is because of my respect for the intricacy and difficulty of engaging in this sort of reading that I do not contend that my interpretation is the definitive presentation of Melville's teaching in "Benito Cereno." Precisely because the careful reader is in the position of being an interlocutor of the text rather than of the author, there is the danger of being led astray by asking either the wrong questions altogether or the right questions at the wrong places.

It is essentially for this reason that I have devised this book as a guide to the serious study of "Benito Cereno." In addition to the interpretive essay, I have included an annotated text of the 1856 version of "Benito Cereno" which appeared as part of *The Piazza Tales* (New York: Dix & Edwards, Inc., 1856). I selected this text because it contained some rather extensive emendations that Melville made in the earlier 1855 version, which had appeared serially in *Putnam's Monthly Magazine*. In a separate section on "Textual Variations," I have identified the hundreds of word and punctuation changes between the two versions. In a few cases, because there were obvious misspellings or other minor printer's errors, I have made changes in the 1856 text, but these alterations have always been placed in brackets. Despite Melville's indication that he was dissatisfied with some of the punctuation of the 1856 text, it is impossible to know which of the punctuation changes found in this later version were attributable to him and which to the overly free hand of the publishers.[3] Consequently, I have accepted the punctuation of the 1856 text as published except for a few instances, which appeared to be clear errors that were not present in the 1855 text. These changes have also been indicated by placing them in brackets.

I have also included a concordance, which identifies key words within the context of the tale. In order to facilitate the accurate use of both the concordance and the textual variations section, I found it desirable to number the paragraphs of the text. Accordingly, all references to the text in these sections as well as in the notes are by paragraph number and not by pagination.

Additionally, I have included Chapter 18 of Amasa Delano's *Narrative*, an 1817 publication which literally provided Melville with the skeleton of a tale which he then proceeded to fill out and enrich to produce "Benito Cereno." As I argue in the interpretive essay, Melville took an autobiographical account and imaginatively used it to reveal man's nature more starkly than the real-life recounting ever could.

Finally, I have added a bibliography which contains a fairly extensive listing of the secondary literature on "Benito Cereno." As even a hasty perusal will show, the secondary literature on this lesser known work of Melville's is vast and, not surprisingly, quite contradictory. The literature's vastness can be seen as clear evidence that Melville has achieved what eluded him during his lifetime: recognition of his greatness as a writer. The disagreements between the commentators may be more an indication of the immense difficulty of attempting to understand properly the complex interplay between the text and the dramatic action than of the commentators' own limitations. Even if he is so inclined, I heartily discourage the reader coming to "Benito Cereno" for the first or even the fifth time from undertaking the Herculean task of reading much of this secondary literature. The effort is likely to result in considerable confusion. It is far better to concentrate on the text and see what questions it raises than to stand too soon on the shoulders of those who later may be found to have been facing in the wrong direction.

I am indebted to a number of individuals and organizations whose collective assistance made this book possible. The Earhart Foundation generously supported my work during the summer of 1980. Without the timely advice, criticisms, and encouragement of Richard H. Cox, Paul Dowling, and Thomas J. Scorza at various points during the preparation of the manuscript, there would not have been a book. Portions of the work have benefitted from the suggestions of David L. Schaefer, James Hurtgen, Phillip J. Cooper, and two anonymous reviewers. Elizabeth P. Stanfield was of considerable assistance in translating several of the characters' names. Kathy Vollmer, Steven Morris, James Smith, Lisa Reed, Brigitte Fessele, Jakki Gaither, and Marilyn Grist either assisted with some of the research or with the tedious task of meticulously proofreading the manuscript. For secretarial assistance, I thank Ginger Bechtold and especially Lucy Hayes, who patiently endured the numerous requests to retype earlier drafts.

Melville's "Benito Cereno"

Annotated Text of "Benito Cereno"*

1. In the year 1799, Captain Amasa Delano, of Duxbury, in Massachusetts, commanding a large sealer and general trader, lay at anchor[,] with a valuable cargo, in the harbor of St. Maria—a small, desert, uninhabited island toward the southern extremity of the long coast of Chili. There he had touched for water.

2. On the second day, not long after dawn, while lying in his berth, his mate came below, informing him that a strange sail was coming into the bay. Ships were then not so plenty in those waters as now. He rose, dressed, and went on deck.

3. The morning was one peculiar to that coast. Everything was mute and calm; everything gray. The sea, though undulated into long roods of swells, seemed fixed, and was sleeked at the surface like waved lead that has cooled and set in the smelter's mould. The sky seemed a gray surtout. Flights of troubled gray fowl, kith and kin with flights of troubled gray vapors among which they were mixed, skimmed low and fitfully over the waters, as swallows over meadows before storms. Shadows present, foreshadowing deeper shadows to come.

4. To Captain Delano's surprise, the stranger, viewed through the glass, showed no colors; though to do so upon entering a haven, however uninhabited in its shores, where but a single other ship might be lying, was the

---

*Text from Herman Melville, *The Piazza Tales* (New York: Dix & Edwards, Inc., 1856).

3

custom among peaceful seamen of all nations. Considering the lawlessness and loneliness of the spot, and the sort of stories, at that day, associated with those seas, Captain Delano's surprise might have deepened into some uneasiness had he not been a person of a singularly undistrustful [good nature], not liable, except on extraordinary and repeated incentives, and hardly then, to indulge in personal alarms, any way involving the imputation of malign evil in man. Whether, in view of what humanity is capable, such a trait implies, along with a benevolent heart, more than ordinary quickness and accuracy of intellectual perception, may be left to the wise to determine.

5.   But whatever misgivings might have obtruded on first seeing the stranger, would almost, in any seaman's mind, have been dissipated by observing that, the ship, in navigating into the harbor, was drawing too near the land; a sunken reef making out off her bow. This seemed to prove her a stranger, indeed, not only to the sealer, but the island; consequently, she could be no wonted freebooter on that ocean. With no small interest, Captain Delano continued to watch her—a proceeding not much facilitated by the vapors partly mantling the hull,[1] through which the far matin light from her cabin streamed equivocally enough; much like the sun— by this time hemisphered on the rim of the horizon, and, apparently, in company with the strange ship entering the harbor—which, wimpled by the same low, creeping clouds, showed not unlike a Lima intriguante's one sinister eye peering across the Plaza[2] from the Indian loop-hole of her dusk *saya-y-manta*.[3]

6.   It might have been but a deception of the vapors, but, the longer the stranger was watched the more singular appeared her manoeuvres. Ere long it seemed hard to decide whether she meant to come in or no—what she wanted, or what she was about. The wind, which had breezed up a little during the night, was now extremely light and baffling, which the more increased the apparent uncertainty of her movements.

7.   Surmising, at last, that it might be a ship in distress, Captain Delano ordered his whale-boat to be dropped, and, much to the wary opposition of his mate, prepared to board her, and, at the least, pilot her in. On the night previous, a fishing-party of the seamen had gone a long distance to some detached rocks out of sight from the sealer, and, an hour or two before day-break, had returned, having met with no small success. Presuming that the stranger might have been long off soundings, the good captain put several baskets of the fish, for presents, into his boat, and so pulled away. From her continuing too near the sunken reef, deeming her in danger, calling to his men, he made all haste to apprise those on board of their situation. But, some time ere the boat came up, the wind, light though it was, having shifted, had headed the vessel off, as well as partly broken the vapors from about her.

8. Upon gaining a less remote view, the ship, when made signally visible on the verge of the leaden-hued swells, with the shreds of fog here and there raggedly furring her, appeared like a white-washed monastery after a thunder- storm, seen perched upon some dun cliff among the Pyrenees.[4] But it was no purely fanciful resemblance which now, for a moment, almost led Captain Delano to think that nothing less than a ship-load of monks was before him. Peering over the bulwarks were what really seemed, in the hazy distance, throngs of dark cowls; while, fitfully revealed through the open port-holes, other dark moving figures were dimly descried, as of Black Friars pacing the cloisters.[5]

9. Upon a still nigher approach, this appearance was modified, and the true character of the vessel was plain—a Spanish merchantman of the first class, carrying negro slaves, amongst other valuable freight, from one colonial port to another. A very large, and, in its time, a very fine vessel, such as in those days were at intervals encountered along that main; sometimes superseded Acapulco treasure-ships, or retired frigates of the Spanish king's navy, which, like superannuated Italian palaces, still, under a decline of masters, preserved signs of former state.

10. As the whale-boat drew more and more nigh, the cause of the peculiar pipe-clayed aspect of the stranger was seen in the slovenly neglect pervading her. The spars, ropes, and great part of the bulwarks, looked woolly, from long unacquaintance with the scraper, tar, and the brush. Her keel seemed laid, her ribs put together, and she launched, from Ezekiel's Valley of Dry Bones.[6]

11. In the present business in which she was engaged, the ship's general model and rig appeared to have undergone no material change from their original warlike and Froissart pattern.[7] However, no guns were seen.

12. The tops were large, and were railed about with what had once been octagonal net-work, all now in sad disrepair. These tops hung overhead like three ruinous aviaries, in one of which was seen perched, on a ratlin, a white noddy, a strange fowl, so called from its lethargic, somnambulistic character, being frequently caught by hand at sea. Battered and mouldy, the castellated forecastle seemed some ancient turret, long ago taken by assault, and then left to decay. Toward the stern, two high-raised quarter galleries—the balustrades here and there covered with dry, tindery seamoss—opening out from the unoccupied state-cabin, whose dead-lights, for all the mild weather, were hermetically closed and calked—these tenantless balconies hung over the sea as if it were the grand Venetian canal.[8] But the principal relic of faded grandeur was the ample oval of the shield-like stern-piece, intricately carved with the arms of Castile and Leon, medallioned about by groups of mythological or symbolical devices; uppermost and central of which was a dark satyr in a mask, holding his foot on the prostrate neck of a writhing figure, likewise masked.[9]

13.   Whether the ship had a figure-head, or only a plain beak, was not quite certain, owing to canvas wrapped about that part, either to protect it while undergoing a re-furbishing, or else decently to hide its decay. Rudely painted or chalked, as in a sailor freak, along the forward side of a sort of pedestal below the canvas, was the sentence, *"Seguid vuestro jefe,"* (follow your leader);[10] while upon the tarnished head-boards, near by, appeared, in stately capitals, once gilt, the ship's name, "SAN DOMINICK,"[11] each letter streakingly corroded with tricklings of copper-spike rust; while, like mourning weeds, dark festoons of sea-grass slimily swept to and fro over the name, with every hearse-like roll of the hull.

14.   As, at last, the boat was hooked from the bow along toward the gangway amidship, its keel, while yet some inches separated from the hull, harshly grated as on a sunken coral reef. It proved a huge bunch of conglobated barnacles adhering below the water to the side like a wen—a token of baffling airs and long calms passed somewhere in those seas.

15.   Climbing the side, the visitor was at once surrounded by a clamorous throng of whites and blacks, but the latter outnumbering the former more than could have been expected, negro transportation-ship as the stranger in port was. But, in one language, and as with one voice,[12] all poured out a common tale of suffering; in which the negresses, of whom there were not a few, exceeded the others in their dolorous vehemence. The scurvy, together with the fever, had swept off a great part of their number, more especially the Spaniards. Off Cape Horn they had narrowly escaped shipwreck; then, for days together, they had lain tranced without wind; their provisions were low; their water next to none; their lips that moment were baked.

16.   While Captain Delano was thus made the mark of all eager tongues, his one eager glance took in all faces, with every other object about him.

17.   Always upon first boarding a large and populous ship at sea, especially a foreign one, with a nondescript crew such as Lascars or Manilla men, the impression varies in a peculiar way from that produced by first entering a strange house with strange inmates in a strange land. Both house and ship— the one by its walls and blinds, the other by its high bulwarks like ramparts —hoard from view their interiors till the last moment: but in the case of the ship there is this addition; that the living spectacle it contains, upon its sudden and complete disclosure, has, in contrast with the blank ocean which zones it, something of the effect of enchantment. The ship seems unreal; these strange costumes, gestures, and faces, but a shadowy tableau just emerged from the deep, which directly must receive back what it gave.

18.   Perhaps it was some such influence, as above is attempted to be described, which, in Captain Delano's mind, heightened whatever, upon a staid scrutiny, might have seemed unusual; especially the conspicuous fig-

6

PLAN OF LOWER DECK WITH THE STOWAGE OF 292 SLAVES

130 OF THESE BEING STOWED <u>UNDER</u> THE SHELVES AS SHEWN IN FIGURE & FIGURE 3.

Fig 2

PLAN SHEWING THE STOWAGE OF 130 ADDITIONAL SLAVES ROUND THE WINGS OR SIDES OF THE LOWER DECK BY MEANS OF PLATFORMS OR SHELVES
(IN THE MANNER OF GALLERIES IN A CHURCH) THE SLAVES STOWED <u>ON</u> THE SHELVES AND BELOW THEM HAVE ONLY A HEIGHT OF 2 FEET 7 INCHES
BETWEEN THE BEAMS AND FAR LESS UNDER THE BEAMS. See Fig I.

Fig 3

ures of four elderly grizzled negroes, their heads like black, doddered willow tops, who, in venerable contrast to the tumult below them, were couched, sphynx-like, one on the starboard cat-head, another on the larboard, and the remaining pair face to face on the opposite bulwarks above the main-chains. They each had bits of unstranded old junk in their hands, and, with a sort of stoical self-content, were picking the junk into oakum, a small heap of which lay by their sides.[13] They accompanied the task with a continuous, low, monotonous chant; droning and druling away like so many gray-headed bag-pipers playing a funeral march.

19.   The quarter-deck rose into an ample elevated poop, upon the forward verge of which, lifted, like the oakum-pickers, some eight feet above the general throng, sat along in a row, separated by regular spaces, the cross-legged figures of six other blacks; each with a rusty hatchet in his hand, which, with a bit of brick and a rag, he was engaged like a scullion in scouring; while between each two was a small stack of hatchets, their rusted edges turned forward awaiting a like operation. Though occasionally the four oakum-pickers would briefly address some person or persons in the crowd below, yet the six hatchet-polishers neither spoke to others, nor breathed a whisper among themselves, but sat intent upon their task, except at intervals, when, with the peculiar love in negroes of uniting industry with pastime, two and two they sideways clashed their hatchets together, like cymbals, with a barbarous din. All six, unlike the generality, had the raw aspect of unsophisticated Africans.

20.   But that first comprehensive glance which took in those ten figures, with scores less conspicuous, rested but an instant upon them, as, impatient of the hubbub of voices, the visitor turned in quest of whomsoever it might be that commanded the ship.

21.   But as if not unwilling to let nature make known her own case among his suffering charge, or else in despair of restraining it for the time, the Spanish captain, a gentlemanly, reserved-looking, and rather young man to a stranger's eye, dressed with singular richness, but bearing plain traces of recent sleepless cares and disquietudes, stood passively by, leaning against the main-mast, at one moment casting a dreary, spiritless look upon his excited people, at the next an unhappy glance toward his visitor. By his side stood a black of small stature, in whose rude face, as occasionally, like a shepherd's dog, he mutely turned it up into the Spaniard's, sorrow and affection were equally blended.

22.   Struggling through the throng, the American advanced to the Spaniard, assuring him of his sympathies, and offering to render whatever assistance might be in his power. To which the Spaniard returned for the present but grave and ceremonious acknowledgments, his national formality dusked by the saturnine mood of ill-health.

23.   But losing no time in mere compliments, Captain Delano, returning to

7

the gangway, had his basket[s] of fish brought up; and as the wind still continued light, so that some hours at least must elapse ere the ship could be brought to the anchorage, he bade his men return to the sealer, and fetch back as much water as the whale-boat could carry, with whatever soft bread the steward might have, all the remaining pumpkins on board, with a box of sugar, and a dozen of his private bottles of cider.

24.   Not many minutes after the boat's pushing off, to the vexation of all, the wind entirely died away, and the tide turning, began drifting back the ship helplessly seaward. But trusting this would not long last, Captain Delano sought, with good hopes, to cheer up the strangers, feeling no small satisfaction that, with persons in their condition, he could—thanks to his frequent voyages along the Spanish main—converse with some freedom in their native tongue.

25.   While left alone with them, he was not long in observing some things tending to heighten his first impressions; but surprise was lost in pity, both for the Spaniards and blacks, alike evidently reduced from scarcity of water and provisions; while long-continued suffering seemed to have brought out the less good-natured qualities of the negroes, besides, at the same time, impairing the Spaniard's authority over them. But, under the circumstances, precisely this condition of things was to have been anticipated. In armies, navies, cities, or families, in nature herself, nothing more relaxes good order than misery. Still, Captain Delano was not without the idea, that had Benito Cereno been a man of greater energy, misrule would hardly have come to the present pass. But the debility, constitutional or induced by hardships, bodily and mental, of the Spanish captain, was too obvious to be overlooked. A prey to settled dejection, as if long mocked with hope he would not now indulge it, even when it had ceased to be a mock, the prospect of that day, or evening at furthest, lying at anchor, with plenty of water for his people, and a brother captain to counsel and befriend, seemed in no perceptible degree to encourage him. His mind appeared unstrung, if not still more seriously affected. Shut up in these oaken walls, chained to one dull round of command, whose unconditionality cloyed him, like some hypochondriac abbot he moved slowly about, at times suddenly pausing, starting, or staring, biting his lip, biting his finger-nail, flushing, paling, twitching his beard, with other symptoms of an absent or moody mind. This distempered spirit was lodged, as before hinted, in as distempered a frame. He was rather tall, but seemed never to have been robust, and now with nervous suffering was almost worn to a skeleton. A tendency to some pulmonary complaint appeared to have been lately confirmed. His voice was like that of one with lungs half gone—hoarsely suppressed, a husky whisper. No wonder that, as in this state he tottered about, his private servant apprehensively followed him. Sometimes the negro gave his master his arm, or took his

8

handkerchief out of his pocket for him; performing these and similar offices with that affectionate zeal which transmutes into something filial or fraternal acts in themselves but menial; and which has gained for the negro the repute of making the most pleasing body- servant in the world; one, too, whom a master need be on no stiffly superior terms with, but may treat with familiar trust; less a servant than a devoted companion.

26.   Marking the noisy indocility of the blacks in general, as well as what seemed the sullen inefficiency of the whites[,] it was not without humane satisfaction that Captain Delano witnessed the steady good conduct of Babo.

27.   But the good conduct of Babo, hardly more than the ill-behavior of others, seemed to withdraw the half-lunatic Don Benito from his cloudy languor. Not that such precisely was the impression made by the Spaniard on the mind of his visitor. The Spaniard's individual unrest was, for the present, but noted as a conspicuous feature in the ship's general affliction. Still, Captain Delano was not a little concerned at what he could not help taking for the time to be Don Benito's unfriendly indifference towards himself. The Spaniard's manner, too, conveyed a sort of sour and gloomy disdain, which he seemed at no pains to disguise. But this the American in charity ascribed to the harassing effects of sickness, since, in former instances, he had noted that there are peculiar natures on whom prolonged physical suffering seems to cancel every social instinct of kindness; as if, forced to black bread themselves, they deemed it but equity that each person coming nigh them should, indirectly, by some slight or affront, be made to partake of their fare.

28.   But ere long Captain Delano bethought him that, indulgent as he was at the first, in judging the Spaniard, he might not, after all, have exercised charity enough. At bottom it was Don Benito's reserve which displeased him; but the same reserve was shown towards all but his faithful personal attendant. Even the formal reports which, according to sea-usage, were, at stated times, made to him by some petty underling, either a white, mulatto or black, he hardly had patience enough to listen to, without betraying contemptuous aversion. His manner upon such occasions was, in its degree, not unlike that which might be supposed to have been his imperial countryman's, Charles V., just previous to the anchoritish retirement of that monarch from the throne.

29.   This splenetic disrelish of his place was evinced in almost every function pertaining to it. Proud as he was moody, he condescended to no personal mandate. Whatever special orders were necessary, their delivery was delegated to his body-servant, who in turn transferred them to their ultimate destination, through runners, alert Spanish boys or slave boys, like pages or pilot-fish within easy call continually hovering round Don Benito. So that to have beheld this undemonstrative invalid gliding about, ap-

athetic and mute, no landsman could have dreamed that in him was lodged a dictatorship beyond which, while at sea, there was no earthly appeal.

30.   Thus, the Spaniard, regarded in his reserve, seemed the involuntary victim of mental disorder. But, in fact, his reserve might, in some degree, have proceeded from design. If so, then here was evinced the unhealthy climax of that icy though conscientious policy, more or less adopted by all commanders of large ships, which, except in signal emergencies, obliterates alike the manifestation of sway with every trace of sociality; transforming the man into a block, or rather into a loaded cannon, which, until there is call for thunder, has nothing to say.

31.   Viewing him in this light, it seemed but a natural token of the perverse habit induced by a long course of such hard self-restraint, that, notwithstanding the present condition of his ship, the Spaniard should still persist in a demeanor, which, however harmless, or, it may be, appropriate, in a well- appointed vessel, such as the San Dominick might have been at the outset of the voyage, was anything but judicious now. But the Spaniard, perhaps, thought that it was with captains as with gods: reserve, under all events, must still be their cue. But probably this appearance of slumbering dominion might have been but an attempted disguise to conscious imbecility—not deep policy, but shallow device. But be all this as it might, whether Don Benito's manner was designed or not, the more Captain Delano noted its pervading reserve, the less he felt uneasiness at any particular manifestation of that reserve towards himself.

32.   Neither were his thoughts taken up by the captain alone. Wonted to the quiet orderliness of the sealer's comfortable family of a crew, the noisy confusion of the San Dominick's suffering host repeatedly challenged his eye. Some prominent breaches, not only of discipline but of decency, were observed. These Captain Delano could not but ascribe, in the main, to the absence of those subordinate deck-officers to whom, along with higher duties, is intrusted what may be styled the police department of a populous ship. True, the old oakum-pickers appeared at times to act the part of monitorial constables to their countrymen, the blacks; but though occasionally succeeding in allaying trifling outbreaks now and then between man and man, they could do little or nothing toward establishing general quiet. The San Dominick was in the condition of a transatlantic emigrant ship, among whose multitude of living freight are some individuals, doubtless, as little troublesome as crates and bales; but the friendly remonstrances of such with their ruder companions are of not so much avail as the unfriendly arm of the mate. What the San Dominick wanted was, what the emigrant ship has, stern superior officers. But on these decks not so much as a fourth-mate was to be seen.

33.   The visitor's curiosity was roused to learn the particulars of those mis-

haps which had brought about such absenteeism, with its consequences; because, though deriving some inkling of the voyage from the wails which at the first moment had greeted him, yet of the details no clear understanding had been had. The best account would, doubtless, be given by the captain. Yet at first the visitor was loth to ask it, unwilling to provoke some distant rebuff. But plucking up courage, he at last accosted Don Benito, renewing the expression of his benevolent interest, adding, that did he (Captain Delano) but know the particulars of the ship's misfortunes, he would, perhaps, be better able in the end to relieve them. Would Don Benito favor him with the whole story[?]

34.   Don Benito faltered; then, like some somnambulist suddenly interfered with, vacantly stared at his visitor, and ended by looking down on the deck. He maintained this posture so long, that Captain Delano, almost equally disconcerted, and involuntarily almost as rude, turned suddenly from him, walking forward to accost one of the Spanish seamen for the desired information. But he had hardly gone five paces, when, with a sort of eagerness, Don Benito invited him back, regretting his momentary absence of mind, and professing readiness to gratify him.

35.   While most part of the story was being given, the two captains stood on the after part of the main-deck, a privileged spot, no one being near but the servant.

36.   "It is now a hundred and ninety days,"[14] began the Spaniard, in his husky whisper, "that this ship, well officered and well manned, with several cabin passengers—some fifty Spaniards in all—sailed from Buenos Ayres bound to Lima, with a general cargo, hardware, Paraguay tea and the like—and," pointing forward, "that parcel of negroes, now not more than a hundred and fifty, as you see, but then numbering over three hundred souls.[15] Off Cape Horn we had heavy gales. In one moment, by night, three of my best officers, with fifteen sailors, were lost, with the main-yard; the spar snapping under them in the slings, as they sought, with heavers, to beat down the icy sail. To lighten the hull, the heavier sacks of mata were thrown into the sea, with most of the water-pipes lashed on deck at the time. And this last necessity it was, combined with the prolonged detentions afterwards experienced, which eventually brought about our chief causes of suffering. When————"

37.   Here there was a sudden fainting attack of his cough, brought on, no doubt, by his mental distress. His servant sustained him, and drawing a cordial from his pocket placed it to his lips. He a little revived. But unwilling to leave him unsupported while yet imperfectly restored, the black with one arm still encircled his master, at the same time keeping his eye fixed on his face, as if to watch for the first sign of complete restoration, or relapse, as the event might prove.

11

38.   The Spaniard proceeded, but brokenly and obscurely, as one in a dream.

39.   —"Oh, my God! rather than pass through what I have, with joy I would have hailed the most terrible gales; but—"

40.   His cough returned and with increased violence; this subsiding, with reddened lips and closed eyes he fell heavily against his supporter.

41.   "His mind wanders. He was thinking of the plague that followed the gales," plaintively sighed the servant; "my poor, poor master!" wringing one hand, and with the other wiping the mouth. "But be patient, Senor,["] again turning to Captain Delano, "these fits do not last long; master will soon be himself."

42.   Don Benito reviving, went on; but as this portion of the story was very brokenly delivered, the substance only will here be set down.[16]

43.   It appeared that after the ship had been many days tossed in storms off the Cape, the scurvy broke out, carrying off numbers of the whites and blacks. When at last they had worked round into the Pacific, their spars and sails were so damaged, and so inadequately handled by the surviving mariners, most of whom were become invalids, that, unable to lay her northerly course by the wind, which was powerful, the unmanageable ship, for successive days and nights, was blown northwestward, where the breeze suddenly deserted her, in unknown waters, to sultry calms. The absence of the water-pipes now proved as fatal to life as before their presence had menaced it. Induced, or at least aggravated, by the more than scanty allowance of water, a malignant fever followed the scurvy; with the excessive heat of the lengthened calm, making such short work of it as to sweep away, as by billows, whole families of the Africans, and a yet larger number, proportionably, of the Spaniards, including, by a luckless fatality, every remaining officer on board. Consequently, in the smart west winds eventually following the calm, the already rent sails, having to be simply dropped, not furled, at need, had been gradually reduced to the beggars' rags they were now. To procure substitutes for his lost sailors, as well as supplies of water and sails, the captain, at the earliest opportunity, had made for Baldivia, the southernmost civilized port of Chili and South America; but upon nearing the coast the thick weather had prevented him from so much as sighting that harbor. Since which period, almost without a crew, and almost without canvas and almost without water, and, at intervals, giving its added dead to the sea, the San Dominick had been battle-dored about by contrary winds, inveigled by currents, or grown weedy in calms. Like a man lost in woods, more than once she had doubled upon her own track.

44.   "But throughout these calamities," huskily continued Don Benito, painfully turning in the half embrace of his servant, "I have to thank those negroes you see, who, though to your inexperienced eyes appearing unruly, have, indeed, conducted themselves with less of restlessness than

even their owner could have thought possible under such circumstances."

45.   Here he again fell faintly back. Again his mind wandered; but he rallied, and less obscurely proceeded.

46.   "Yes, their owner was quite right in assuring me that no fetters would be needed with his blacks; so that while, as is wont in this transportation, those negroes have always remained upon deck—not thrust below, as in the Guinea- men—they have, also, from the beginning, been freely permitted to range within given bounds at their pleasure."

47.   Once more the faintness returned—his mind roved—but, recovering, he resumed:

48.   "But it is Babo here to whom, under God, I owe not only my own preservation, but likewise to him, chiefly, the merit is due, of pacifying his more ignorant brethren, when at intervals tempted to murmurings."

49.   "Ah, master," sighed the black, bowing his face, "don't speak of me; Babo is nothing; what Babo has done was but duty."

50.   "Faithful fellow!" cried Captain Delano. "Don Benito, I envy you such a friend; slave I cannot call him."

51.   As master and man stood before him, the black upholding the white, Captain Delano could not but bethink him of the beauty of that relationship which could present such a spectacle of fidelity on the one hand and confidence on the other. The scene was heightened by the contrast in dress, denoting their relative positions. The Spaniard wore a loose Chili jacket of dark velvet; white small-clothes and stockings, with silver buckles at the knee and instep; a high-crowned sombrero, of fine grass; a slender sword, silver mounted, hung from a knot in his sash—the last being an almost invariable adjunct, more for utility than ornament, of a South American gentleman's dress to this hour.[17] Excepting when his occasional nervous contortions brought about disarray, there was a certain precision in his attire curiously at variance with the unsightly disorder around; especially in the belittered Ghetto, forward of the main-mast, wholly occupied by the blacks.

52.   The servant wore nothing but wide trowsers, apparently, from their coarseness and patches, made out of some old topsail; they were clean, and confined at the waist by a bit of unstranded rope, which, with his composed, deprecatory air at times, made him look something like a begging friar of St. Francis.[18]

53.   However unsuitable for the time and place, at least in the blunt-thinking American's eyes, and however strangely surviving in the midst of all his afflictions, the toilette of Don Benito might not, in fashion at least, have gone beyond the style of the day among South Americans of his class. Though on the present voyage sailing from Buenos Ayres, he had avowed himself a native and resident of Chili, whose inhabitants had not so generally adopted the plain coat and once plebeian pantaloons; but, with a

becoming modification, adhered to their provincial costume, picturesque as any in the world. Still, relatively to the pale history of the voyage, and his own pale face, there seemed something so incongruous in the Spaniard's apparel, as almost to suggest the image of an invalid courtier tottering about London streets in the time of the plague.

54.   The portion of the narrative which, perhaps, most excited interest, as well as some surprise, considering the latitudes in question, was the long calms spoken of, and more particularly the ship's so long drifting about. Without communicating the opinion, of course, the American could not but impute at least part of the detentions both to clumsy seamanship and faulty navigation. Eying Don Benito's small, yellow hands, he easily inferred that the young captain had not got into command at the hawse-hole, but the cabin-window; and if so, why wonder at incompetence, in youth, sickness, and gentility united?

55.   But drowning criticism in compassion, after a fresh repetition of his sympathies, Captain Delano, having heard out his story, not only engaged, as in the first place, to see Don Benito and his people supplied in their immediate bodily needs, but, also, now further promised to assist him in procuring a large permanent supply of water, as well as some sails and rigging; and, though it would involve no small embarrassment to himself, yet he would spare three of his best seamen for temporary deck officers; so that without delay the ship might proceed to Conception, there fully to refit for Lima, her destined port.

56.   Such generosity was not without its effect, even upon the invalid. His face lighted up; eager and hectic, he met the honest glance of his visitor. With gratitude he seemed overcome.

57.   "This excitement is bad for master," whispered the servant, taking his arm, and with soothing words gently drawing him aside.

58.   When Don Benito returned, the American was pained to observe that his hopefulness, like the sudden kindling in his cheek, was but febrile and transient.

59.   Ere long, with a joyless mien, looking up towards the poop, the host invited his guest to accompany him there, for the benefit of what little breath of wind might be stirring.

60.   As, during the telling of the story, Captain Delano had once or twice started at the occasional cymballing of the hatchet-polishers, wondering why such an interruption should be allowed, especially in that part of the ship, and in the ears of an invalid; and moreover, as the hatchets had anything but an attractive look, and the handlers of them still less so, it was, therefore, to tell the truth, not without some lurking reluctance, or even shrinking, it may be, that Captain Delano, with apparent complaisance, acquiesced in his host's invitation. The more so, since, with an untimely caprice of punctilio, rendered distressing by his cadaverous aspect, Don

14

Benito, with Castilian bows, solemnly insisted upon his guest's preceding him up the ladder leading to the elevation; where, one on each side of the last step, sat for armorial supporters and sentries two of the ominous file. Gingerly enough stepped good Captain Delano between them, and in the instant of leaving them behind, like one running the gauntlet, he felt an apprehensive twitch in the calves of his legs.

61.   But when, facing about, he saw the whole file, like so many organ-grinders, still stupidly intent on their work, unmindful of everything beside, he could not but smile at his late fidgety panic.

62.   Presently, while standing with his host, looking forward upon the decks below, he was struck by one of those instances of insubordination previously alluded to. Three black boys, with two Spanish boys, were sitting together on the hatches, scraping a rude wooden platter, in which some scanty mess had recently been cooked. Suddenly, one of the black boys, enraged at a word dropped by one of his white companions, seized a knife, and, though called to forbear by one of the oakum-pickers, struck the lad over the head, inflicting a gash from which blood flowed.

63.   In amazement, Captain Delano inquired what this meant. To which the pale Don Benito dully muttered, that it was merely the sport of the lad.

64.   "Pretty serious sport, truly," rejoined Captain Delano. "Had such a thing happened on board the Bachelor's Delight, instant punishment would have followed."

65.   At these words the Spaniard turned upon the American one of his sudden, staring, half-lunatic looks; then, relapsing into his torpor, answered, "Doubtless, doubtless, Senor."

66.   Is it, thought Captain Delano, that this hapless man is one of those paper captains I've known, who by policy wink at what by power they cannot put down? I know no sadder sight than a commander who has little of command but the name.

67.   "I should think, Don Benito," he now said, glancing towards the oakum- picker who had sought to interfere with the boys, "that you would find it advantageous to keep all your blacks employed, especially the younger ones, no matter at what useless task, and no matter what happens to the ship. Why, even with my little band, I find such a course indispensable. I once kept a crew on my quarter-deck thrumming mats for my cabin, when, for three days, I had given up my ship—mats, men, and all—for a speedy loss, owing to the violence of a gale, in which we could do nothing but helplessly drive before it."

68.   "Doubtless, doubtless," muttered Don Benito.

69.   "But," continued Captain Delano, again glancing upon the oakum-pickers and then at the hatchet-polishers, near by, "I see you keep some, at least, of your host employed."

70.   "Yes," was again the vacant response.

15

71.   "Those old men there, shaking their pows from their pulpits," continued Captain Delano, pointing to the oakum-pickers, "seem to act the part of old dominies to the rest, little heeded as their admonitions are at times. Is this voluntary on their part, Don Benito, or have you appointed them shepherds to your flock of black sheep?"

72.   "What posts they fill, I appointed them," rejoined the Spaniard, in an acrid tone, as if resenting some supposed satiric reflection.

73.   "And these others, these Ashantee conjurors here," continued Captain Delano, rather uneasily eying the brandished steel of the hatchet-polishers, where, in spots, it had been brought to a shine, "this seems a curious business they are at, Don Benito?"

74.   "In the gales we met," answered the Spaniard, "what of our general cargo was not thrown overboard was much damaged by the brine. Since coming into calm weather, I have had several cases of knives and hatchets daily brought up for overhauling and cleaning."

75.   "A prudent idea, Don Benito. You are part owner of ship and cargo, I presume; but none of the slaves, perhaps?"

76.   ["]I am owner of all you see," impatiently returned Don Benito, "except the main company of blacks, who belonged to my late friend, Alexandro Aranda."

77.   As he mentioned this name, his air was heart-broken; his knees shook; his servant supported him.

78.   Thinking he divined the cause of such unusual emotion, to confirm his surmise, Captain Delano, after a pause, said: "And may I ask, Don Benito, whether—since awhile ago you spoke of some cabin passengers —the friend, whose loss so afflicts you, at the outset of the voyage accompanied his blacks?"

79.   "Yes."

80.   "But died of the fever?"

81.   ["]Died of the fever. Oh, could I but—"

82.   Again quivering, the Spaniard paused.

83.   "Pardon me," said Captain Delano, lowly, "but I think that, by a sympathetic experience, I conjecture, Don Benito, what it is that gives the keener edge to your grief. It was once my hard fortune to lose, at sea, a dear friend, my own brother, then supercargo. Assured of the welfare of his spirit, its departure I could have borne like a man; but that honest eye, that honest hand—both of which had so often met mine—and that warm heart; all, all—like scraps to the dogs—to throw all to the sharks! It was then I vowed never to have for fellow-voyager a man I loved, unless, unbeknown to him, I had provided every requisite, in case of a fatality, for embalming his mortal part for interment on shore. Were your friend's remains now on board this ship, Don Benito, not thus strangely would the mention of his name affect you."

16

84. "On board this ship?" echoed the Spaniard. Then, with horrified gestures, as directed against some spectre, he unconsciously fell into the ready arms of his attendant, who, with a silent appeal toward Captain Delano, seemed beseeching him not again to broach a theme so unspeakably distressing to his master.

85. This poor fellow now, thought the pained American, is the victim of that sad superstition which associates goblins with the deserted body of man, as ghosts with an abandoned house. How unlike are we made! What to me, in like case, would have been a solemn satisfaction, the bare suggestion, even, terrifies the Spaniard into this trance. Poor Alexandro Aranda! what would you say could you here see your friend—who, on former voyages, when you, for months, were left behind, has, I dare say, often longed, and longed, for one peep at you—now transported with terror at the least thought of having you anyway nigh him.

86. At this moment, with a dreary grave-yard toll, betokening a flaw, the ship's forecastle bell, smote by one of the grizzled oakum-pickers, proclaimed ten o'clock, through the leaden calm; when Captain Delano's attention was caught by the moving figure of a gigantic black, emerging from the general crowd below, and slowly advancing towards the elevated poop. An iron collar was about his neck, from which depended a chain, thrice wound round his body; the terminating links padlocked together at a broad band of iron, his girdle.

87. "How like a mute Atufal moves," murmured the servant.

88. The black mounted the steps of the poop, and, like a brave prisoner, brought up to receive sentence, stood in unquailing muteness before Don Benito, now recovered from his attack.

89. At the first glimpse of his approach, Don Benito had started, a resentful shadow swept over his face; and, as with the sudden memory of bootless rage, his white lips glued together.

90. This is some mulish mutineer, thought Captain Delano, surveying, not without a mixture of admiration, the colossal form of the negro.

91. "See, he waits your question, master," said the servant.

92. Thus reminded, Don Benito, nervously averting his glance, as if shunning, by anticipation, some rebellious response, in a disconcerted voice, thus spoke:—

93. "Atufal, will you ask my pardon, now?"

94. The black was silent.

95. "Again, master," murmured the servant, with bitter upbraiding eyeing his countryman, "Again, master; he will bend to master yet."

96. "Answer," said Don Benito, still averting his glance, "say but the one word, *pardon*, and your chains shall be off."

97. Upon this, the black, slowly raising both arms, let them lifelessly fall, his links clanking, his head bowed; as much as to say, "no, I am content."

17

98.   "Go," said Don Benito, with inkept and unknown emotion.

99.   Deliberately as he had come, the black obeyed.

100.   "Excuse me, Don Benito," said Captain Delano, "but this scene surprises me; what means it, pray?"

101.   "It means that that negro alone, of all the band, has given me peculiar cause of offense. I have put him in chains; I—"

102.   Here he paused; his hand to his head, as if there were a swimming there, or a sudden bewilderment of memory had come over him; but meeting his servant's kindly glance seemed reassured, and proceeded:—

103.   "I could not scourge such a form. But I told him he must ask my pardon. As yet he has not. At my command, every two hours he stands before me."

104.   "And how long has this been?"

105.   "Some sixty days."

106.   "And obedient in all else? And respectful?"

107.   "Yes."

108.   "Upon my conscience, then," exclaimed Captain Delano, impulsively, "[he has] a royal spirit in him, this fellow."

109.   "He may have some right to it," bitterly returned Don Benito, "he says he was king in his own land."

110.   "Yes," said the servant, entering a word, "those slits in Atufal's ears once held wedges of gold; but poor Babo here, in his own land, was only a poor slave; a black man's slave was Babo, who now is the white's."

111.   Somewhat annoyed by these conversational familiarities, Captain Delano turned curiously upon the attendant, then glanced inquiringly at his master; but, as if long wonted to these little informalities, neither master nor man seemed to understand him.

112.   "What, pray, was Atufal's offense, Don Benito?" asked Captain Delano; "if it was not something very serious, take a fool's advice, and, in view of his general docility, as well as in some natural respect for his spirit, remit him his penalty."

113.   "No, no, master never will do that," here murmured the servant to himself, "proud Atufal must first ask master's pardon. The slave there carries the padlock, but master here carries the key."

114.   His attention thus directed, Captain Delano now noticed for the first [time], that, suspended by a slender silken cord, from Don Benito's neck, hung a key. At once, from the servant's muttered syllables, divining the key's purpose, he smiled and said:—"So, Don Benito—padlock and key—significant symbols, truly."

115.   Biting his lip, Don Benito faltered.

116.   Though the remark of Captain Delano, a man of such native simplicity as to be incapable of satire or irony, had been dropped in playful allusion

18

to the Spaniard's singularly evidenced lordship over the black; yet the hypochondriac seemed some way to have taken it as a malicious reflection upon his confessed inability thus far to break down, at least, on a verbal summons, the entrenched will of the slave. Deploring this supposed misconception, yet despairing of correcting it, Captain Delano shifted the subject; but finding his companion more than ever withdrawn, as if still sourly digesting the lees of the presumed affront above-mentioned, by-and-by Captain Delano likewise became less talkative, oppressed, against his own will, by what seemed the secret vindictiveness of the morbidly sensitive Spaniard. But the good sailor, himself of a quite contrary disposition, refrained, on his part, alike from the appearance as from the feeling of resentment, and if silent, was only so from contagion.

117.   Presently the Spaniard, assisted by his servant[,] somewhat discourteously crossed over from his guest; a procedure which, sensibly enough, might have been allowed to pass for idle caprice of ill-humor, had not master and man, lingering round the corner of the elevated skylight, began whispering together in low voices. This was unpleasing. And more; the moody air of the Spaniard, which at times had not been without a sort of valetudinarian stateliness, now seemed anything but dignified; while the menial familiarity of the servant lost its original charm of simple-hearted attachment.

118.   In his embarrassment, the visitor turned his face to the other side of the ship. By so doing, his glance accidentally fell on a young Spanish sailor, a coil of rope in his hand, just stepped from the deck to the first round of the mizzen-rigging. Perhaps the man would not have been particularly noticed, were it not that, during his ascent to one of the yards, he, with a sort of covert intentness, kept his eye fixed on Captain Delano, from whom, presently, it passed, as if by a natural sequence, to the two whisperers.

119.   His own attention thus redirected to that quarter, Captain Delano gave a slight start. From something in Don Benito's manner just then, it seemed as if the visitor had, at least partly, been the subject of the withdrawn consultation going on—a conjecture as little agreeable to the guest as it was little flattering to the host.

120.   The singular alternations of courtesy and ill-breeding in the Spanish captain were unaccountable, except on one of two suppositions—innocent lunacy, or wicked imposture.

121.   But the first idea, though it might naturally have occurred to an indifferent observer, and, in some respect, had not hitherto been wholly a stranger to Captain Delano's mind, yet, now that, in an incipient way, he began to regard the stranger's conduct something in the light of an intentional affront, of course the idea of lunacy was virtually vacated. But if not a lunatic, what then? Under the circumstances, would a gentleman, nay,

19

any honest boor, act the part now acted by his host? The man was an impostor. Some low-born adventurer, masquerading as an oceanic grandee; yet so ignorant of the first requisites of mere gentlemanhood as to be betrayed into the present remarkable indecorum. That strange ceremoniousness, too, at other times evinced, seemed not uncharacteristic of one playing a part above his real level. Benito Cereno—Don Benito Cereno—a sounding name. One, too, at that period, not unknown, in the surname, to supercargoes and sea captains trading along the Spanish Main, as belonging to one of the most enterprising and extensive mercantile families in all those provinces; several members of it having titles; a sort of Castilian Rothschild, with a noble brother, or cousin, in every great trading town of South America.[19] The alleged Don Benito was in early manhood, about twenty-nine or thirty. To assume a sort of roving cadetship in the maritime affairs of such a house, what more likely scheme for a young knave of talent and spirit? But the Spaniard was a pale invalid. Never mind. For even to the degree of simulating mortal disease, the craft of some tricksters had been known to attain. To think that, under the aspect of infantile weakness, the most savage energies might be couched—those velvets of the Spaniard but the silky paw to his fangs.

122.   From no train of thought did these fancies come; not from within, but from without; suddenly, too, and in one throng, like hoar frost; yet as soon to vanish as the mild sun of Captain Delano's good-nature regained its meridian.

123.   Glancing over once more towards his host—whose side-face, revealed above the skylight, was now turned towards him—he was struck by the profile, whose clearness of cut was refined by the thinness, incident to ill-health, as well as ennobled about the chin by the beard. Away with suspicion. He was a true off-shoot of a true hidalgo Cereno.[20]

124.   Relieved by these and other better thoughts, the visitor, lightly humming a tune, now began indifferently pacing the poop, so as not to betray to Don Benito that he had at all mistrusted incivility, much less duplicity; for such mistrust would yet be proved illusory, and by the event; though, for the present, the circumstance which had provoked that distrust remained unexplained. But when that little mystery should have been cleared up, Captain Delano thought he might extremely regret it, did he allow Don Benito to become aware that he had indulged in ungenerous surmises. In short, to the Spaniard's black-letter text, it was best, for awhile, to leave open margin.

125.   Presently, his pale face twitching and overcast, the Spaniard, still supported by his attendant, moved over towards his guest, when, with even more than his usual embarrassment, and a strange sort of intriguing intonation in his husky whisper, the following conversation began:—

126.   "Senor, may I ask how long you have lain at this isle?"

20

127.   "Oh, but a day or two, Don Benito."

128.   "And from what port are you last?"

129.   "Canton."

130.   "And there, Senor, you exchanged your seal-skins for teas and silks, I think you said?"

131.   "Yes. Silks, mostly."

132.   "And the balance you took in specie, perhaps?"

133.   Captain Delano, fidgeting a little, answered—

134.   "Yes; some silver; not a very great deal, though."

135.   "Ah—well. May I ask how many men have you, Senor?"

136.   Captain Delano slightly started, but answered—

137.   "About five-and-twenty, all told."

138.   "And at present, Senor, all on board, I suppose?"

139.   "All on board, Don Benito," replied the Captain, now with satisfaction.

140.   "And will be to-night, Senor?"

141.   At this last question, following so many pertinacious ones, for the soul of him Captain Delano could not but look very earnestly at the questioner, who, instead of meeting the glance, with every token of craven discomposure dropped his eyes to the deck; presenting an unworthy contrast to his servant, who, just then, was kneeling at his feet, adjusting a loose shoe-buckle; his disengaged face meantime, with humble curiosity, turned openly up into his master's downcast one.

142.   The Spaniard, still with a guilty shuffle, repeated his question:

143.   "And—and will be to-night, Senor?"

144.   "Yes, for aught I know," returned Captain Delano—"but nay," rallying himself into fearless truth, "some of them talked of going off on another fishing party about midnight."

145.   "Your ships generally go—go more or less armed, I believe, Senor?"

146.   "Oh, a six-pounder or two, in case of emergency," was the intrepidly indifferent reply, "with a small stock of muskets, sealing-spears, and cutlasses, you know."

147.   As he thus responded, Captain Delano again glanced at Don Benito, but the latter's eyes were averted; while abruptly and awkwardly shifting the subject, he made some peevish allusion to the calm, and then, without apology, once more, with his attendant, withdrew to the opposite bulwarks, where the whispering was resumed.

148.   At this moment, and ere Captain Delano could cast a cool thought upon what had just passed, the young Spanish sailor, before mentioned, was seen descending from the rigging. In act of stooping over to spring inboard to the deck, his voluminous, unconfined frock, or shirt, of coarse woolen, much spotted with tar, opened out far down the chest, revealing a soiled under garment of what seemed the finest linen, edged, about the

21

neck, with a narrow blue ribbon, sadly faded and worn.[21] At this moment the young sailor's eye was again fixed on the whisperers, and Captain Delano thought he observed a lurking significance in it, as if silent signs, of some Freemason sort, had that instant been interchanged.[22]

149.   This once more impelled his own glance in the direction of Don Benito, and, as before, he could not but infer that himself formed the subject of the conference. He paused. The sound of the hatchet-polishing fell on his ears. He cast another swift side-look at the two. They had the air of conspirators. In connection with the late questionings, and the incident of the young sailor, these things now begat such return of involuntary suspicion, that the singular guilelessness of the American could not endure it. Plucking up a gay and humorous expression, he crossed over to the two rapidly, saying:—"Ha, Don Benito, your black here seems high in your trust; a sort of privy-counselor, in fact."

150.   Upon this, the servant looked up with a good-natured grin, but the master started as from a venomous bite. It was a moment or two before the Spaniard sufficiently recovered himself to reply; which he did, at last, with cold constraint:—"Yes, Senor, I have trust in Babo."

151.   Here Babo, changing his previous grin of mere animal humor into an intelligent smile, not ungratefully eyed his master.

152.   Finding that the Spaniard now stood silent and reserved, as if involuntarily, or purposely giving hint that his guest's proximity was inconvenient just then, Captain Delano, unwilling to appear uncivil even to incivility itself, made some trivial remark and moved off; again and again turning over in his mind the mysterious demeanor of Don Benito Cereno.

153.   He had descended from the poop, and, wrapped in thought, was passing near a dark hatchway, leading down into the steerage, when, perceiving motion there, he looked to see what moved. The same instant there was a sparkle in the shadowy hatchway, and he saw one of the Spanish sailors, prowling there[,] hurriedly placing his hand in the bosom of his frock, as if hiding something. Before the man could have been certain who it was that was passing, he slunk below out of sight. But enough was seen of him to make it sure that he was the same young sailor before noticed in the rigging.

154.   What was that which so sparkled? thought Captain Delano. It was no lamp—no match—no live coal. Could it have been a jewel? But how come sailors with jewels?—or with silk-trimmed under-shirts either? Has he been robbing the trunks of the dead cabin-passengers? But if so, he would hardly wear one of the stolen articles on board ship here. Ah, ah—if, now, that was, indeed, a secret sign I saw passing between this suspicious fellow and his captain awhile since; if I could only be certain that, in my uneasiness, my senses did not deceive me, then—

155.   Here, passing from one suspicious thing to another, his mind revolved

22

the strange questions put to him concerning his ship.

156.   By a curious coincidence, as each point was recalled, the black wizards of Ashantee would strike up with their hatchets, as in ominous comment on the white stranger's thoughts. Pressed by such enigmas and portents, it would have been almost against nature, had not, even into the least distrustful heart, some ugly misgivings obtruded.

157.   Observing the ship, now helplessly fallen into a current, with enchanted sails, drifting with increased rapidity seaward; and noting that, from a lately intercepted projection of the land, the sealer was hidden, the stout mariner began to quake at thoughts which he barely durst confess to himself. Above all, he began to feel a ghostly dread of Don Benito. And yet, when he roused himself, dilated his chest, felt himself strong on his legs, and coolly considered it—what did all these phantoms amount to?
amount to?

158.   Had the Spaniard any sinister scheme, it must have reference not so much to him (Captain Delano) as to his ship (the Bachelor's Delight). Hence the present drifting away of the one ship from the other, instead of favoring any such possible scheme, was, for the time, at least, opposed to it. Clearly any suspicion, combining such contradictions, must need be delusive. Beside, was it not absurd to think of a vessel in distress—a vessel by sickness almost dismanned of her crew—a vessel whose inmates were parched for water—was it not a thousand times absurd that such a craft should, at present, be of a piratical character; or her commander, either for himself or those under him, cherish any desire but for speedy relief and refreshment? But then, might not general distress, and thirst in particular, be affected? And might not that same undiminished Spanish crew, alleged to have perished off to a remnant, be at that very moment lurking in the hold? On heart-broken pretense of entreating a cup of cold water, fiends in human form had got into lonely dwellings, nor retired until a dark deed had been done. And among the Malay pirates, it was no unusual thing to lure ships after them into their treacherous harbors, or entice boarders from a declared enemy at sea, by the spectacle of thinly manned or vacant decks, beneath which prowled a hundred spears with yellow arms ready to upthrust them through the mats. Not that Captain Delano had entirely credited such things. He had heard of them—and now, as stories, they recurred. The present destination of the ship was the anchorage. There she would be near his own vessel. Upon gaining that vicinity, might not the San Dominick, like a slumbering volcano, suddenly let loose energies now hid?

159.   He recalled the Spaniard's manner while telling his story. There was a gloomy hesitancy and subterfuge about it. It was just the manner of one making up his tale for evil purposes, as he goes. But if that story was not true, what was the truth? That the ship had unlawfully come into the

Spaniard's possession? But in many of its details, especially in reference to the more calamitous parts, such as the fatalities among the seamen, the consequent prolonged beating about, the past sufferings from obstinate calms, and still continued suffering from thirst; in all these points, as well as others, Don Benito's story had corroborated not only the wailing ejaculations of the indiscriminate multitude, white and black, but likewise—what seemed impossible to be counterfeit—by the very expression and play of every human feature, which Captain Delano saw. If Don Benito's story was, throughout, an invention, then every soul on board, down to the youngest negress, was his carefully drilled recruit in the plot: an incredible inference. And yet, if there was ground for mistrusting his veracity, that inference was a legitimate one.

160.   But those questions of the Spaniard. There, indeed, one might pause. Did they not seem put with much the same object with which the burglar or assassin, by day-time, reconnoitres the walls of a house? But, with ill purposes, to solicit such information openly of the chief person endangered, and so, in effect, setting him on his guard; how unlikely a procedure was that? Absurd, then, to suppose that those questions had been prompted by evil designs. Thus, the same conduct, which, in this instance, had raised the alarm, served to dispel it. In short, scarce any suspicion or uneasiness, however apparently reasonable at the time, which was not now, with equal apparent reason, dismissed.

161.   At last he began to laugh at his former forebodings; and laugh at the strange ship for, in its aspect, someway siding with them, as it were; and laugh, too, at the odd-looking blacks, particularly those old scissors-grinders, the Ashantees; and those bed-ridden old knitting women, the oakum-pickers; and almost at the dark Spaniard himself, the central hobgoblin of all.

162.   For the rest, whatever in a serious way seemed enigmatical, was now good- naturedly explained away by the thought that, for the most part, the poor invalid scarcely knew what he was about; either sulking in black vapors, or putting idle questions without sense or object. Evidently, for the present, the man was not fit to be intrusted with the ship. On some benevolent plea withdrawing the command from him, Captain Delano would yet have to send her to Conception, in charge of his second mate, a worthy person and good navigator—a plan not more convenient for the San Dominick than for Don Benito; for, relieved from all anxiety, keeping wholly to his cabin, the sick man, under the good nursing of his servant, would, probably, by the end of the passage, be in a measure restored to health, and with that he should also be restored to authority.

163.   Such were the American's thoughts. They were tranquilizing. There was a difference between the idea of Don Benito's darkly pre-ordaining Captain Delano's fate, and Captain Delano's lightly arranging Don Ben-

ito's. Nevertheless, it was not without something of relief that the good seaman presently perceived his whale-boat in the distance. Its absence had been prolonged by unexpected detention at the sealer's side, as well as its returning trip lengthened by the continual recession of the goal.

164.   The advancing speck was observed by the blacks. Their shouts attracted the attention of Don Benito, who, with a return of courtesy, approaching Captain Delano, expressed satisfaction at the coming of some supplies, slight and temporary as they must necessarily prove.

165.   Captain Delano responded; but while doing so, his attention was drawn to something passing on the deck below: among the crowd climbing the landward bulwarks, anxiously watching the coming boat, two blacks, to all appearances accidentally incommoded by one of the sailors, violently pushed him aside, which the sailor someway resenting, they dashed him to the deck, despite the earnest cries of the oakum-pickers.

166.   "Don Benito," said Captain Delano quickly, "do you see what is going on there? Look!"

167.   But, seized by his cough, the Spaniard staggered, with both hands to his face, on the point of falling. Captain Delano would have supported him, but the servant was more alert, who, with one hand sustaining his master, with the other applied the cordial. Don Benito restored, the black withdrew his support, slipping aside a little, but dutifully remaining within call of a whisper. Such discretion was here evinced as quite wiped away, in the visitor's eyes, any blemish of impropriety which might have attached to the attendant, from the indecorous conferences before mentioned; showing, too, that if the servant were to blame, it might be more the master's fault than his own, since, when left to himself, he could conduct thus well.

168.   His glance called away from the spectacle of disorder to the more pleasing one before him, Captain Delano could not avoid again congratulating his host upon possessing such a servant, who, though perhaps a little too forward now and then, must upon the whole be invaluable to one in the invalid's situation.

169.   "Tell me, Don Benito," he added, with a smile—"I should like to have your man here, myself—what will you take for him? Would fifty doubloons be any object?"[23]

170.   "Master wouldn't part with Babo for a thousand doubloons," murmured the black, overhearing the offer, and taking it in earnest, and, with the strange vanity of a faithful slave, appreciated by his master, scorning to hear so paltry a valuation put upon him by a stranger. But Don Benito, apparently hardly yet completely restored, and again interrupted by his cough, made but some broken reply.

171.   Soon his physical distress became so great, affecting his mind, too, apparently, that, as if to screen the sad spectacle, the servant

gently conducted his master below.

172.   Left to himself, the American, to while away the time till his boat should arrive, would have pleasantly accosted some one of the few Spanish seamen he saw; but recalling something that Don Benito had said touching their ill conduct, he refrained; as a ship-master indisposed to countenance cowardice or unfaithfulness in seamen.

173.   While, with these thoughts, standing with eye directed forward towards that handful of sailors, suddenly he thought that one or two of them returned the glance and with a sort of meaning. He rubbed his eyes, and looked again; but again seemed to see the same thing. Under a new form, but more obscure than any previous one, the old suspicions recurred, but, in the absence of Don Benito, with less of panic than before. Despite the bad account given of the sailors, Captain Delano resolved forthwith to accost one of them. Descending the poop, he made his way through the blacks, his movement drawing a queer cry from the oakum-pickers, prompted by whom, the negroes, twitching each other aside, divided before him; but, as if curious to see what was the object of this deliberate visit to their Ghetto, closing in behind, in tolerable order, followed the white stranger up. His progress thus proclaimed as by mounted kings-at-arms, and escorted as by a Caffre guard of honor, Captain Delano, assuming a good-humored, off-handed air, continued to advance; now and then saying a blithe word to the negroes, and his eye curiously surveying the white faces, here and there sparsely mixed in with the blacks, like stray white pawns venturously involved in the ranks of the chess-men opposed.[24]

174.   While thinking which of them to select for his purpose, he chanced to observe a sailor seated on the deck engaged in tarring the strap of a large block, a circle of blacks squatted round him inquisitively eying the process.

175.   The mean employment of the man was in contrast with something superior in his figure. His hand, black with continually thrusting it into the tar-pot held for him by a negro, seemed not naturally allied to his face, a face which would have been a very fine one but for its haggardness. Whether this haggardness had aught to do with criminality, could not be determined; since, as intense heat and cold, though unlike, produce like sensations, so innocence and guilt, when, through casual association with mental pain, stamping any visible impress, use one seal—a hacked one.

176.   Not again that this reflection occurred to Captain Delano at the time, charitable man as he was. Rather another idea. Because observing so singular a haggardness combined with a dark eye, averted as in trouble and shame, and then again recalling Don Benito's confessed ill opinion of his crew, insensibly he was operated upon by certain general notions which, while disconnecting pain and abash-

ment from virtue, invariably link them with vice.[25]

177.   If, indeed, there be any wickedness on board this ship, thought Captain Delano, be sure that man there has fouled his hand in it, even as now he fouls it in the pitch. I don't like to accost him. I will speak to this other, this old Jack here on the windlass.[26]

178.   He advanced to an old Barcelona tar, in ragged red breeches and dirty night-cap, cheeks trenched and bronzed, whiskers dense as thorn hedges. Seated between two sleepy-looking Africans, this mariner, like his younger shipmate, was employed upon some rigging—splicing a cable—the sleepy-looking blacks performing the inferior function of holding the outer parts of the ropes for him.[27]

179.   Upon Captain Delano's approach, the man at once hung his head below its previous level; the one necessary for business. It appeared as if he desired to be thought absorbed, with more than common fidelity, in his task. Being addressed, he glanced up, but with what seemed a furtive, diffident air, which sat strangely enough on his weather-beaten visage, much as if a grizzly bear, instead of growling and biting, should simper and cast sheep's eyes. He was asked several questions concerning the voyage—questions purposely referring to several particulars in Don Benito's narrative, not previously corroborated by those impulsive cries greeting the visitor on first coming on board. The questions were briefly answered, confirming all that remained to be confirmed of the story. The negroes about the windlass joined in with the old sailor; but, as they became talkative, he by degrees became mute, and at length quite glum, seemed morosely unwilling to answer more questions, and yet, all the while, this ursine air was somehow mixed with his sheepish one.

180.   Despairing of getting into unembarrassed talk with such a centaur, Captain Delano, after glancing round for a more promising countenance, but seeing none, spoke pleasantly to the blacks to make way for him; and so, amid various grins and grimaces, returned to the poop, feeling a little strange at first, he could hardly tell why, but upon the whole with regained confidence in Benito Cereno.

181.   How plainly, thought he, did that old whiskerando yonder betray a consciousness of ill desert.[28] No doubt, when he saw me coming, he dreaded lest I, apprised by his Captain of the crew's general misbehavior, came with sharp words for him, and so down with his head. And yet—and yet, now that I think of it, that very old fellow, if I err not, was one of those who seemed so earnestly eying me here awhile since. Ah, these currents spin one's head round almost as much as they do the ship. Ha, there now's a pleasant sort of sunny sight; quite sociable, too.

182.   His attention had been drawn to a slumbering negress, partly disclosed through the lacework of some rigging, lying, with youthful limbs carelessly disposed, under the lee of the bulwarks, like a doe in the shade of a

woodland rock. Sprawling at her lapped [breasts was] her wide-awake fawn, stark naked, its black little body half lifted from the deck, crosswise with its dam's; its hands, like two paws, clambering upon her; its mouth and nose ineffectually rooting to get at the mark; and meantime giving a vexatious half-grunt, blending with the composed snore of the negress.

183.   The uncommon vigor of the child at length roused the mother. She started up, at a distance facing Captain Delano. But as if not at all concerned at the attitude in which she had been caught, delightedly she caught the child up, with maternal transports, covering it with kisses.

184.   There's naked nature, now; pure tenderness and love, thought Captain Delano, well pleased.

185.   This incident prompted him to remark the other negresses more particularly than before. He was gratified with their manners: like most uncivilized women, they seemed at once tender of heart and tough of constitution; equally ready to die for their infants or fight for them. Unsophisticated as leopardesses; loving as doves.[29] Ah! thought Captain Delano, these, perhaps, are some of the very women whom Ledyard saw in Africa, and gave such a noble account of.[30]

186.   These natural sights somehow insensibly deepened his confidence and ease. At last he looked to see how his boat was getting on; but it was still pretty remote. He turned to see if Don Benito had returned; but he had not.

187.   To change the scene, as well as to please himself with a leisurely observation of the coming boat, stepping over into the mizzen-chains, he clambered his way into the starboard quarter-gallery—one of those abandoned Venetian- looking water-balconies previously mentioned—retreats cut off from the deck. As his foot pressed the half-damp, half-dry sea-mosses matting the place, and a chance phantom cats- paw—an islet of breeze, unheralded, unfollowed— as this ghostly cats paw came fanning his cheek; as his glance fell upon the row of small, round dead-lights—all closed like coppered eyes of the coffined —and the state-cabin door, once connecting with the gallery, even as the dead- lights had once looked out upon it, but now calked fast like a sarcophagus lid; and to a purple-black[,] tarred-[over panel], threshold, and post; and he bethought him of the time, when that state-cabin and this state-balcony had heard the voices of the Spanish king's officers, and the forms of the Lima viceroy's daughters had perhaps leaned where he stood—as these and other images flitted through his mind, as the cats-paw through the calm, gradually he felt rising a dreamy inquietude, like that of one who alone on the prairie feels unrest from the repose of the noon.[31]

188.   He leaned against the carved balustrade, again looking off toward his boat; but found his eye falling upon the ribbon grass, trailing along the

ship's water-line, straight as a border of green box; and parterres of sea-weed, broad ovals and crescents, floating nigh and far, with what seemed long formal alleys between, crossing the terraces of swells, and sweeping round as if leading to the grottoes below.[32] And overhanging all was the balustrade by his arm, which, partly stained with pitch and partly embossed with moss, seemed the charred ruin of some summer-house in a grand garden long running to waste.

189.   Trying to break one charm, he was but becharmed anew. Though upon the wide sea, he seemed in some far inland country; prisoner in some deserted château, left to stare at empty grounds, and peer out at vague roads, where never wagon or wayfarer passed.

190.   But these enchantments were a little disenchanted as his eye fell on the corroded mainchains. Of an ancient style, massy and rusty in link, shackle and bolt, they seemed even more fit for the ship's present business than the one for which she had been built.

191.   Presently he thought something moved nigh the chains. He rubbed his eyes, and looked hard. Groves of rigging were about the chains; and there, peering from behind a great stay, like an Indian from behind a hemlock, a Spanish sailor, a marlingspike in his hand, was seen, who made what seemed an imperfect gesture towards the balcony, but immediately[,] as if alarmed by some advancing step along the deck within, vanished into the recesses of the hempen forest, like a poacher.

192.   What meant this? Something the man had sought to communicate, unbeknown to any one, even to his captain. Did the secret involve aught unfavorable to his captain? Were those previous misgivings of Captain Delano's about to be verified? Or, in his haunted mood at the moment, had some random, unintentional motion of the man, while busy with the stay, as if repairing it, been mistaken for a significant beckoning?

193.   Not unbewildered, again he gazed off for his boat. But it was temporarily hidden by a rocky spur of the isle. As with some eagerness he bent forward, watching for the first shooting view of its beak, the balustrade gave way before him like charcoal. Had he not clutched an outreaching rope he would have fallen into the sea. The crash, though feeble, and the fall, though hollow, of the rotten fragments, must have been overheard. He glanced up. With sober curiosity peering down upon him was one of the old oakum-pickers, slipped from his perch to an outside boom; while below the old negro, and, invisible to him, reconnoitering from a port-hole like a fox from the mouth of its den, crouched the Spanish sailor again. From something suddenly suggested by the man's air, the mad idea now darted into Captain Delano's mind, that Don Benito's plea of indisposition, in withdrawing below, was but a pretense: that he was engaged there maturing his plot, of which the sailor, by some means gaining an inkling, had a mind to warn the stranger against; incited, it may be, by gratitude

for a kind word on first boarding the ship. Was it from foreseeing some possible interference like this, that Don Benito had, beforehand, given such a bad character of his sailors, while praising the negroes; though, indeed, the former seemed as docile as the latter the contrary? The whites, too, by nature, were the shrewder race. A man with some evil design, would he not be likely to speak well of that stupidity which was blind to his depravity, and malign that intelligence from which it might not be hidden? Not unlikely, perhaps. But if the whites had dark secrets concerning Don Benito, could then Don Benito be any way in complicity with the blacks? But they were too stupid. Besides, who ever heard of a white so far a renegade as to apostatize from his very species almost, by leaguing in against it with negroes? These difficulties recalled former ones. Lost in their mazes, Captain Delano, who had now regained the deck, was uneasily advancing along it, when he observed a new face; an aged sailor seated cross-legged near the main hatchway. His skin was shrunk up with wrinkles like a pelican's empty pouch; his hair frosted; his countenance grave and composed. His hands were full of ropes, which he was working into a large knot. Some blacks were about him obligingly dipping the strands for him, here and there, as the exigencies of the operation demanded.

194. Captain Delano crossed over to him, and stood in silence surveying the knot; his mind, by a not uncongenial transition, passing from its own entanglements to those of the hemp. For intricacy, such a knot he had never seen in an American ship, nor indeed any other. The old man looked like an Egyptian priest, making Gordian knots for the temple of Ammon.[33] The knot seemed a combination of double-bowline-knot, treble-crown-knot, back-handed-well- knot, knot-in-and-out-knot, and jamming-knot.

195. At last, puzzled to comprehend the meaning of such a knot, Captain Delano addressed the knotter:—

196. "What are you knotting there, my man?"

197. "The knot," was the brief reply, without looking up.

198. "So it seems; but what is it for?"

199. "For some one else to undo," muttered back the old man, plying his fingers harder than ever, the knot being now nearly completed.

200. While Captain Delano stood watching him, suddenly the old man threw the knot towards him, saying in broken English—the first heard in the ship —something to this effect: "Undo it, cut it, quick." It was said lowly, but with such condensation of rapidity, that the long, slow words in Spanish, which had preceded and followed, almost operated as covers to the brief English between.

201. For a moment, knot in hand, and knot in head, Captain Delano stood mute; while, without further heeding him, the old man was now intent upon other ropes. Presently there was a slight stir behind Captain Delano. Turning, he saw the chained negro, Atufal, standing quietly there.

30

The next moment the old sailor rose, muttering, and, followed by his subordinate negroes, removed to the forward part of the ship, where in the crowd he disappeared.

202.   An elderly negro, in a clout like an infant's, and with a pepper and salt head, and a kind of attorney air, now approached Captain Delano. In tolerable Spanish, and with a good-natured, knowing wink, he informed him that the old knotter was simple-witted, but harmless; often playing his odd tricks. The negro concluded by begging the knot, for of course the stranger would not care to be troubled with it. Unconsciously, it was handed to him. With a sort of congé, the negro received it, and, turning his back, ferreted into it like a detective custom-house officer after smuggled laces. Soon, with some African word, equivalent to pshaw, he tossed the knot overboard.

203.   All this is very queer now, thought Captain Delano, with a qualmish sort of emotion; but, as one feeling incipient sea-sickness, he strove, by ignoring the symptoms, to get rid of the malady. Once more he looked off for his boat. To his delight, it was now again in view, leaving the rocky spur astern.

204.   The sensation here experienced, after at first relieving his uneasiness, with unforeseen efficacy soon began to remove it. The less distant sight of that well-known boat—showing it, not as before, half blended with the haze, but with outline defined, so that its individuality, like a man's, was manifest; that boat, Rover by name, which, though now in strange seas, had often pressed the beach of Captain Delano's home, and, brought to its threshold for repairs, had familiarly lain there, as a Newfoundland dog; the sight of that household boat evoked a thousand trustful associations, which, contrasted with previous suspicions, filled him not only with lightsome confidence, but somehow with half humorous self-reproaches at his former lack of it.[34]

205.   "What, I, Amasa Delano—Jack of the Beach, as they called me when a lad—I, Amasa; the same that, duck-satchel in hand, used to paddle along the water-side to the school-house made from the old hulk—I, little Jack of the Beach, that used to go berrying with cousin Nat and the rest; I to be murdered here at the ends of the earth, on board a haunted pirate-ship by a horrible Spaniard? Too nonsensical to think of! Who would murder Amasa Delano? His conscience is clean. There is some one above. Fie, fie, Jack of the Beach! you are a child indeed; a child of the second childhood, old boy; you are beginning to dote and drule, I'm afraid."

206.   Light of heart and foot, he stepped aft, and there was met by Don Benito's servant, who, with a pleasing expression, responsive to his own present feelings, informed him that his master had recovered from the effects of his coughing fit, and had just ordered him to go present his compliments to his good guest, Don Amasa, and say that he (Don Benito) would

soon have the happiness to rejoin him.

207.   There now, do you mark that? again thought Captain Delano, walking the poop. What a donkey I was. This kind gentleman who here sends me his kind compliments, he, but ten minutes ago, dark-lantern in [hand], was dodging round some old grind-stone in the hold, sharpening a hatchet for me, I thought. Well, well; these long calms have a morbid effect on the mind, I've often heard, though I never believed it before. Ha! glancing towards the boat; there's Rover; good dog; a white bone in her mouth. A pretty big bone though, seems to me.—What? Yes, she has fallen afoul of the bubbling tide-rip there. It sets her the other way, too, for the time. Patience.

208.   It was now about noon, though, from the grayness of everything, it seemed to be getting towards dusk.

209.   The calm was confirmed. In the far distance, away from the influence of land, the leaden ocean seemed laid out and leaded up, its course finished, soul gone, defunct. But the current from landward, where the ship was, increased; silently sweeping her further and further towards the tranced waters beyond.

210.   Still, from his knowledge of those latitudes, cherishing hopes of a breeze, and a fair and fresh one, at any moment, Captain Delano, despite present prospects, buoyantly counted upon bringing the San Dominick safely to anchor ere night. The distance swept over was nothing; since, with a good wind, ten minutes' sailing would retrace more than sixty minutes, drifting. Meantime, one moment turning to mark "Rover" fighting the tide-rip, and the next to see Don Benito approaching, he continued walking the poop.

211.   Gradually he felt a vexation arising from the delay of his boat; this soon merged into uneasiness; and at last—his eye falling continually, as from a stage-box into the pit, upon the strange crowd before and below him, and, by-and-by, recognizing there the face—now composed to indifference— of the Spanish sailor who had seemed to beckon from the main-chains— something of his old trepidations returned.

212.   Ah, thought he—gravely enough—this is like the ague: because it went off, it follows not that it won't come back.

213.   Though ashamed of the relapse, he could not altogether subdue it; and so, exerting his good-nature to the utmost, insensibly he came to a compromise.

214.   Yes, this is a strange craft; a strange history, too, and strange folks on board. But—nothing more.

215.   By way of keeping his mind out of mischief till the boat should arrive, he tried to occupy it with turning over and over, in a purely speculative sort of way, some lesser peculiarities of the captain and crew. Among others, four curious points recurred:

216.   First, the affair of the Spanish lad assailed with a knife by the slave boy; an act winked at by Don Benito. Second, the tyranny in Don Benito's treatment of Atufal, the black; as if a child should lead a bull of the Nile by the ring in his nose. Third, the trampling of the sailor by the two negroes; a piece of insolence passed over without so much as a reprimand. Fourth, the cringing submission to their [master of] all the ship's underlings, mostly blacks; as if by the least inadvertence they feared to draw down his despotic displeasure.

217.   Coupling these points, they seemed somewhat contradictory. But what then, thought Captain Delano, glancing towards his now nearing boat— what then? Why, Don Benito is a very capricious commander. But he is not the first of the sort I have seen; though it's true he rather exceeds any other. But as a nation—continued he in his reveries—these Spaniards are all an odd set; the very word Spaniard has a curious, conspirator, Guy-Fawkish twang to it.[35] And yet, I dare say, Spaniards in the main are as good folks as any in Duxbury, Massachusetts. Ah good! At last "Rover" has come.

218.   As, with its welcome freight, the boat touched the side, the oakum-pickers, with venerable gestures, sought to restrain the blacks, who, at the sight of three gurried water-casks in its bottom, and a pile of wilted pumpkins in its bow, hung over the bulwarks in disorderly raptures.

219.   Don Benito, with his servant, now appeared; his coming, perhaps, hastened by hearing the noise. Of him Captain Delano sought permission to serve out the water, so that all might share alike, and none injure themselves by unfair excess. But sensible, and, on Don Benito's account, kind as this offer was, it was received with what seemed impatience; as if aware that he lacked energy as a commander, Don Benito, with the true jealousy of weakness, resented as an affront any interference. So, at least, Captain Delano inferred.

220.   In another moment the casks were being hoisted in, when some of the eager negroes accidentally jostled Captain Delano, where he stood by the gangway; so that, unmindful of Don Benito, yielding to the impulse of the moment, with good-natured authority he bade the blacks stand back; to enforce his words making use of a half-mirthful, half-menacing gesture. Instantly the blacks paused, just where they were, each negro and negress suspended in his or her posture, exactly as the word had found them—for a few seconds continuing so—while, as between the responsive posts of a telegraph, an unknown syllable ran from man to man among the perched oakum-pickers. While the visitor's attention was fixed by this scene, suddenly the hatchet-polishers half rose, and a rapid cry came from Don Benito.

221.   Thinking that at the signal of the Spaniard he was about to be massacred, Captain Delano would have sprung for his boat, but paused, as the

oakum-pickers, dropping down into the crowd with earnest exclamations, forced every white and every negro back, at the same moment, with gestures friendly and familiar, almost jocose, bidding him, in substance, not be a fool. Simultaneously the hatchet-polishers resumed their seats, quietly as so many tailors, and at once, as if nothing had happened, the work of hoisting in the casks was resumed, whites and blacks singing at the tackle.

222. Captain Delano glanced towards Don Benito. As he saw his meagre form in the act of recovering itself from reclining in the servant's arms, into which the agitated invalid had fallen, he could not but marvel at the panic by which himself had been surprised, on the darting supposition that such a commander, who, upon a legitimate occasion, so trivial, too, as it now appeared, could lose all self-command, was, with energetic iniquity, going to bring about his murder.

223. The casks being on deck, Captain Delano was handed a number of jars and cups by one of the steward's aids, who, in the name of his captain, entreated him to do as he had proposed—dole out the water. He complied, with republican impartiality as to this republican element, which always seeks one level, serving the oldest white no better than the youngest black; excepting, indeed, poor Don Benito, whose condition, if not rank, demanded an extra allowance. To him, in the first place, Captain Delano presented a fair pitcher of the fluid; but, thirsting as he was for it, the Spaniard quaffed not a drop until after several grave bows and salutes. A reciprocation of courtesies which the sight-loving Africans hailed with clapping of hands.

224. Two of the less wilted pumpkins being reserved for the cabin table, the residue were minced up on the spot for the general regalement. But the soft bread, sugar, and bottled cider, Captain Delano would have given the whites alone, and in chief Don Benito; but the latter objected; which disinterestedness not a little pleased the American; and so mouthfuls all around were given alike to whites and blacks; excepting one bottle of cider, which Babo insisted upon setting aside for his master.[36]

225. Here it may be observed that as, on the first visit of the boat, the American had not permitted his men to board the ship, neither did he now; being unwilling to add to the confusion of the decks.

226. Not uninfluenced by the peculiar good-humor at present prevailing, and for the time oblivious of any but benevolent thoughts, Captain Delano, who, from recent indications, counted upon a breeze within an hour or two at furthest, dispatched the boat back to the sealer, with orders for all the hands that could be spared immediately to set about rafting casks to the watering-place and filling them. Likewise he bade word be carried to his chief officer, that if, against present expectation, the ship was not brought to anchor by sunset, he need be under no concern; for as there

was to be a full moon that night, he (Captain Delano) would remain on board ready to play the pilot, come the wind soon or late.

227.   As the two Captains stood together, observing the departing boat—the servant, as it happened, having just spied a spot on his master's velvet sleeve, and silently engaged rubbing it out—the American expressed his regrets that the San Dominick had no boats; none, at least, but the unseaworthy old hulk of the long-boat, which, warped as a camel's skeleton in the desert, and almost as bleached, lay pot-wise inverted amid-ships, one side a little tipped, furnishing a subterranean sort of den for family groups of the blacks, mostly women and small children; who, squatting on old mats below, or perched above in the dark dome, on the elevated seats, were descried, some distance within, like a social circle of bats, sheltering in some friendly cave; at intervals, ebon flights of naked boys and girls, three or four years old, darting in and out of the den's mouth.

228.   "Had you three or four boats now, Don Benito," said Captain Delano, "I think that, by tugging at the oars, your negroes here might help along matters some. Did you sail from port without boats, Don Benito?"

229.   "They were stove in the gales, Senor."

230.   "That was bad. Many men, too, you lost then. Boats and men. Those must have been hard gales, Don Benito."

231.   "Past all speech," cringed the Spaniard.

232.   "Tell me, Don Benito," continued his companion with increased interest, "tell me, were these gales immediately off the pitch of Cape Horn?"

233.   "Cape Horn?—who spoke of Cape Horn?"

234.   "Yourself did, when giving me an account of your voyage," answered Captain Delano, with almost equal astonishment at this eating of his own words, even as he ever seemed eating his own heart, on the part of the Spaniard. "You yourself, Don Benito, spoke of Cape Horn," he emphatically repeated.

235.   The Spaniard turned, in a sort of stooping posture, pausing an instant, as one about to make a plunging exchange of elements, as from air to water.

236.   At this moment a messenger-boy, a white, hurried by, in the regular performance of his function carrying the last expired half hour forward to the forecastle, from the cabin time-piece, to have it struck at the ship's large bell.

237.   "Master," said the servant, discontinuing his work on the coat sleeve, and addressing the rapt Spaniard with a sort of timid apprehensiveness, as one charged with a duty, the discharge of which, it was foreseen, would prove irksome to the very person who had imposed it, and for whose benefit it was intended, "master told me never mind where he was, or how engaged, always to remind him, to a minute, when shaving-time comes. Miguel has gone to strike the half-hour afternoon. It is

now, master. Will master go into the cuddy?"

238.   "Ah—yes," answered the Spaniard, starting, as from dreams into realities; then turning upon Captain Delano, he said that ere long he would resume the conversation.

239.   "Then if master means to talk more to Don Amasa," said the servant, "why not let Don Amasa sit by master in the cuddy, and master can talk, and Don Amasa can listen, while Babo here lathers and strops."

240.   "Yes," said Captain Delano, not unpleased with this sociable plan, "yes, Don Benito, unless you had rather not, I will go with you."

241.   "Be it so, Senor."

242.   As the three passed aft, the American could not but think it another strange instance of his host's capriciousness, this being shaved with such uncommon punctuality in the middle of the day. But he deemed it more than likely that the servant's anxious fidelity had something to do with the matter; inasmuch as the timely interruption served to rally his master from the mood which had evidently been coming upon him.

243.   The place called the cuddy was a light deck-cabin formed by the poop, a sort of attic to the large cabin below. Part of it had formerly been the quarters of the officers; but since their death all the partitionings had been thrown down, and the whole interior converted into one spacious and airy marine hall; for absence of fine furniture and picturesque disarray of odd appurtenances, somewhat answering to the wide, cluttered hall of some eccentric bachelor-squire in the country, who hangs his shooting-jacket and tobacco- pouch on deer antlers, and keeps his fishing-rod, tongs, and walking-stick in the same corner.

244.   The similitude was heightened, if not originally suggested, by glimpses of the surrounding sea; since, in one aspect, the country and the ocean seem cousins-german.

245.   The floor of the cuddy was matted. Overhead, four or five old muskets were stuck into horizontal holes along the beams. On one side was a claw-footed old table lashed to the deck; a thumbed missal on it, and over it a small, meagre crucifix attached to the bulk-head. Under the table lay a dented cutlass or two, with a hacked harpoon, among some melancholy old rigging, like a heap of poor friars' girdles. There were also two long, sharp-ribbed settees of Malacca cane, black with age, and uncomfortable to look at as inquisitors' racks, with a large, misshapen arm-chair, which, furnished with a rude barber's crotch at the back, working with a screw, seemed some grotesque engine of torment. A flag locker was in one corner, open, exposing various colored bunting, some rolled up, others half unrolled, still others tumbled. Opposite was a cumbrous washstand, of black mahogany, all of one block, with a pedestal, like a font, and over it a railed shelf, containing combs, brushes, and other implements of the toilet. A torn hammock of stained grass swung near; the sheets tossed, and the pil-

low wrinkled up like a brow, as if who ever slept here slept but illy, with alternate visitations of sad thoughts and bad dreams.[37]

246. The further extremity of the cuddy, overhanging the ship's stern, was pierced with three openings, windows or port-holes, according as men or cannon might peer, socially or unsocially, out of them. At present neither men nor cannon were seen, though huge ring-bolts and other rusty iron fixtures of the wood-work hinted of twenty-four-pounders.

247. Glancing towards the hammock as he entered, Captain Delano said, "You sleep here, Don Benito?"

248. "Yes, Senor, since we got into mild weather."

249. "This seems a sort of dormitory, sitting-room, sail-loft, chapel, armory, and private closet all together, Don Benito," added Captain Delano, looking round.[38]

250. "Yes, Senor; events have not been favorable to much order in my arrangements."

251. Here the servant, napkin on arm, made a motion as if waiting his master's good pleasure. Don Benito signified his readiness, when, seating him in the Malacca arm-chair, and for the guest's convenience drawing opposite one of the settees, the servant commenced operations by throwing back his master's collar and loossening his cravat.

252. There is something in the negro which, in a peculiar way, fits him for avocations about one's person. Most negroes are natural valets and hairdressers; taking to the comb and brush congenially as to the castinets, and flourishing them apparently with almost equal satisfaction. There is, too, a smooth tact about them in this employment, with a marvelous, noiseless, gliding briskness, not ungraceful in its way, singularly pleasing to behold, and still more so to be the manipulated subject of. And above all is the great gift of good-humor. Not the mere grin or laugh is here meant. Those were unsuitable. But a certain easy cheerfulness, harmonious in every glance and gesture; as though God had set the whole negro to some pleasant tune.

253. When to this is added the docility arising from the unaspiring contentment of a limited mind, and that susceptibility of blind attachment sometimes inhering in indisputable inferiors, one readily perceives why those hypochondriacs, Johnson and Byron—it may be, something like the hypochondriac Benito Cereno—took to their hearts, almost to the exclusion of the entire white race, their serving men, the negroes, Barber and Fletcher.[39] But if there be that in the negro which exempts him from the inflicted sourness of the morbid or cynical mind, how, in his most prepossessing aspects, must he appear to a benevolent one? When at ease with respect to exterior things, Captain Delano's nature was not only benign, but familiarly and humorously so. At home, he had often taken rare satisfaction in sitting in his door, watching some free man of color at his work

or play. If on a voyage he chanced to have a black sailor, invariably he was on chatty and half-gamesome terms with him. In fact, like most men of a good, blithe heart, Captain Delano took to negroes, not philanthropically, but genially, just as other men to Newfoundland dogs.

254.   Hitherto, the circumstances in which he found the San Dominick had repressed the tendency. But in the cuddy, relieved from his former uneasiness, and, for various reasons, more sociably inclined than at any previous period of the day, and seeing the colored servant, napkin on arm, so debonair about his master, in a business so familiar as that of shaving, too, all his old weakness for negroes returned.

255.   Among other things, he was amused with an odd instance of the African love of bright colors and fine shows, in the black's informally taking from the flag-locker a great piece of bunting of all hues, and lavishly tucking it under his master's chin for an apron.

256.   The mode of shaving among the Spaniards is a little different from what it is with other nations. They have a basin, specifically called a barber's basin, which on one side is scooped out, so as accurately to receive the chin, against which it is closely held in lathering; which is done, not with a brush, but with soap dipped in the water of the basin and rubbed on the face.

257.   In the present instance salt-water was used for lack of better; and the parts lathered were only the upper lip, and low down under the throat, all the rest being cultivated beard.

258.   The preliminaries being somewhat novel to Captain Delano, he sat curiously eying them, so that no conversation took place, nor, for the present, did Don Benito appear disposed to renew any.

259.   Setting down his basin, the negro searched among the razors, as for the sharpest, and having found it, gave it an additional edge by expertly strapping it on the firm, smooth, oily skin of his open palm; he then made a gesture as if to begin, but midway stood suspended for an instant, one hand elevating the razor, the other professionally dabbling among the bubbling suds on the Spaniard's lank neck. Not unaffected by the close sight of the gleaming steel, Don Benito nervously shuddered; his usual ghastliness was heightened by the lather, which lather, again, was intensified in its hue by the contrasting sootiness of the negro's body. Altogether the scene was somewhat peculiar, at least to Captain Delano, nor, as he saw the two thus postured, could he resist the vagary, that in the black he saw a headsman, and in the white a man at the block. But this was one of those antic conceits, appearing and vanishing in a breath, from which, perhaps, the best regulated mind is not always free.

260.   Meantime the agitation of the Spaniard had a little loosened the bunting from around him, so that one broad fold swept curtain-like over the chair-arm to the floor, revealing, amid a profusion of armorial bars and ground-

colors —black, blue, and yellow—a closed castle in a blood red field diagonal with a lion rampant in a white.

261. "The castle and the lion" exclaimed Captain Delano—"why, Don Benito, this is the flag of Spain you use here. It's well it's only I, and not the King, that sees this," he added, with a smile, "but"—turning towards the black— "it's all one, I suppose, so the colors be gay;" which playful remark did not fail somewhat to tickle the negro.

262. "Now, master," he said, readjusting the flag, and pressing the head gently further back into the crotch of the chair; "now, master," and the steel glanced nigh the throat.

263. Again Don Benito faintly shuddered.

264. "You must not shake so, master. See, Don Amasa, master always shakes when I shave him. And yet master knows I never yet have drawn blood, though it's true, if master will shake so, I may some of these times. Now master," he continued. "And now, Don Amasa, please go on with your talk about the gale, and all that; master can hear, and, between times, master can answer."

265. "Ah yes, these gales," said Captain Delano; "but the more I think of your voyage, Don Benito, the more I wonder, not at the gales, terrible as they must have been, but at the disastrous interval following them. For here, by your account, have you been these two months and more getting from Cape Horn to St. Maria, a distance which I myself, with a good wind, have sailed in a few days. True, you had calms, and long ones, but to be becalmed for two months, that is, at least, unusual. Why, Don Benito, had almost any other gentleman told me such a story, I should have been half disposed to a little incredulity."

266. Here an involuntary expression came over the Spaniard, similar to that just before on the deck, and whether it was the start he gave, or a sudden gawky roll of the hull in the calm, or a momentary unsteadiness of the servant's hand, however it was, just then the razor drew blood, spots of which stained the creamy lather under the throat: immediately the black barber drew back his steel, and, remaining in his professional attitude, back to Captain Delano, and face to Don Benito, held up the trickling razor, saying, with a sort of half humorous sorrow, "See, master—you shook so—here's Babo's first blood."

267. No sword drawn before James the First of England, no assassination in that timid King's presence, could have produced a more terrified aspect than was now presented by Don Benito.[40]

268. Poor fellow, thought Captain Delano, so nervous he can't even bear the sight of barber's blood; and this unstrung, sick man, is it credible that I should have imagined he meant to spill all my blood, who can't endure the sight of one little drop of his own? Surely, Amasa Delano, you have been beside yourself this day. Tell it not when you get home, sappy Amasa.

Well, well, he looks like a murderer, doesn't he? More like as if himself were to be done for. Well, well, this day's experience shall be a good lesson.

269.   Meantime, while these things were running through the honest seaman's mind, the servant had taken the napkin from his arm, and to Don Benito had said—"But answer Don Amasa, please, master, while I wipe this ugly stuff off the razor, and strop it again."

270.   As he said the words, his face was turned half round, so as to be alike visible to the Spaniard and the American, and seemed, by its expression, to hint, that he was desirous, by getting his master to go on with the conversation, considerately to withdraw his attention from the recent annoying accident. As if glad to snatch the offered relief, Don Benito resumed, rehearsing to Captain Delano, that not only were the calms of unusual duration, but the ship had fallen in with obstinate currents; and other things he added, some of which were but repetitions of former statements, to explain how it came to pass that the passage from Cape Horn to St. Maria had been so exceedingly long; now and then mingling with his words, incidental praises, less qualified than before, to the blacks, for their general good conduct. These particulars were not given consecutively, the servant, at convenient times, using his razor, and so, between the intervals of shaving, the story and panegyric went on with more than usual huskiness.

271.   To Captain Delano's imagination, now again not wholly at rest, there was something so hollow in the Spaniard's manner, with apparently some reciprocal hollowness in the servant's dusky comment of silence, that the idea flashed across him, that possibly master and man, for some unknown purpose, were acting out, both in word and deed, nay, to the very tremor of Don Benito's limbs, some juggling play before him. Neither did the suspicion of collusion lack apparent support, from the fact of those whispered conferences before mentioned. But then, what could be the object of enacting this play of the barber before him? At last, regarding the notion as a whimsy, insensibly suggested, perhaps, by the theatrical aspect of Don Benito in his harlequin ensign, Captain Delano speedily banished it.[41]

272.   The shaving over, the servant bestirred himself with a small bottle of scented waters, pouring a few drops on the head, and then diligently rubbing; the vehemence of the exercise causing the muscles of his face to twitch rather strangely.

273.   His next operation was with comb, scissors, and brush; going round and round, smoothing a curl here, clipping an unruly whisker-hair there, giving a graceful sweep to the temple-lock, with other impromptu touches evincing the hand of a master; while, like any resigned gentleman in barber's hands, Don Benito bore all, much less uneasily, at least, than he had

done the razoring; indeed, he sat so pale and rigid now, that the negro seemed a Nubian sculptor finishing off a white statue-head.[42]

274.   All being over at last, the standard of Spain removed, tumbled up, and tossed back into the flag-locker, the negro's warm breath blowing away any stray hair which might have lodged down his master's neck; collar and cravat readjusted; a speck of lint whisked off the velvet lapel; all this being done; backing off a little space, and pausing with an expression of sub- dued self- complacency, the servant for a moment surveyed his master, as, in toilet at least, the creature of his own tasteful hands.

275.   Captain Delano playfully complimented him upon his achievement; at the same time congratulating Don Benito.

276.   But neither sweet waters, nor shampooing, nor fidelity, nor sociality, delighted the Spaniard. Seeing him relapsing into forbidding gloom, and still remaining seated, Captain Delano, thinking that his presence was undesired just then, withdrew, on pretense of seeing whether, as he had prophesied, any signs of a breeze were visible.

277.   Walking forward to the main-mast, he stood awhile thinking over the scene, and not without some undefined misgivings, when he heard a noise near the cuddy, and turning, saw the negro, his hand to his cheek. Advancing, Captain Delano perceived that the cheek was bleeding. He was about to ask the cause, when the negro's wailing soliloquy enlightened him.

278.   "Ah, when will master get better from his sickness; only the sour heart that sour sickness breeds made him serve Babo so; cutting Babo with the razor, because, only by accident, Babo had given master one little scratch; and for the first time in so many a day, too. Ah, ah, ah," holding his hand to his face.

279.   Is it possible, thought Captain Delano; was it to wreak in private his Spanish spite against this poor friend of his, that Don Benito, by his sullen manner, impelled me to withdraw? Ah[,] this slavery breeds ugly passions in man.—Poor fellow!

280.   He was about to speak in sympathy to the negro, but with a timid reluctance he now re-entered the cuddy.

281.   Presently master and man came forth; Don Benito leaning on his servant as if nothing had happened.

282.   But a sort of love-quarrel, after all, thought Captain Delano.

283.   He accosted Don Benito, and they slowly walked together. They had gone but a few paces, when the steward—a tall, rajah-looking mulatto, orientally set off with a pagoda turban formed by three or four Madras handkerchiefs wound about his head, tier on tier—approaching with a saalam, announced lunch in the cabin.[43]

284.   On their way thither, the two captains were preceded by the mulatto, who, turning round as he advanced, with continual smiles and bows, ush-

ered them on, a display of elegance which quite completed the insignificance of the small bare-headed Babo, who, as if not unconscious of inferiority, eyed askance the graceful steward. But in part, Captain Delano
imputed his jealous watchfulness to that peculiar feeling which the full-
blooded African entertains for the adulterated one. As for the steward, his
manner, if not bespeaking much dignity of self-respect, yet evidenced his
extreme desire to please; which is doubly meritorious, as at once Christian
and Chesterfieldian.[44]

285.   Captain Delano observed with interest that while the complexion of the
mulatto was hybrid, his physiognomy was European—classically so.

286.   "Don Benito," whispered he, "I am glad to see this usher-of-the-
golden-rod of yours;[45] the sight refutes an ugly remark once made to me
by a Barbadoes planter; that when a mulatto has a regular European face,
look out for him; he is a devil. But see, your steward here has features
more regular than King George's of England; and yet there he nods, and
bows, and smiles; a king, indeed—the king of kind hearts and polite fellows.[46] What a pleasant voice he has, too?["]

287.   "He has, Senor."

288.   "But tell me, has he not, so far as you have known him, always proved
a good, worthy fellow?" said Captain Delano, pausing, while with a final
genuflexion the steward disappeared into the cabin; "come, for the reason
just mentioned, I am curious to know."

289.   "Francesco is a good man," a sort of sluggishly responded Don Benito,
like a phlegmatic appreciator, who would neither find fault nor flatter.[47]

290.   "Ah, I thought so. For it were strange, indeed, and not very creditable
to us white-skins, if a little of our blood mixed with the African's, should,
far from improving the latter's quality, have the sad effect of pouring vit-
riolic acid into black broth; improving the hue, perhaps, but not the
wholesomeness."

291.   "Doubtless, doubtless, Senor, but"—glancing at Babo—"not to speak
of negroes, your planter's remark I have heard applied to the Spanish and
Indian intermixtures in our provinces. But I know nothing about the matter," he listlessly added.

292.   And here they entered the cabin.

293.   The lunch was a frugal one. Some of Captain Delano's fresh fish and
pumpkins, biscuit and salt beef, the reserved bottle of cider, and the San
Dominick's last bottle of Canary.[48]

294.   As they entered, Francesco, with two or three colored aids, was hovering over the table giving the last adjustments. Upon perceiving their master they withdrew, Francesco making a smiling congé, and the Spaniard,
without condescending to notice it, fastidiously remarking to his companion that he relished not superfluous attendance.

295.   Without companions, host and guest sat down, like a childless married

couple, at opposite ends of the table, Don Benito waving Captain Delano to his place, and, weak as he was, insisting upon that gentleman being seated before himself.

296.   The negro placed a rug under Don Benito's feet, and a cushion behind his back, and then stood behind, not his master's chair, but Captain Delano's. At first, this a little surprised the latter. But it was soon evident that, in taking his position, the black was still true to his master; since by facing him he could the more readily anticipate his slightest want.

297.   "This is an uncommonly intelligent fellow of yours, Don Benito," whispered Captain Delano across the table.

298.   "You say true, Senor."

299.   During the repast, the guest again reverted to parts of Don Benito's story, begging further particulars here and there. He inquired how it was that the scurvy and fever should have committed such wholesale havoc upon the whites, while destroying less than half of the blacks. As if this question reproduced the whole scene of plague before the Spaniard's eyes, miserably reminding him of his solitude in a cabin where before he had had so many friends and officers round him, his hand shook, his face became hueless, broken words escaped; but directly the sane memory of the past seemed replaced by insane terrors of the present. With starting eyes he stared before him at vacancy. For nothing was to be seen but the hand of his servant pushing the Canary over towards him.[49] At length a few sips served partially to restore him. He made random reference to the different constitution of races, enabling one to offer more resistance to certain maladies than another. The thought was new to his companion.

300.   Presently Captain Delano, intending to say something to his host concerning the pecuniary part of the business he had undertaken for him, especially—since he was strictly accountable to his owners—with reference to the new suit of sails, and other things of that sort; and naturally preferring to conduct such affairs in private, was desirous that the servant should withdraw; imagining that Don Benito for a few minutes could dispense with his attendance. He, however, waited awhile; thinking that, as the conversation proceeded, Don Benito, without being prompted, would perceive the propriety of the step.

301.   But it was otherwise. At last catching his host's eye, Captain Delano, with a slight backward gesture of his thumb, whispered, "Don Benito, pardon me, but there is an interference with the full expression of what I have to say to you."

302.   Upon this the Spaniard changed countenance; which was imputed to his resenting the hint, as in some way a reflection upon his servant. After a moment's pause, he assured his guest that the black's remaining with them could be of no disservice; because since losing his officers he had made Babo (whose original office, it now appeared, had been captain of

the slaves) not only his constant attendant and companion, but in all things his confidant.

303.   After this, nothing more could be said; though, indeed, Captain Delano could hardly avoid some little tinge of irritation upon being left ungratified in so inconsiderable a wish, by one, too, for whom he intended such solid services. But it is only his querulousness, thought he; and so filling his glass he proceeded to business.

304.   The price of the sails and other matters was fixed upon. But while this was being done, the American observed that, though his original offer of assistance had been hailed with hectic animation, yet now when it was reduced to a business transaction, indifference and apathy were betrayed. Don Benito, in fact, appeared to submit to hearing the details more out of regard to common propriety, than from any impression that weighty benefit to himself and his voyage was involved.

305.   Soon, his manner became still more reserved. The effort was vain to seek to draw him into social talk. Gnawed by his splenetic mood, he sat twitching his beard, while to little purpose the hand of his servant, mute as that on the wall, slowly pushed over the Canary.

306.   Lunch being over, they sat down on the cushioned transom; the servant placing a pillow behind his master. The long continuance of the calm had now affected the atmosphere. Don Benito sighed heavily, as if for breath.

307.   "Why not adjourn to the cuddy," said Captain Delano; "there is more air there." But the host sat silent and motionless.

308.   Meantime his servant knelt before him, with a large fan of feathers. And Francesco coming in on tiptoes, handed the negro a little cup of aromatic waters, with which at intervals he chafed his master's brow; smoothing the hair along the temples as a nurse does a child's. He spoke no word. He only rested his eye on his master's, as if, amid all Don Benito's distress, a little to refresh his spirit by the silent sight of fidelity.

309.   Presently the ship's bell sounded two o'clock; and through the cabin windows a slight rippling of the sea was discerned; and from the desired direction.

310.   "There," exclaimed Captain Delano, "I told you so, Don Benito, look!"

311.   He had risen to his feet, speaking in a very animated tone, with a view the more to rouse his companion. But though the crimson curtain of the stern- window near him that moment fluttered against his pale cheek, Don Benito seemed to have even less welcome for the breeze than the calm.

312.   Poor fellow, thought Captain Delano, bitter experience has taught him that one ripple does not make a wind, any more than one swallow a summer. But he is mistaken for once. I will get his ship in for him, and prove it.

44

313.   Briefly alluding to his weak condition, he urged his host to remain quietly where he was, since he (Captain Delano) would with pleasure take
upon himself the responsibility of making the best use of the wind.

314.   Upon gaining the deck, Captain Delano started at the unexpected figure of Atufal, monumentally fixed at the threshold, like one of those
sculptured porters of black marble guarding the porches of Egyptian
tombs.

315.   But this time the start was, perhaps, purely physical. Atufal's presence,
singularly attesting docility even in sullenness, was contrasted with that
of the hatchet-polishers, who in patience evinced their industry; while
both spectacles showed, that lax as Don Benito's general authority might
be, still, whenever he chose to exert it, no man so savage or colossal but
must, more or less, bow.

316.   Snatching a trumpet which hung from the bulwarks, with a free step
Captain Delano advanced to the forward edge of the poop, issuing his orders in his best Spanish. The few sailors and many negroes, all equally
pleased, obediently set about heading the ship towards the harbor.

317.   While giving some directions about setting a lower stu'n'-sail,[50] suddenly Captain Delano heard a voice faithfully repeating his orders. Turning, he saw Babo, now for the time acting, under the pilot, his original
part of captain of the slaves.[51] This assistance proved valuable. Tattered
sails and warped yards were soon brought into some trim. And no brace
or halyard was pulled but to the blithe songs of the inspirited negroes.

318.   Good fellows, thought Captain Delano, a little training would make fine
sailors of them. Why see, the very women pull and sing too. These must
be some of those Ashantee negresses that make such capital soldiers, I've
heard. But who's at the helm. I must have a good hand there.

319.   He went to see.

320.   The San Dominick steered with a cumbrous tiller, with large horizontal
pullies attached. At each pully-end stood a subordinate black, and between them, at the tiller-head, [the responsible] post, a Spanish seaman,
whose countenance evinced his due share in the general hopefulness and
confidence at the coming of the breeze.

321.   He proved the same man who had behaved with so shame-faced an air
on the windlass.

322.   "Ah,—it is you, my man," exclaimed Captain Delano—"well, no
more sheep's-eyes now;—look straight forward and keep the ship so.[52]
Good hand, I trust? And want to get into the harbor, don't you?"

323.   The man assented with an inward chuckle, grasping the tiller-head
firmly. Upon this, unperceived by the American, the two blacks eyed the
sailor intently.

324.   Finding all right at the helm, the pilot went forward to the forecastle, to
see how matters stood there.

325.   The ship now had way enough to breast the current. With the approach of evening, the breeze would be sure to freshen.

326.   Having done all that was needed for the present, Captain Delano, giving his last orders to the sailors, turned aft to report affairs to Don Benito in the cabin; perhaps additionally incited to rejoin him by the hope of snatching a moment's private chat while the servant was engaged upon deck.

327.   From opposite sides, there were, beneath the poop, two approaches to the cabin; one further forward than the other, and consequently communicating with a longer passage. Marking the servant still above, Captain Delano, taking the nighest entrance—the one last named, and at whose porch Atufal still stood—hurried on his way, till, arrived at the cabin threshold, he paused an instant, a little to recover from his eagerness. Then, with the words of his intended business upon his lips, he entered. As he advanced toward the seated Spaniard, he heard another footstep, keeping time with his. From the opposite door, a salver in hand, the servant was likewise advancing.

328.   "Confound the faithful fellow," thought Captain Delano; "what a vexatious coincidence."

329.   Possibly, the vexation might have been something different, were it not for the brisk confidence inspired by the breeze. But even as it was, he felt a slight twinge, from a sudden indefinite association in his mind of Babo with Atufal.

330.   "Don Benito," said he, "I give you joy; the breeze will hold, and will increase. By the way, your tall man and time-piece, Atufal, stands without. By your order, of course?"

331.   Don Benito recoiled, as if at some bland satirical touch, delivered with such adroit garnish of apparent good breeding as to present no handle for retort.

332.   He is like one flayed alive, thought Captain Delano; where may one touch him without causing a shrink?

333.   The servant moved before his master, adjusting a cushion; recalled to civility, the Spaniard stiffly replied: "you are right. The slave appears where you saw him, according to my command; which is, that if at the given hour I am below, he must take his stand and abide my coming."

334.   "Ah now, pardon me, but that is treating the poor fellow like an ex-king indeed. Ah, Don Benito," smiling, "for all the license you permit in some things, I fear lest, at bottom, you are a bitter hard master."

335.   Again Don Benito shrank; and this time, as the good sailor thought, from a genuine twinge of his conscience.

336.   Again conversation became constrained. In vain Captain Delano called attention to the now perceptible motion of the keel gently cleaving the sea; with lack-lustre eye, Don Benito returned words few and reserved.

46

337.   By-and-by, the wind having steadily risen, and still blowing right into the harbor, bore the San Dominick swiftly on. Rounding a point of land, the sealer at distance came into open view.

338.   Meantime Captain Delano had again repaired to the deck, remaining there some time. Having at last altered the ship's course, so as to give the reef a wide berth, he returned for a few moments below.

339.   I will cheer up my poor friend, this time, thought he.

340.   "Better and better, [Don Benito,"] he cried as he blithely re-entered: "there will soon be an end to your cares, at least for awhile. For when, after a long, sad voyage, you know, the anchor drops into the haven, all its vast weight seems lifted from the captain's heart. We are getting on famously, Don Benito. My ship is in sight. Look through this side-light here; there she is; all a-taunt-o![53] The Bachelor's Delight, my good friend. Ah, how this wind braces one up. Come, you must take a cup of coffee with me this evening. My old steward will give you as fine a cup as ever any sultan tasted. What say you, Don Benito, will you?"

341.   At first, the Spaniard glanced feverishly up, casting a longing look towards the sealer, while with mute concern his servant gazed into his face. Suddenly the old ague of coldness returned, and dropping back to his cushions he was silent.

342.   "You do not answer. Come, all day you have been my host; would you have hospitality all on one side?"

343.   "I cannot go," was the response.

344.   "What? it will not fatigue you. The ships will lie together as near as they can, without swinging foul. It will be little more than stepping from deck to deck; which is but as from room to room. Come, come, you must not refuse me."

345.   "I cannot go," decisively and repulsively repeated Don Benito.

346.   Renouncing all but the last appearance of courtesy, with a sort of cadaverous sullenness, and biting his thin nails to the quick, he glanced, almost glared, at his guest, as if impatient that a stranger's presence should interfere with the full indulgence of his morbid hour. Meantime the sound of the parted waters came more and more gurglingly and merrily in at the windows; as reproaching him for his dark spleen; as telling him that, sulk as he might, and go mad with it, nature cared not a jot; since, whose fault was it, pray?[54]

347.   But the foul mood was now at its depth, as the fair wind at its height.

348.   There was something in the man so far beyond any mere unsociality or sourness previously evinced, that even the forbearing good-nature of his guest could no longer endure it. Wholly at a loss to account for such demeanor, and deeming sickness with eccentricity, however extreme, no adequate excuse, well satisfied, too, that nothing in his own conduct could justify it, Captain Delano's pride began to be roused. Himself became

reserved. But all seemed one to the Spaniard. Quitting him, therefore, Captain Delano once more went to the deck.

349. The ship was now within less than two miles of the sealer. The whale-boat was seen darting over the interval.

350. To be brief, the two vessels, thanks to the pilot's skill, ere long in neighborly style lay anchored together.

351. Before returning to his own vessel, Captain Delano had intended communicating to Don Benito the smaller details of the proposed services to be rendered. But, as it was, unwilling anew to subject himself to rebuffs, he resolved, now that he had seen the San Dominick safely moored, immediately to quit her, without further allusion to hospitality or business. Indefinitely postponing his ulterior plans, he would regulate his future actions according to future circumstances. His boat was ready to receive him; but his host still tarried below. Well, thought Captain Delano, if he has little breeding, the more need to show mine. He descended to the cabin to bid a ceremonious, and, it may be, tacitly rebukeful adieu. But to his great satisfaction, Don Benito, as if he began to feel the weight of that treatment with which his slighted guest had, not indecorously, retaliated upon him, now supported by his servant, rose to his feet, and grasping Captain Delano's hand, stood tremulous; too much agitated to speak. But the good augury hence drawn was suddenly dashed, by his resuming all his previous reserve, with augmented gloom, as, with half-averted eyes, he silently reseated himself on his cushions. With a corresponding return of his own chilled feelings, Captain Delano bowed and withdrew.

352. He was hardly midway in the narrow corridor, dim as a tunnel, leading from the cabin to the stairs, when a sound, as of the tolling for execution in some jail-yard, fell on his ears. It was the echo of the ship's flawed bell, striking the hour, drearily reverberated in this subterranean vault.[55] Instantly, by a fatality not to be withstood, his mind, responsive to the portent, swarmed with superstitious suspicions. He paused. In images far swifter than these sentences, the minutest details of all his former distrusts swept through him.

353. Hitherto, credulous good-nature had been too ready to furnish excuses for reasonable fears. Why was the Spaniard, so superfluously punctilious at times, now heedless of common propriety in not accompanying to the side his departing guest? Did indisposition forbid? Indisposition had not forbidden more irksome exertion that day. His last equivocal demeanor recurred. He had risen to his feet, grasped his guest's hand, motioned toward his hat; then, in an instant, all was eclipsed in sinister muteness and gloom. Did this imply one brief, repentant relenting at the final moment, from some iniquitous plot, followed by remorseless return to it? His last glance seemed to express a calamitous, yet acquiescent farewell to Captain Delano forever. Why decline the invitation to visit the sealer that

evening? Or was the Spaniard less hardened than the Jew, who refrained not from supping at the board of him whom the same night he meant to betray?[56] What imported all those day-long enigmas and contradictions, except they were intended to mystify, preliminary to some stealthy blow? Atufal, the pretended rebel, but punctual shadow, that moment lurked by the threshold without. He seemed a sentry, and more. Who, by his own confession, had stationed him there? Was the negro now lying in wait?

354.   The Spaniard behind—his creature before: to rush from darkness to light was the involuntary choice.

355.   The next moment, with clenched jaw and hand, he passed Atufal, and stood unharmed in the light. As he saw his trim ship lying peacefully at anchor, and almost within ordinary call; as he saw his household boat, with familiar faces in it, patiently rising and falling on the short waves by the San Dominick's side; and then, glancing about the decks where he stood, saw the oakum-pickers still gravely plying their fingers; and heard the low, buzzing whistle and industrious hum of the hatchet-polishers, still bestirring themselves over their endless occupation; and more than all, as he saw the benign aspect of nature, taking her innocent repose in the evening; the screened sun in the quiet camp of the west shining out like the mild light from Abraham's tent; as charmed eye and ear took in all these, with the chained figure of the black, clenched jaw and hand re-laxed. Once again he smiled at the phantoms which had mocked him, and felt something like a tinge of remorse, that, by harboring them even for a moment, he should, by implication, have betrayed an atheist doubt of the ever-watchful Providence above.

356.   There was a few minutes' delay, while, in obedience to his orders, the boat was being hooked along to the gangway. During this interval, a sort of saddened satisfaction stole over Captain Delano, at thinking of the kindly offices he had that day discharged for a stranger. Ah, thought he, after good actions one's conscience is never ungrateful, however much so the benefited party may be.

357.   Presently, his foot, in the first act of descent into the boat, pressed the first round of the side-ladder, his face presented inward upon the deck. In the same moment, he heard his name courteously sounded; and, to his pleased surprise, saw Don Benito advancing—an unwonted energy in his air, as if, at the last moment, intent upon making amends for his recent discourtesy. With instinctive good feeling, Captain Delano, withdrawing his foot, turned and reciprocally advanced. As he did so, the Spaniard's nervous eagerness increased, but his vital energy failed; so that, the better to support him, the servant, placing his master's hand on his naked shoul-der, and gently holding it there, formed himself into a sort of crutch.

358.   When the two captains met, the Spaniard again fervently took the hand of the American, at the same time casting an earnest glance into his eyes,

but, as before, too much overcome to speak.

359.   I have done him wrong, self-reproachfully thought Captain Delano; his apparent coldness has deceived me; in no instance has he meant to offend.

360.   Meantime, as if fearful that the continuance of the scene might too much unstring his master, the servant seemed anxious to terminate it. And so, still presenting himself as a crutch, and walking between the two captains, he advanced with them towards the gangway; while still, as if full of kindly contrition, Don Benito would not let go the hand of Captain Delano, but retained it in his, across the black's body.

361.   Soon they were standing by the side, looking over into the boat, whose crew turned up their curious eyes. Waiting a moment for the Spaniard to relinquish his hold, the now embarrassed Captain Delano lifted his foot, to overstep the threshold of the open gangway; but still Don Benito would not let go his hand. And yet, with an agitated tone, he said, "I can go no further; here I must bid you adieu. Adieu, my dear, dear Don Amasa. Go—go!" suddenly tearing his hand loose, "go, and God guard you better than me, my best friend."

362.   Not unaffected, Captain Delano would now have lingered; but catching the meekly admonitory eye of the servant, with a hasty farewell he descended into his boat, followed by the continual adieus of Don Benito, standing rooted in the gangway.

363.   Seating himself in the stern, Captain Delano, making a last salute, ordered the boat shoved off. The crew had their oars on end. The bowsmen pushed the boat a sufficient distance for the oars to be lengthwise dropped. The instant that was done, Don Benito sprang over the bulwarks, falling at the feet of Captain Delano; at the same time calling towards his ship, but in tones so frenzied, that none in the boat could understand him. But, as if not equally obtuse, three sailors, from three different and distant parts of the ship, splashed into the sea, swimming after their captain, as if intent upon his rescue.

364.   The dismayed officer of the boat eagerly asked what this meant. To which, Captain Delano, turning a disdainful smile upon the unaccountable Spaniard, answered that, for his part, he neither knew nor cared; but it seemed as if Don Benito had taken it into his head to produce the impression among his people that the boat wanted to kidnap him. "Or else—give way for your lives," he wildly added, starting at a clattering hubbub in the ship, above which rang the tocsin of the hatchet-polishers; and seizing Don Benito by the throat he added, "this plotting pirate means murder!"[57] Here, in apparent verification of the words, the servant, a dagger in his hand, was seen on the rail overhead, poised, in the act of leaping, as if with desperate fidelity to befriend his master to the last; while, seemingly to aid the black, the three white sailors were trying to clamber into the hampered bow. Meantime, the whole host of negroes, as

if inflamed at the sight of their jeopardized captain, impended in one sooty avalanche over the bulwarks.

365. All this, with what preceded, and what followed, occurred with such involutions of rapidity, that past, present, and future seemed one.

366. Seeing the negro coming, Captain Delano had flung the Spaniard aside, almost in the very act of clutching him, and, by the unconscious recoil, shifting his place, with arms thrown up, so promptly grappled the servant in his descent, that with dagger presented at Captain Delano's heart, the black seemed of purpose to have leaped there as to his mark. But the weapon was wrenched away, and the assailant dashed down into the bottom of the boat, which now, with disentangled oars, began to speed through the sea.

367. At this juncture, the left hand of Captain Delano, on one side, again clutched the half-reclined Don Benito, heedless that he was in a speechless faint, while his right foot, on the other side, ground the prostrate negro; and his right arm pressed for added speed on the after oar, his eye bent forward, encouraging his men to their utmost.[58]

368. But here, the officer of the boat, who had at last succeeded in beating off the towing sailors, and was now, with face turned aft, assisting the bowsman at his oar, suddenly called to Captain Delano, to see what the black was about; while a Portuguese oarsman shouted to him to give heed to what the Spaniard was saying.

369. Glancing down at his feet, Captain Delano saw the freed hand of the servant aiming with a second dagger—a small one, before concealed in his wool —with this he was snakishly writhing up from the boat's bottom, at the heart of his master, his countenance lividly vindictive, expressing the centred purpose of his soul; while the Spaniard, half-choked, was vainly shrinking away, with husky words, incoherent to all but the Portuguese.

370. That moment, across the long-benighted mind of Captain Delano, a flash of revelation swept, illuminating, in unanticipated clearness, his host's whole mysterious demeanor, with every enigmatic event of the day, as well as the entire past voyage of the San Dominick. He smote Babo's hand down, but his own heart smote him harder. With infinite pity he withdrew his hold from Don Benito. Not Captain Delano, but Don Benito, the black, in leaping into the boat, had intended to stab.

371. Both the black's hands were held, as, glancing up towards the San Dominick, Captain Delano, now with scales dropped from his eyes, saw the negroes, not in misrule, not in tumult, not as if frantically concerned for Don Benito, but with mask torn away, flourishing hatchets and knives, in ferocious piratical revolt. Like delirious black dervishes, the six Ashantees danced on the poop.[59] Prevented by their foes from springing into the water, the Spanish boys were hurrying up to the topmost spars, while such

of the few Spanish sailors, not already in the sea, less alert, were descried, helplessly mixed in, on deck, with the blacks.

372.　Meantime Captain Delano hailed his own vessel, ordering the ports up, and the guns run out. But by this time the cable of the San Dominick had been cut; and the fag-end, in lashing out, whipped away the canvas shroud about the beak, suddenly revealing, as the bleached hull swung round towards the open ocean, death for the figure-head, in a human skeleton; chalky comment on the chalked words below, *"Follow your leader."*

373.　At the sight, Don Benito, covering his face, wailed out: "'Tis he, Aranda! my murdered, unburied friend!"

374.　Upon reaching the sealer, calling for ropes, Captain Delano bound the negro, who made no resistance, and had him hoisted to the deck. He would then have assisted the now almost helpless Don Benito up the side; but Don Benito, wan as he was, refused to move, or be moved, until the negro should have been first put below out of view. When, presently assured that it was done, he no more shrank from the ascent.

375.　The boat was immediately dispatched back to pick up the three swimming sailors. Meantime, the guns were in readiness, though, owing to the San Dominick having glided somewhat astern of the sealer, only the aftermost one could be brought to bear. With this, they fired six times; thinking to cripple the fugitive ship by bringing down her spars. But only a few inconsiderable ropes were shot away. Soon the ship was beyond the gun's range, steering broad out of the bay; the blacks thickly clustering round the bowsprit, one moment with taunting cries towards the whites, the next with upthrown gestures hailing the now dusky moors of ocean— cawing crows escaped from the hand of the fowler.

376.　The first impulse was to slip the cables and give chase. But, upon second thoughts, to pursue with whale-boat and yawl seemed more promising.

377.　Upon inquiring of Don Benito what firearms they had on board the San Dominick, Captain Delano was answered that they had none that could be used; because, in the earlier stages of the mutiny, a cabin-passenger, since dead, had secretly put out of order the locks of what few muskets there were. But with all his remaining strength, Don Benito entreated the American not to give chase, either with ship or boat; for the negroes had already proved themselves such desperadoes, that, in case of a present assault, nothing but a total massacre of the whites could be looked for. But, regarding this warning as coming from one whose spirit had been crushed by misery[,] the American did not give up his design.

378.　The boats were got ready and armed. Captain Delano ordered his men into them. He was going himself when Don Benito grasped his arm.

379.　"What! have you saved my life, Senor, and are you now going to throw away your own?"

52

380.   The officers also, for reasons connected with their interests and those of the voyage, and a duty owing to the owners, strongly objected against their commander's going. Weighing their remonstrances a moment, Captain Delano felt bound to remain; appointing his chief mate—an athletic and resolute man, who had been a privateer's-man—to head the party. The more to encourage the sailors, they were told, that the Spanish captain considered his ship good as lost; that she and her cargo, including some gold and silver, were worth more than a thousand doubloons.[60] Take her, and no small part should be theirs. The sailors replied with a shout.

381.   The fugitives had now almost gained an offing. It was nearly night; but the moon was rising. After hard, prolonged pulling, the boats came up on the ship's quarters, at a suitable distance laying upon their oars to discharge their muskets. Having no bullets to return, the negroes sent their yells. But, upon the second volley, Indian-like, they hurtled their hatchets. One took off a sailor's fingers. Another struck the whale-boat's bow, cutting off the rope there, and remaining stuck in the gunwale like a woodman's axe. Snatching it, quivering from its lodgment, the mate hurled it back. The returned gauntlet now stuck in the ship's broken quarter-gallery, and so remained.

382.   The negroes giving too hot a reception, the whites kept a more respectful distance. Hovering now just out of reach of the hurtling hatchets, they, with a view to the close encounter which must soon come, sought to decoy the blacks into entirely disarming themselves of their most murderous weapons in a hand-to-hand fight, by foolishly flinging them, as missiles, short of the mark, into the sea. But, ere long, perceiving the stratagem, the negroes desisted, though not before many of them had to replace their lost hatchets with handspikes; an exchange which, as counted upon, proved, in the end, favorable to the assailants.

383.   Meantime, with a strong wind, the ship still clove the water; the boats alternately falling behind, and pulling up, to discharge fresh volleys.

384.   The fire was mostly directed towards the stern, since there, chiefly, the negroes, at present, were clustering. But to kill or maim the negroes was not the object. To take them, with the ship, was the object. To do it, the ship must be boarded; which could not be done by boats while she was sailing so fast.

385.   A thought now struck the mate. Observing the Spanish boys still aloft, high as they could get, he called to them to descend to the yards, and cut adrift the sails. It was done. About this time, owing to causes hereafter to be shown, two Spaniards, in the dress of sailors, and conspicuously showing themselves, were killed; not by volleys, but by deliberate marksman's shots; while, as it afterwards appeared, by one of the general discharges, Atufal, the black, and the Spaniard at the helm likewise were killed.[61] What now, with the loss of the sails, and loss of leaders, the ship became

unmanageable to the negroes.

386.　　With creaking masts, she came heavily round to the wind; the prow slowly swinging into view of the boats, its skeleton gleaming in the horizontal moonlight, and casting a gigantic ribbed shadow upon the water. One extended arm of the ghost seemed beckoning the whites to avenge it.[62]

387.　　"Follow your leader!" cried the mate; and, one on each bow, the boats boarded.[63] Sealing-spears and cutlasses crossed hatchets and handspikes. Huddled upon the long-boat amidships, the negresses raised a wailing chant, whose chorus was the clash of the steel.

388.　　For a time, the attack wavered; the negroes wedging themselves to beat it back; the half-repelled sailors, as yet unable to gain a footing, fighting as troopers in the saddle, one leg sideways flung over the bulwarks, and one without, plying their cutlasses like carters' whips.[64] But in vain. They were almost overborne, when, rallying themselves into a squad as one man, with a huzza, they sprang inboard, where, entangled, they involuntarily separated again. For a few breaths' space, there was a vague, muffled, inner sound, as of submerged sword-fish rushing hither and thither through shoals of black-fish. Soon, in a reunited band, and joined by the Spanish seamen, the whites came to the surface, irresistibly driving the negroes toward the stern. But a barricade of casks and sacks, from side to side, had been thrown up by the mainmast. Here the negroes faced about, and though scorning peace or truce, yet fain would have had respite. But, without pause, overleaping the barrier, the unflagging sailors again closed. Exhausted, the blacks now fought in despair. Their red tongues lolled, wolf-like, from their black mouths. But the pale sailors' teeth were set; not a word was spoken; and, in five minutes more, the ship was won.

389.　　Nearly a score of the negroes were killed. Exclusive of those by the balls, many were mangled; their wounds—mostly inflicted by the long-edged sealing-spears, resembling those shaven ones of the English at Preston Pans, made by the poled scythes of the Highlanders.[65] On the other side, none were killed, though several were wounded; some severely, including the mate. The surviving negroes were temporarily secured, and the ship, towed back into the harbor at midnight, once more lay anchored.

390.　　Omitting the incidents and arrangements ensuing, suffice it that, after two days spent in refitting, the ships sailed in company for Conception, in Chili, and thence for Lima, in Peru; where, before the vice-regal courts, the whole affair, from the beginning, underwent investigation.

391.　　Though, midway on the passage, the ill-fated Spaniard, relaxed from constraint, showed some signs of regaining health with free-will; yet, agreeably to his own foreboding, shortly before arriving at Lima, he relapsed, finally becoming so reduced as to be carried ashore in arms. Hearing of his story and plight, one of the many religious institutions of the City of Kings opened an hospitable refuge to him, where both physician and priest were his nurses, and a member of the order volunteered to be his one special guardian and consoler, by night and by day.

392.   The following extracts, translated from one of the official Spanish documents, will, it is hoped, shed light on the preceding narrative, as well as, in the first place, reveal the true port of departure and true history of the San Dominick's voyage, down to the time of her touching at the island of St. Maria.

393.   But, ere the extracts come, it may be well to preface them with a remark.

394.   The document selected, from among many others, for partial translation, contains the deposition of Benito Cereno; the first taken in the case. Some disclosures therein were, at the time, held dubious for both learned and natural reasons. The tribunal inclined to the opinion that the deponent, not undisturbed in his mind by recent events, raved of some things which could never have happened. But subsequent depositions of the surviving sailors, bearing out the revelations of their captain in several of the strangest particulars, gave credence to the rest. So that the tribunal, in its final decision, rested its capital sentences upon statements which, had they lacked confirmation, it would have deemed it but duty to reject.[66]

---

395.   I, DON JOSE DE ABOS AND PADILLA, His Majesty's Notary for the Royal Revenue, and Register of this Province, and Notary Public of the Holy Crusade of this Bishopric, etc.

396.   Do certify and declare, as much as is requisite in law, that, in the criminal cause commenced the twenty-fourth of the month of September, in the year seventeen hundred and ninety-nine, against the negroes of the ship San Dominick,[67] the following declaration before me was made:

397.   *Declaration of the first witness,* DON BENITO CERENO.

398.   The same day, and month, and year, His Honor, Doctor Juan Martinez de Rozas,[68] Councilor of the Royal Audience of this Kingdom, and learned in the law of this Intendency, ordered the captain of the ship San Dominick, Don Benito Cereno,[69] to appear; which he did in his litter, attended by the monk Infelez;[70] of whom he received the oath, which he took by God, our Lord, and a sign of the Cross; under which he promised to tell the truth of whatever he should know and should be asked;—and being interrogated agreeably to the tenor of the act commencing the process, he said, that on the twentieth of May last, he set sail with his ship from the port of Valparaiso, bound to that of Callao; loaded with the produce of the

country beside thirty cases of hardware and one hundred and sixty blacks, of both sexes, mostly belonging to Don Alexandro Aranda, gentleman, of the city of Mendoza; that the crew of the ship consisted of thirty-six men, beside the persons who went as passengers; that the negroes were in part as follows:

399.   *[Here, in the original, follows a list of some fifty names, descriptions, and ages, compiled from certain recovered documents of Aranda's, and also from recollections of the deponent, from which portions only are extracted.]*

400.   —One, from about eighteen to nineteen years, named José, and this was the man that waited upon his master, Don Alexandro, and who speaks well the Spanish, having served him four or five years;* * * a mulatto, named Francesco,[71] the cabin steward, of a good person and voice, having sung in the Valparaiso churches, native of the province of Buenos Ayres, aged about thirty-five years. * * * A smart negro, named Dago,[72] who had been for many years a grave-digger among the Spaniards, aged forty-six years. * * * Four old negroes, born in Africa, from sixty to seventy, but sound, calkers by trade, whose names are as follows:—the first was named Muri, and he was killed (as was also his son named Diamelo); the second, Nacta;[73] the third, Yola, likewise killed; the fourth, Ghofan;[74] and six full-grown negroes, aged from thirty to forty-five, all raw, and born among the Ashantees—Matiluqui, Yan,[75] Lecbe, Mapenda,[76] Yambaio, Akim;[77] four of whom were killed; * * * a powerful negro named Atufal, who being supposed to have been a chief in Africa, his owner set great store by him. * * * And a small negro of Senegal, but some years among the Spaniards, aged about thirty, which negro's name was Babo;* * * that he does not remember the names of the others, but that still expecting the residue of Don Alexandro's papers will be found, will then take due account of them all, and remit to the court; * * * and thirty-nine women and children of all ages.

401.   *[The catalogue over, the deposition goes on.]*

402.   * * * That all the negroes slept upon deck, as is customary in this navigation, and none wore fetters, because the owner, his friend Aranda, told him that they were all tractable; * * * that on the seventh day after leaving port, at three o'clock in the morning, all the Spaniards being asleep except the two officers on the watch, who were the boatswain, Juan Robles, and the carpenter, Juan Bautista Gayete,[78] and the helmsman and his boy, the negroes revolted suddenly, wounded dangerously the boatswain and the carpenter, and successively killed eighteen men of those who were sleeping upon deck, some with hand-spikes and hatchets, and others by

56

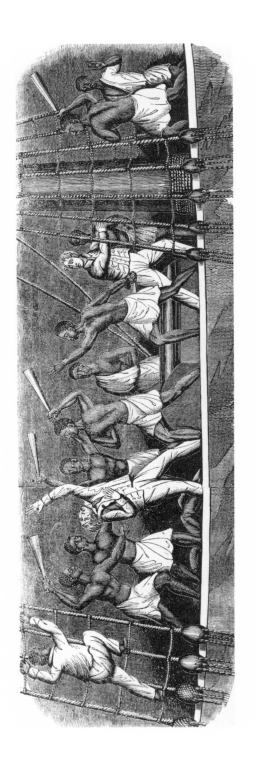

throwing them alive overboard, after tying them; that of the Spaniards upon deck, they left about seven, as he thinks, alive and tied, to manoeuvre the ship, and three or four more, who hid themselves, remained also alive. Although in the act of revolt the negroes made themselves masters of the hatchway, six or seven wounded went through it to the cockpit, without any hindrance on their part; that during the act of revolt, the mate and another person, whose name he does not recollect, attempted to come up through the hatchway, but being quickly wounded, were obliged to return to the cabin; that the deponent resolved at break of day to come up the companion-way, where the negro Babo was, being the ringleader, and Atufal, who assisted him, and having spoken to them, exhorted them to cease committing such atrocities, asking them, at the same time, what they wanted and intended to do, offering, himself, to obey their commands; that[,] notwithstanding this, they threw, in his presence, three men, alive and tied, overboard; that they told the deponent to come up, and that they would not kill him; which having done, the negro Babo asked him whether there were in those seas any negro countries where they might be carried, and he answered them, No; that the negro Babo afterwards told him to carry them to Senegal, or to the neighboring islands of St. Nicholas;[79] and he answered, that this was impossible, on account of the great distance, the necessity involved of rounding Cape Horn, the bad condition of the vessel, the want of provisions, sails, and water; but that the negro Babo replied to him he must carry them in any way; that they would do and conform themselves to everything the deponent should require as to eating and drinking; that after a long conference, being absolutely compelled to please them, for they threatened to kill all the whites if they were not, at all events, carried to Senegal, he told them that what was most wanting for the voyage was water; that they would go near the coast to take it, and thence they would proceed on their course; that the negro Babo agreed to it; and the deponent steered towards the intermediate ports, hoping to meet some Spanish or foreign vessel that would save them; that within ten or eleven days they saw the land, and continued their course by it in the vicinity of Nasca; that the deponent observed that the negroes were now restless and mutinous, because he did not effect the taking in of water, the negro Babo having required, with threats, that it should be done, without fail, the following day; he told him he saw plainly that the coast was steep, and the rivers designated in the maps were not to be found, with other reasons suitable to the circumstances; that the best way would be to go to the island of Santa Maria, where they might water easily, it being a solitary island, as the foreigners did; that the deponent did not go to Pisco, that was near, nor make any other port of the coast, because the negro Babo had intimated to him several times, that he would kill all the whites the very moment he should perceive any city, town, or settlement of any kind on the shores to which they should be carried: that having determined to go to the island of Santa Maria, as the deponent had planned, for the purpose of trying whether, on the passage or near the island itself, they could find any vessel that should favor them, or whether he could escape from it in a boat to the neighboring coast of Arruco, to adopt the necessary means he immediately changed his course, steering for the island; that the negroes Babo and Atufal held daily conferences, in which they discussed what was necessary for their design of returning to Senegal, whether they were to kill all the Spaniards, and particularly the deponent; that eight days after parting from the coast of Nasca, the deponent being on the watch a little after day-break, and soon after the negroes had their meeting, the negro Babo came to the place where the deponent was, and told him that he had determined to kill his master, Don Alexandro Aranda, both because he and his companions could not otherwise be sure of their liberty, and that to keep the seamen in subjection, he wanted to prepare a warning of what road they should be made to take did they or any of them oppose him; and that, by means of the death of Don Alexandro, that warning would best be given; but, that what this last meant, the deponent did not at the time comprehend, nor could not, further than that the death of Don Alexandro was intended; and moreover the negro Babo proposed to the deponent to call the mate Raneds, who was sleeping in the cabin, before the thing was done, for fear, as the deponent understood it, that the mate, who was a good navigator, should be killed with Don Alexandro and the rest; that the deponent, who was the friend, from youth, of Don Alexandro, prayed and conjured, but all was useless; for the negro Babo answered him that the thing could not be prevented, and that all the Spaniards risked their death if they should attempt to frustrate his will in this matter, or any other; that, in this conflict, the deponent called the mate, Raneds,[80] who was forced to go apart, and immediately the negro Babo commanded the Ashantee Martinqui and the Ashantee Lecbe to go and commit the murder; that those two went down with hatchets to the berth of Don Alexandro; that, yet half alive and mangled, they dragged him on deck; that they were going to throw him overboard in that state, but the negro Babo stopped them, bidding the murder be completed on the deck before him, which was done, when, by his orders, the body was carried below, forward; that nothing more was seen of it by the deponent for three days; * * * that Don Alonzo Sidonia,[81] an old man, long resident at Valparaiso, and lately appointed to a civil office in Peru, whither he had taken passage, was at the time sleeping in the berth opposite Don Alexandro's; that awakening at his cries, surprised by them, and at the sight of the negroes with their bloody hatchets in their hands, he threw himself into the sea through a window which was near him, and was drowned, without it

being in the power of the deponent to assist or take him up; * * * that[,]
a short time after killing Aranda, they brought upon deck his german-
cousin, of middle-age, Don Francisco Masa, of Mendoza, and the young
Don Joaquin, Marques de Aramboalaza,[82] then lately from Spain, with
his Spanish servant Ponce,[83] and the three young clerks of Aranda, José
Mozairi,[84] Lorenzo Bargas, and Hermenegildo Gandix,[85] all of Cadiz;
that Don Joaquin and Hermenegildo Gandix, the negro Babo, for purposes hereafter to appear, preserved alive; but Don Francisco Masa, José
Mozairi, and Lorenzo Bargas, with Ponce the servant, beside the boatswain, Juan Robles, the boatswain's mates, Manuel Viscaya[86] and Roderigo Hurta,[87] and four of the sailors, the negro Babo ordered to be thrown
alive into the sea, although they made no resistance, nor begged for anything else but mercy; that the boatswain, Juan Robles, who knew how to
swim, kept the longest above water, making acts of contrition, and, in the
last words he uttered, charged this deponent to cause mass to be said for
his soul to our Lady of Succor: * * * that, during the three days which
followed, the deponent, uncertain what fate had befallen the remains of
Don Alexandro, frequently asked the negro Babo where they were, and,
if still on board, whether they were to be preserved for interment ashore,
entreating him so to order it; that the negro Babo answered nothing till
the fourth day, when at sunrise, the deponent coming on deck, the negro
Babo showed him a skeleton, which had been substituted for the ship's
proper figure-head—the image of Christopher Colon,[88] the discoverer of
the New World; that the negro Babo asked him whose skeleton that was,
and whether, from its whiteness, he should not think it a white's; that,
upon [his covering] his face, the negro Babo, coming close said words to
this effect: "Keep faith with the blacks from here to Senegal, or you shall
in spirit, as now in body, follow your leader," pointing to the prow; * * *
that the same morning the negro Babo took by succession each Spaniard
forward, and asked him whose skeleton that was, and whether, from its
whiteness, he should not think it a white's; that each Spaniard covered his
face; that then to each the negro Babo repeated the words in the first place
said to the deponent; * * * that they (the Spaniards), being then assembled
aft, the negro Babo harangued them, saying that he had now done all; that
the deponent (as navigator for the negroes) might pursue his course, warning him and all of them that they should, soul and body, go the way of Don
Alexandro, if he saw them (the Spaniards) speak or plot anything against
them (the negroes)—a threat which was repeated every day; that, before
the events last mentioned, they had tied the cook to throw him overboard,
for it is not known what thing they heard him speak, but finally the negro
Babo spared his life, at the request of the deponent; that a few days after,
the deponent, endeavoring not to omit any means to preserve the lives of
the remaining whites, spoke to the negroes peace and tranquillity, and

agreed to draw up a paper, signed by the deponent and the sailors who could write, as also by the negro Babo, for himself and all the blacks, in which the deponent obliged himself to carry them to Senegal, and they not to kill any more, and he formally to make over to them the ship, with the cargo, with which they were for that time satisfied and quieted. ★ ★ But the next day, the more surely to guard against the sailors' escape, the negro Babo commanded all the boats to be destroyed but the long-boat, which was unseaworthy, and another, a cutter in good condition, which[,] knowing it would yet be wanted for towing the water casks, he had it lowered down into the hold.

★★★

403.   [*Various particulars of the prolonged and perplexed navigation ensuing here follow, with incidents of a calamitous calm, from which portion one passage is extracted, to wit:*]

★★★

404.   —That on the fifth day of the calm, all on board suffering much from the heat, and want of water, and five having died in fits, and mad, the negroes became irritable, and for a chance gesture, which they deemed suspicious —though it was harmless—made by the mate, Raneds, to the deponent in the act of handing a quadrant, they killed him; but that for this they afterwards were sorry, the mate being the only remaining navigator on board, except the deponent.

405.   —That omitting other events, which daily happened, and which can only serve uselessly to recall past misfortunes and conflicts, after seventy-three days' navigation, reckoned from the time they sailed from Nasca, during which they navigated under a scanty allowance of water, and were afflicted with the calms before mentioned, they at last arrived at the island of Santa Maria, on the seventeenth of the month of August, at about six o'clock in the afternoon, at which hour they cast anchor very near the American ship, Bachelor's Delight,[89] which lay in the same bay, commanded by the generous Captain Amasa Delano; but at six o'clock in the morning, they had already descried the port, and the negroes became uneasy, as soon as at a distance they saw the ship, not having expected to see one there; that the negro Babo pacified them, assuring them that no fear need be had; that straightway he ordered the figure on the bow to be covered with canvas, as for repairs, and had the decks a little set in order; that for a time the negro Babo and the negro Atufal conferred; that the negro Atufal was for sailing away, but the negro Babo would not, and, by himself, cast about what to do; that at last he came to the deponent, proposing to him to say and do all that the deponent declares to have said and done to the American captain; ★ ★ ★ ★ ★ ★ ★ ★ ★ that the negro Babo warned him that if he varied in the least, or uttered any word, or gave any look that should give the least intimation of the past events or present state, he

would instantly kill him, with all his companions, showing a dagger, which he carried hid, saying something which, as he understood it, meant that that dagger would be alert as his eye; that the negro Babo then announced the plan to all his companions, which pleased them; that he then, the better to disguise the truth, devised many expedients, in some of them uniting deceit and defense; that of this sort was the device of the six Ashantees before named, who were his bravoes; that them he stationed on the break of the poop, as if to clean certain hatchets (in cases, which were part of the cargo), but in reality to use them, and distribute them at need, and at a given word he told them; that, among other devices, was the device of presenting Atufal, his right hand man, as chained, though in a moment the chains could be dropped; that in every particular he informed the deponent what part he was expected to enact in every device, and what story he was to tell on every occasion, always threatening him with instant death if he varied in the least: that, conscious that many of the negroes would be turbulent, the negro Babo appointed the four aged negroes, who were calkers, to keep what domestic order they could on the decks; that again and again he harangued the Spaniards and his companions, informing them of his intent, and of his devices, and of the invented story that this deponent was to tell[,] charging them lest any of them varied from that story; that these arrangements were made and matured during the interval of two or three hours, between their first sighting the ship and the arrival on board of Captain Amasa Delano; that this happened about half-past seven o'clock in the morning, Captain Amasa Delano coming in his boat, and all gladly receiving him; that the deponent, as well as he could force himself, acting then the part of principal owner, and a free captain of the ship, told Captain Amasa Delano, when called upon, that he came from Buenos Ayres, bound to Lima, with three hundred negroes; that off Cape Horn, and in a subsequent fever, many negroes had died; that also, by similar casualties, all the sea officers and the greatest part of the crew had died.

★★★

406.   *[And so the deposition goes on, circumstantially recounting the fictitious story dictated to the deponent by Babo, and through the deponent imposed upon Captain Delano; and also recounting the friendly offers of Captain Delano, with other things, but all of which is here omitted. After the fictitious story, etc. the deposition proceeds:]*

★★★

407.   —that the generous Captain Amasa Delano remained on board all the day, till he left the ship anchored at six o'clock in the evening, deponent speaking to him always of his pretended misfortunes, under the fore-mentioned principles, without having had it in his power to tell a single word, or give him the least hint, that he might know the truth and state of

things; because the negro Babo, performing the office of an officious serv-ant with all the appearance of submission of the humble slave, did not leave the deponent one moment; that this was in order to observe the de-ponent's actions and words, for the negro Babo understands well the Spanish; and besides, there were thereabout some others who were con-stantly on the watch, and likewise understood the Spanish; ✱ ✱ ✱ that upon one occasion, while deponent was standing on the deck conversing with Amasa Delano, by a secret sign the negro Babo drew him (the deponent) aside, the act appearing as if originating with the deponent; that then, he being drawn aside, the negro Babo proposed to him to gain from Amasa Delano full particulars about his ship, and crew, and arms; that the de-ponent asked "For what?" that the negro Babo answered he might con-ceive; that, grieved at the prospect of what might overtake the generous Captain Amasa Delano, the deponent at first refused to ask the desired questions, and used every argument to induce the negro Babo to give up this new design; that the negro Babo showed the point of his dagger; that, after the information had been obtained[,] the negro Babo again drew him aside, telling him that that very night he (the deponent) would be captain of two ships, instead of one, for that, great part of the American's ship's crew being to be absent fishing, the six Ashantees, without any one else, would easily take it; that at this time he said other things to the same pur-pose; that no entreaties availed; that, before Amasa Delano's coming on board, no hint had been given touching the capture of the American ship: that to prevent this project the deponent was powerless; ✱ ✱ ✱ —that in some things his memory is confused, he cannot distinctly recall every event; ✱ ✱ ✱ —that as soon as they had cast anchor at six of the clock in the evening, as has before been stated, the American Captain took [leave to] return to his vessel; that upon a sudden impulse, which the deponent believes to have come from God and his angels, he, after the farewell had been said, followed the generous Captain Amasa Delano as far as the gun-wale, where he stayed, under pretense of taking leave, until Amasa Delano should have been seated in his boat; that on shoving off, the deponent sprang from the gunwale into the boat, and fell into it, he knows not how, God guarding him; that—

✱✱

408.   [*Here, in the original, follows the account of what further happened at the escape, and how the San Dominick was retaken, and of the passage to the coast; including in the recital many expressions of "eternal gratitude" to the "generous Captain Amasa Delano." The deposition then proceeds with recap-itulatory remarks, and a partial renumeration of the negroes, making record of their individual part in the past events, with a view to furnishing, according to command of the court, the data whereon to found the criminal sentences to be pronounced. From this portion is the following;*]

409.   —That he believes that all the negroes, though not in the first place knowing to the design of revolt, when it was accomplished, approved it. * * * That the negro, José, eighteen years old, and in the personal service of Don Alexandro, was the one who communicated the information to the negro Babo, about the state of things in the cabin, before the revolt; that this is known, because, in the preceding midnight, he use to come from his berth, which was under his master's, in the cabin, to the deck where the ringleader and his associates were, and had secret conversations with the negro Babo, in which he was several times seen by the mate; that, one night, the mate drove him away twice; * * that this same negro José was the one who, without being commanded to do so by the negro Babo, as Lecbe and Martinqui were, stabbed his master, Don Alexandro, after he had been dragged half-lifeless to the deck; * * that the mulatto steward, Francesco, was of the first band of revolters, that he was, in all things, the creature and tool of the negro Babo; that, to make his court, he, just before a repast in the cabin, proposed, to the negro Babo, poisoning a dish for the generous Captain Amasa Delano; this is known and believed, because the negroes have said it; but that the negro Babo, having another design, forbade Francesco; * * that the Ashantee Lecbe was one of the worst of them; for that, on the day the ship was retaken, he assisted in the defense of her, with a hatchet in each hand, with one of which he wounded, in the breast, the chief mate of Amasa Delano, in the first act of boarding; this all knew; that, in sight of the deponent, Lecbe struck, with a hatchet, Don Francisco Masa, when, by the negro Babo's orders, he was carrying him to throw him overboard, alive, beside participating in the murder, before mentioned, of Don Alexandro Aranda, and others of the cabin-passengers; that, owing to the fury with which the Ashantees fought in the engagement with the boats, but this Lecbe and Yan survived; that Yan was bad as Lecbe; that Yan was the man who, by Babo's command, willingly prepared the skeleton of Don Alexandro, in a way the negroes afterwards told the deponent, but which he, so long as reason is left him, can never divulge; that Yan and Lecbe were the two who, in a calm by night, riveted the skeleton to the bow; this also the negroes told him; that the negro Babo was he who traced the inscription below it; that the negro Babo was the plotter from first to last; he ordered every murder, and was the helm and keel of the revolt; that Atufal was his lieutenant in all; but Atufal, with his own hand, committed no murder; nor did the negro Babo; * * that Atufal was shot, being killed in the fight with the boats, ere boarding; * * that the negresses, of age, were knowing to the revolt, and testified themselves satisfied at the death of their master, Don Alexandro; that, had the negroes not restrained them, they would have tortured to death, instead of simply killing, the Spaniards slain by command of the negro Babo; that the negresses used their utmost influence to

63

have the deponent made away with; that, in the various acts of murder, they sang songs and danced—not gaily, but solemnly; and before the engagement with the boats, as well as during the action, they sang melancholy songs to the negroes, and that this melancholy tone was more inflaming than a different one would have been, and was so intended; that all this is believed, because the negroes have said it.

—that of the thirty-six men of the crew, exclusive of the passengers (all of whom are now dead), which the deponent had knowledge of, six only remained alive, with four cabin-boys and ship-boys, not included with the crew; ★ ★ —that the negroes broke an arm of one of the cabin-boys and gave him strokes with hatchets.

★★★

410.   *[Then follow various random disclosures referring to various periods of time. The following are extracted;]*

★★★

411.   —That during the presence of Captain Amasa Delano on board, some attempts were made by the sailors, and one by Hermenegildo Gandix, to convey hints to him of the true state of affairs; but that these attempts were ineffectual, owing to fear of incurring death, and, furthermore, owing to the devices which offered contradictions to the true state of affairs, as well as owing to the generosity and piety of Amasa Delano incapable of sounding such wickedness; ★ ★ ★ that Luys Galgo,[90] a sailor about sixty years of age, and formerly of the king's navy, was one of those who sought to convey tokens to Captain Amasa Delano; but his intent, though undiscovered, being suspected, he was, on a pretense, made to retire out of sight, and at last into the hold, and there was made away with. This the negroes have since said; ★ ★ ★ that one of the ship-boys feeling, from Captain Amasa Delano's presence, some hopes of release, and not having enough prudence, dropped some chance-word respecting his expectations, which being overheard and understood by a slave-boy with whom he was eating at the time, the latter struck him on the head with a knife, inflicting a bad wound, but of which the boy is now healing; that likewise, not long before the ship was brought to anchor, one of the seamen, steering at the time, endangered himself by letting the blacks remark some expression in his countenance, arising from a cause similar to the above; but this sailor, by his heedful after conduct, escaped; ★ ★ ★ that these statements are made to show the court that from the beginning to the end of the revolt, it was impossible for the deponent and his men to act otherwise than they did; ★ ★ ★ —that the third clerk, Hermenegildo Gandix, who before had been forced to live among the seamen, wearing a seaman's habit, and in all respects appearing to be one for the time; he, Gandix, was killed by a musket ball fired through mistake from the boats before boarding; having in his fright run up the mizzen-rigging, calling to the boats—"don't

board;" lest upon their boarding the negroes should kill him; that this inducing the Americans to believe he some way favored the cause of the negroes, they fired two balls at him, so that he fell wounded from the rigging, and was drowned in the sea; ✶ ✶ ✶ —that the young Don Joaquin, Marques de Aramboalaza, like Hermenegildo Gandix, the third clerk, was degraded to the office and appearance of a common seaman; that upon one occasion when Don Joaquin shrank, the negro Babo commanded the Ashantee Lecbe to take tar and heat it, and pour it upon Don Joaquin's hands; ✶ ✶ ✶ —that Don Joaquin was killed owing to another mistake of the Americans, but one impossible to be avoided, as upon the approach of the boats, Don Joaquin, with a hatchet tied edge out and upright to his hand, was made by the negroes to appear on the bulwarks; whereupon, seen with arms in his hands and in a questionable attitude, he was shot for a renegade seaman; ✶ ✶ ✶ —that on the person of Don Joaquin was found secreted a jewel, which, by papers that were discovered, proved to have been meant for the shrine of our Lady of Mercy in Lima; a votive offering, beforehand prepared and guarded, to attest his gratitude, when he should have landed in Peru, his last destination, for the safe conclusion of his entire voyage from Spain; ✶ ✶ ✶ —that the jewel, with the other effects of the late Don Joaquin, is in the custody of the brethren of the Hospital de Sacerdotes,[91] awaiting the disposition of the honorable court; ✶ ✶ ✶ —that, owing to the condition of the deponent, as well as the haste in which the boats departed for the attack, the Americans were not forewarned that there were, among the apparent crew, a passenger and one of the clerks disguised by the negro Babo; ✶ ✶ ✶ —that, beside the negroes killed in the action, some were killed after the capture and reanchoring at night, when shackled to the ring-bolts on deck; that these deaths were committed by the sailors, ere they could be prevented. That so soon as informed of it, Captain Amasa Delano used all his authority, and, in particular with his own hand, struck down Martinez Gola,[92] who, having found a razor in the pocket of an old jacket of his, which one of the shackled negroes had on, was aiming it at the negro's throat; that the noble Captain Amasa Delano also wrenched from the hand of Bartholomew Barlo[93] a dagger, secreted at the time of the massacre of the whites, with which he was in the act of stabbing a shackled negro, who, the same day, with another negro, had thrown him down and jumped upon him; ✶ ✶ ✶ —that, for all the events, befalling through so long a time, during which the ship was in the hands of the negro Babo, he cannot here give account; but that, what he has said is the most substantial of what occurs to him at present, and is the truth under the oath which he has taken; which declaration he affirmed and ratified, after hearing it read to him.

412.   He said that he is twenty-nine years of age, and broken in body and mind; that when finally dismissed by the court, he shall not return home

to Chili, but betake himself to the monastery on Mount Agonia[94] without; and signed with his honor, and crossed himself, and, for the time, departed as he came, in his litter, with the monk Infelez, to the Hospital de Sacerdotes.

DOCTOR ROZAS.   BENITO CERENO.

413.   If the Deposition [has] served as the key to fit into the lock of the complications which precede it, then, as a vault whose door has been flung back, the San Dominick's hull lies open today.

414.   Hitherto the nature of this narrative, besides rendering the intricacies in the beginning unavoidable, has more or less required that many things, instead of being set down in the order of occurrence, should be retrospectively, or irregularly given; this last is the case with the following passages, which will conclude the account:

415.   During the long, mild voyage to Lima, there was, as before hinted, a period during which the sufferer a little recovered his health, or, at least in some degree, his tranquillity. Ere the decided relapse which came, the two captains had many cordial conversations—their fraternal unreserve in singular contrast with former withdrawments.

416.   Again and again it was repeated, how hard it had been to enact the part forced on the Spaniard by Babo.

417.   "Ah, my dear friend," Don Benito once said, "at those very times when you thought me so morose and ungrateful, nay, when, as you now admit, you half thought me plotting your murder, at those very times my heart was frozen; I could not look at you, thinking of what, both on board this ship and your own, hung, from other hands, over my kind benefactor. And as God lives, Don Amasa, I know not whether desire for my own safety alone could have nerved me to that leap into your boat, had it not been for the thought that, did you, unenlightened, return to your ship, you, my best friend, with all who might be with you, stolen upon, that night, in your hammocks, would never in this world have wakened again. Do but think how you walked this deck, how you sat in this cabin, every inch of ground mined into honey-combs under you. Had I dropped the least hint, made the least advance towards an understanding between us, death, explosive death—yours as mine—would have ended the scene."

418.   "True, true," cried Captain Delano, starting, "you have saved my life, Don Benito, more than I yours; saved it, too, against my knowledge and will."

419.   "Nay, my friend," rejoined the Spaniard, courteous even to the point of religion, "God charmed your life, but you saved mine. To think of some things you did—those smilings and chattings, rash pointings and gestur-

ings. For less than these, they slew my mate, Raneds; but you had the Prince of Heaven's safe-conduct through all ambuscades."

420. "Yes, all is owing to Providence, I know[;] but the temper of my mind that morning was more than commonly pleasant, while the sight of so much suffering, more apparent than real, added to my good-nature, compassion, and charity, happily interweaving the three. Had it been otherwise, doubtless, as you hint some of my interferences might have ended unhappily enough. Besides, those feelings I spoke of enabled me to get the better of momentary distrust, at times when acuteness might have cost me my life, without saving another's. Only at the end did my suspicions get the better of me, and you know how wide of the mark they then proved."

421. "Wide, indeed," said Don Benito, sadly; "you were with me all day; stood with me, sat with me, talked with me, looked at me, ate with me, drank with me; and yet, your last act was to clutch for a monster, not only an innocent man, but the most pitiable of all men. To such degree may malign machinations and deceptions impose. So far may even the best man err, in judging the conduct of one with the recesses of whose condition he is not acquainted. But you were forced to it; and you were in time undeceived. Would that, in both respects, it was so ever, and with all men."

422. "You generalize, Don Benito; and mournfully enough. But the past is passed; why moralize upon it? Forget it. See, yon bright sun has forgotten it all, and the blue sea, and the blue sky; these have turned over new leaves."

423. "Because they have no memory," he dejectedly replied; "because they are not human."

424. "But these mild trades that now fan your cheek, do they not come with a human-like healing to you? Warm friends, steadfast friends are the trades."

425. "With their steadfastness they but waft me to my tomb, Senor," was the foreboding response.

426. "You are saved," cried Captain Delano, more and more astonished and pained; "you are saved: what has cast such a shadow upon you?"

427. "The negro."

428. There was silence, while the moody man sat, slowly and unconsciously gathering his mantle about him, as if it were a pall.

429. There was no more conversation that day.

430. But if the Spaniard's melancholy sometimes ended in muteness upon topics like the above, there were others upon which he never spoke at all; on which, indeed, all his old reserves were piled. Pass over the worst, and, only to elucidate, let an item or two of these be cited. The dress, so precise and costly, worn by him on the day whose events have been narrated, had not willingly been put on. And that silver-mounted sword, apparent sym-

bol of despotic command, was not, indeed, a sword, but the ghost of one. The scabbard, artificially stiffened, was empty.

431.   As for the black—whose brain, not body, had schemed and led the revolt, with the plot—his slight frame, inadequate to that which it held, had at once yielded to the superior muscular strength of his captor, in the boat. Seeing all was over, he uttered no sound, and could not be forced to. His aspect seemed to say, since I cannot do deeds, I will not speak words. Put in irons in the hold, with the rest, he was carried to Lima. During the passage, Don Benito did not visit him. Nor then, nor at any time after, would he look at him. Before the tribunal he refused. When pressed by the judges he fainted. On the testimony of the sailors alone rested the legal identity of Babo.

432.   Some months after, dragged to the gibbet at the tail of a mule, the black met his voiceless end. The body was burned to ashes; but for many days, the head, that hive of subtlety, fixed on a pole in the Plaza, met, unabashed, the gaze of the whites; and across the Plaza looked towards St. Bartholomew's church,[95] in whose vaults slept then, as now, the recovered bones of Aranda[;] and across the Rimac bridge[96] looked towards the monastery, on Mount Agonia without; where, three months after being dismissed by the court, Benito Cereno, borne on the bier, did, indeed, follow his leader.

68

Interpretive Essay

Melville's "Benito Cereno," a tale of a shipboard slave rebellion, has an obvious political theme: the clash between modern civilization and barbarism. Within the context of this theme, Melville addresses some of the most fundamental political problems confronting man—problems involving the tensions between conventional and natural inequality; between the preservation of existing political orders and revolution; between the demands of a secular state and those of a state captivated by religion; between democracy and aristocracy; between the requirements of justice and those of the law; and, finally, between the dictates of reason and those of unreasoning forces such as prejudice—particularly racial prejudice.[1]

The subtle way in which Melville treats the civilization-barbarism theme may explain why many reviewers of "Benito Cereno" fail to perceive either the number and complexity of the political problems addressed in the work or Melville's teachings about them.[2] In addressing these problems, particularly that of racial prejudice, Melville approaches them on two different levels. On the surface of the work, he seems to be speaking to the ordinary citizen of America—the white, Northern or Southern man of commerce who is the product of modern political philosophy's overwhelming sway in America. This citizen reader of "Benito Cereno" derives a simple meaning from the tale: slave uprisings are unquestionably wrong and their participants, accordingly, inevitably must succumb to such superior white men of commerce as Captain Amasa Delano. In this view, Delano is the tale's hero; he embodies those qualities which the average American citizen admires: hard work, Protestantism, bravery, loyalty, honesty, frugality, and a sense of justice. This citizen perspective of "Benito Cereno" largely explains why the tale consistently evoked such encomiums as "thrilling" and "powerful" from reviewers who were themselves average citizens addressing like audiences.

However, the very art for which Melville is praised (writing a good short story) is also responsible for veiling another meaning of the tale—one which is sympathetic to portions of what I will term the "citizen perspective," but antipathetic to much of it. This other, deeper meaning reveals itself only through the most painstaking attention to Melville's use of symbolism, contradiction, and structure. It is veiled partly because its teaching does not support the citizen perspective addressed on the tale's surface and, for that reason, it could be dangerous to and subversive of the American regime. Another reason the deeper meaning remains veiled is related to but nonetheless separate from the first: Melville seeks to address and teach those individuals who possess the capacity of mind to unravel the hidden meaning, a dedication to the pursuit of truth, and the strength of character requisite to a proper understanding and use of the veiled teaching. It would appear that those to whom this knowledge would be most appropriate would be either statesmen or the teachers of statesmen. Consequently, this hidden meaning hereafter will be referred to as the "statesman perspective." Before one can attempt to understand this statesman perspective, however, it is necessary that one comprehend the simple or citizen perspective as fully as possible. The surmounting of this preliminary obstacle is facilitated by an understanding of the political environment of the 1850s.[3]

In brief, the United States of that period was being severely buffeted by the controversy over admitting sections of the territories as either slave or free states.[4] As a consequence of the various recurring disagreements over this issue, many citizens coalesced into two violently opposed camps: the abolitionists, composed primarily of Northerners from regions (such as Massachusetts) that no longer derived much or any commercial benefit from slavery, and the proslavery faction, composed largely, but certainly not exclusively, of Southern slave owners who obviously had a large investment in slaves. Another part of the American citizenry was uncommitted to either extreme but was nonetheless affected by the turbulence produced by the contending factions. It was this large group of citizens occupying an uncertain middle ground that each of the two extreme factions sought either to win to their respective positions or, failing that, to manipulate to their partisan advantage.

As a result of this factional conflict, the political climate was such that a prudent man would have been ill-advised to attempt to reason with his fellow citizens about, for example, the merits of the black slaves; and only a fool would have been so bold as to speak openly to whites about black equality or, worse, black superiority. Similarly, discussion about the justice or injustice of slavery was also likely to deprive one of an attentive audience. A reasonable man who desired to teach his fellow citizens had to have the ability to manipulate the contending passions of the moment in such a way that he could get and keep the attention of his intended audience; that accomplished, the skillful teacher could then carefully attempt to dampen those passions in such a way as to permit reason to state its case.

To understand both the way in which Melville attempts to present his teaching in these volatile times as well as that teaching itself, it is necessary to be meticulous in one's reading of "Benito Cereno." This effort is enhanced, to a considerable extent, by the knowledge that the tale is woven around a published account of an actual event which occurred in 1805. The initial entrance into the mysteries of "Benito Cereno," therefore, lies outside its text in part of a work by the real-life Captain Amasa Delano entitled *A Narrative of Voyages and Travels*.[5] On their surfaces, Delano's autobiographical account and Melville's "Benito Cereno" seem very similar. For example, both versions have narrative sections which are bolstered by depositions from courts of law, some of the names in both tales are identical, and the main story-lines are very similar. These similarities, however, in no way detract either from Melville's stature as an author and teacher or from the greatness of "Benito Cereno." Melville obviously came upon Delano's account and was intrigued by what it said (and could be made to say) about man. The real-life Delano, the hero of his own tale and a main character in Melville's, certainly appears to have been blind to the lessons Melville saw in the autobiographical account. For Melville, the real-life incident contained the necessary ingredients to reveal man more starkly than any purely fictional account ever could.[6]

The real usefulness of Delano's account becomes apparent when one looks at the differences, rather than the similarities, between the two narratives. In other words, in those places where Melville chose not to follow Delano's account but instead deviated from it, the reader is justified in assuming that he attached some importance to those deviations. Close attention to these alterations reveals some interesting things. For instance, one of the most obvious changes Melville makes in Delano's account involves the dating of the events: Delano contended that, up until the time he encountered it, the rebellious slave-transporter had been at sea from December 20, 1804, until February 20, 1805, a period of 62 days. In Melville's tale, however, the slave-transporter is at sea from May 20, 1799, until its meeting with the American ship on August 17, 1799, a period of 89 days. With this manipulation of the dates, Melville brings several things into focus for the reader. First of all, when one considers the immediate subject matter of the tale—blacks rebelling against their enslavement by whites—this change to the year 1799 assumes considerable importance, for that year was the midpoint of the French Revolution and its famous struggle in the name of the rights of man. The year is also significant in that it was the midpoint of the American Constitution's 20-year ban on the prohibition of slavery[7]—a ban which permitted, and to an extent increased, the enslavement and transportation of black slaves aboard vessels such as that depicted in "Benito Cereno." Lastly and most significantly, if one calculates the midpoint between May 20th, and the date the slave-transporter left port, and August 17th, the date of its fateful meeting with Delano, a startling discovery is made: the exact center of the 89 day voyage falls on July 4th. Thus, on the day that whites throughout America were celebrating their liberation from the comparatively mild tyranny of Great Britain, the blacks on board the slave-transporter were not only free from the tyranny of the whites, but were also exercising self-government.

The final important change Melville makes in Delano's account that will concern us at the moment is a "rechristening" of the two ships involved. The American ship's name is changed from the Perseverance to the Bachelor's Delight. The new name may be intended to convey a sense of Delano's character. The American captain is portrayed as a fastidious bachelor who delights in "the comfortable family of a crew" on board his orderly ship.[8] In terms of the rebellion that occurs aboard the slave-transporter, the change of its name from the Tryal to the San Dominick seems to be laden with much more significance. For instance, there is an island off the southern shore of the United States which bears the same name as the slave-ship in Melville's tale. This island of Santo Domingo was the first land of the New World discovered by Christopher Columbus. (Fittingly, Melville makes this discoverer serve as the figurehead of the San Dominick.) It was also on this island that the Spanish first introduced slavery into the Western Hemisphere in 1493. Lastly, this island was the scene of devastating and—to the whites in neighboring America—fearsome slave rebellions from the late 1790s until the mid-1800s.[9] That the significance of the name San Dominick should have been recognizable by the average citizen of the 1850s can be surmised from the fact that mention of these slave rebellions was not uncommon in the popular press; there is even mention of them in one of the same issues of the monthly magazine in which "Benito Cereno" initially appeared.[10]

The Citizen Perspective

The first thing that strikes the reader's eye in any work is the title. In the case of "Benito Cereno," the title is unusual, one could even say strange. How does one pronounce it? What does it mean? It turns out to be a Spanish name, specifically, the name of one of the three main characters in the tale. It translates as "Pallid Benedictine (monk)." One who has read the story may be inclined to ask why the author did not give it a good American title, such as "Captain Delano." After all, the American captain appears to be the good-hearted, courageous hero. (Would a reader of the 1850s even have bothered to wonder why the tale was not named after the apparent anti-hero, Babo?) As we will see, the strangeness of the title is indicative of the tale itself, for neither it nor any of its main characters are really what they seem to be.

Unlike the title, the text of "Benito Cereno" is in English. It is divided into two main parts: a long narrative of the dramatic action and a relatively short deposition before a vice-regal court by Benito Cereno, the captain of the San

Dominick. A close examination of each of these parts, however, reveals some interesting things. First of all, it is not entirely correct to state that there are only two main parts; actually, the deposition is situated so as to sever the narrative into two unequal parts. Consequently, it could be said that "Benito Cereno" is composed of three parts: a long narrative describing events from the time of the San Dominick's meeting with Delano's ship, the Bachelor's Delight, until the latter's crew retakes it; the deposition; and a short narrative describing, among other things, a conversation between Delano and Benito Cereno enroute to Conception after the Spaniard's rescue. Chronologically, most of this final narrative belongs with the first part, for it relates events which occurred prior to the deposition. (Only its final two paragraphs describe events occurring subsequent to the deposition.)

The first long narrative can be readily subdivided into two very unequal parts: Delano's actions prior to boarding the San Dominick (pars. 1–14) and after boarding it (pars. 15–361). This extensive last portion then can be subdivided further according to the seven cycles of suspicion Delano experiences while on board the San Dominick: first cycle (pars. 15–61), second cycle (pars. 62–123), third cycle (pars. 124–63), fourth cycle (pars. 164–205), fifth cycle (pars. 206–17), sixth cycle (pars. 218–71), and seventh cycle (pars. 272–355). (The remaining thirty-nine paragraphs of the narrative detail Delano's discovery of the rebellion, the whites' recapture of the San Dominick, and the journey to the vice-regal court.) This subdivision reveals a series of interrelated suspicions in which each suspicion, building upon those which precede it, is progressively more alarming (and nearer to the "truth"). Interestingly, the central cycle (pars. 164–205), which is also one of the shortest, concerns an intriguing Gordian-like knot tossed to Delano by Luys Galgo, an old knotmaker. In the midst of rapidly spoken words of Spanish, Galgo utters the only words of English heard on board the San Dominick on August 17th; clearly and unmistakably he urges Delano, who is perplexedly holding the knot, to "Undo it, cut it, quick" (par. 200).

Subdividing the main narrative in this manner does not alter its most distinctive feature; it still reveals little to the first-time reader that is not also being revealed to Delano. Thus, while presented in the past tense, the narrative slowly takes the reader through the same labyrinth confronting (and generally confounding) the American. As with Delano, the reader's opinions, passions, prejudices, and reason are alternately both hindrances to and vehicles for a true understanding of the events occurring on board the San Dominick. In this sense, the narrative presents the tale from the perspective of an American citizen, that is, it corresponds more closely with reality than does the deposition and, in a limited sense, it is analogous to the sources from which the citizen-reader would normally receive his information about events which he has not witnessed. It is through such sources—newspapers, eyewitness accounts, biographies, hearsay—that his opinions and prejudices are either reinforced, left unchanged, or altered. From the surface or citizen perspective of "Benito Cereno," Captain Amasa Delano readily can be seen to be the tale's hero, for it is through his actions that the San Dominick is both put in a position to be rescued (by means of his Good Samaritan act of piloting it to an anchorage) and then actually rescued by means of the Americans' ingenuity, weaponry, and courage. It is also from the citizen perspective that one might be inclined to praise lavishly the defeat and punishment of the treacherous blacks. The fact that Delano remains unaffected in both body and mind by his experiences may merely indicate the American's superior strength of character; in the manner of Theseus, he can journey (albeit unwittingly) into the maw of Hades and emerge unscathed.

Delano's suspicions while aboard the San Dominick could be described as the reactions of a typical good-hearted American; such men normally do not expect nefarious treacheries at the hands of other white men, and they certainly do not expect them from docile black slaves. However, it is sufficiently reassuring to the citizen-reader to know that, once he is made aware of duplicity and wrong-doing, the American is more than equal to the task of setting matters right.

The Statesman Perspective

In addition to the citizen perspective, "Benito Cereno" also has a deeper meaning—one which I have termed "the statesman perspective." At this deeper level, Melville attempts to impart an important political teaching. It is at the level of the statesman perspective that the reader confronts the main theme of "Benito Cereno": the confrontation between modern civilization and barbarism as played out by the blacks and whites on board the San Dominick and in the Lima courtroom. To understand this theme properly, we must examine the tale from its beginning with great care. That this may be the way in which Melville expected —even required—the work to be approached seems to be indicated by the narrator's remark at the conclusion of the deposition:

> (T)he nature of this narrative, besides rendering the intricacies in the beginning unavoidable, has more or less required that many things, instead of being set down in the order of occurrence, should be retrospectively, or irregularly given... (par. 414).

The dramatic action in "Benito Cereno" concerning the relations between men of different colors is presaged by a conspicuous absence or at least a muddying of colors in the opening paragraphs:

> The morning was one peculiar to that coast. Everything was mute and calm; everything gray. The sea, though undulated into long roods of swells, seemed fixed, and was sleeked at the surface like waved lead that has cooled and set in the smelter's mould. The sky seemed a gray surtout. Flights of troubled gray fowl, kith and kin with flights of troubled gray vapors among which they were mixed, skimmed low and fitfully over the waters, as swallows over meadows

before storms. *Shadows present, foreshadowing deeper shadows to come* (par. 3, emphasis added).

Even the San Dominick, upon entering the harbor, displays no colors.[11] The only exceptions to this scene are the white noddy ("strange fowl") somnambulistically perched in the San Dominick's rigging, and the black figures at its portholes (who appear to be "Black Friars" to the approaching Delano). Even these vivid examples of the extremes of white and black, however, seem to blend together in the overall picture to form a veil of gray.

My examination of the relations between men of different races will be patterned after Melville's treatment of the main characters in "Benito Cereno," that is, I first will discuss Delano, then Benito, and, finally, Babo. Aside from these men, there are only two other characters—the Spanish knotmaker and Delano's mate—who actually speak in the narrative. The order in which the various characters will be treated also reflects the number of speeches each of them makes.[12] Babo stands out in this treatment both because he is the only black man to speak directly and because he speaks so little in comparison to Delano and Benito Cereno.

Captain Amasa Delano

Captain Delano, a "good sailor" who heads a "comfortable family of a crew" (par. 32), has been castigated for proving "to be amazingly stupid . . . aboard the San Dominick."[13] Admittedly, Delano does fail to perceive the reality behind the charade Babo, the slave leader, causes to be acted out before him. However, an important point to be made about Delano's obtuseness is that, once he steps on board the San Dominick, he is removed from all of his familiar guideposts. The San Dominick is strange to the American in many ways. Aside from its lack of any identifying ensign, there is the slovenly and— to Delano, who is used to the orderliness of his sealer—disturbing physical neglect of the ship. The strangeness is heightened by the conditions on board, which produce "something of the effect of enchantment. The ship seems unreal."[14] Amasa Delano is cast adrift; as a man whose actions are directed by his expectations and whose expectations are governed by that which he has experienced, he flounders when the actions of other men do not closely conform to his own past experiences.[15] Thus, when his mind is swimming with strange suspicions, Delano continually seeks some standard, some familiar object, by which to judge them. The most obvious example of this involves Rover, his household whaleboat. When Delano's anxieties about the situation on board the San Dominick force him to confront the possibility that what seems to be true may not be true at all, the sight of Rover, as reliable and predictable as a Newfoundland dog, serves to calm him and to dispel his unsettling thoughts.[16] When threatened by the strange, Delano's recourse is to reject it and to take confident refuge in the familiar.

That Delano is not stupid can be readily seen by his actions once the strange or "seeming" finally conforms to the familiar or "being." When, with the assistance of a Portuguese sailor manning the oars of Rover, the "scales drop . . . from his eyes" (par. 371) and he is able to see Babo and the other blacks as mutineers, Delano takes immediate and decisive action. The American is, first and foremost, a man of action. His extensive experience as a sea-captain enables him to use known nature; he confronts the previously experienced terrors of the sea courageously and skillfully. This is his world. When Benito continues to be dejected after having been saved, Delano, in urging him not to "moralize" about the past, refers to known nature, his "Warm friends, steadfast friends . . . the trades."[17]

Delano's knowledge of and faith in the predictable, useful ways of nature (along with his corresponding ignorance of the natures of men) befit a modern American. Delano is a representative of a regime which is unsurpassed in its production of wealth, technology, and all manner of things which tend to make man's life on earth easier. This image of Delano as a representative of modernity is depicted in "Benito Cereno" in at least two important ways.

First, of course, there is Delano's occupation: he is preeminently a man of commerce, an activity which is capable of procuring for a nation the necessary wealth that enables other citizens to pursue such time-consuming and expensive enterprises as technological development. Delano displays both the fruits of his occupation (when he twice has excess provisions brought to the San Dominick) and the moneymaking art which is that occupation's chief concern (when he arranges for payment from Benito Cereno for all of those provisions which the reader initially may have assumed were being provided free by a Good Samaritan).

Second, the technological superiority of the Americans is displayed to the reader. The knowledge of nature which enabled technological marvels to be produced was not gained merely by diligent observation of nature's ways; in Francis Bacon's apt word, nature obviously was "vexed" at some point into revealing her secrets. Thus, when it finally comes to a battle between the less civilized (or less modern) Africans and the Americans, the former are armed only with hatchets (which, incidentally, they procured from the whites), while the latter possess the great equalizers, cannons and muskets. Consequently, the whites are able to lay back out of any considerable danger and relentlessly direct accurate fire at the blacks massed on the San Dominick's stern. Once the blacks have been considerably reduced in both arms and numbers, the whites board and eventually overcome them. (It is one of the paradoxes of the confrontation between the civilized whites and the barbaric blacks that the combination of commerce and technological progress which here results in the blacks' re-enslavement also ultimately made it politically feasible to move for the abolition of that institution. Machines eventually rendered slave labor uneconomical, inefficient, and then undesirable.)

A more subtle presentation of what may be referred to as the art versus nature aspect of black-white relations aboard the San Dominick involves Delano's
boat, Rover. On the second and central of the three roundtrips Rover makes
between the Bachelor's Delight and the San Dominick, there is a revealing incident involving the distribution of its cargo of foodstuffs. Before Cereno stops
him, Delano intends to dispense only fish, water (the "republican element"),
and pumpkins to the blacks, while reserving the soft bread, cider, and sugar
exclusively for the whites. In other words, the blacks are to be limited to those
goods which are wholly the products of nature while the whites feast on those
goods which are produced by man's art (pars. 220–24).

In essence, the crucial difference between the blacks and the whites (and that
which most distinguishes the less civilized from the more civilized men in the
modern world) involves the blacks' ignorance of art or the useful sciences.[18]
Babo, for example, may know well the art of ruling men, but this knowledge
ultimately proves insufficient when he is confronted by Delano who, while de-
ficient in his knowledge of men, nevertheless possesses a sufficient knowledge
of the useful sciences to vanquish the blacks.[19]

The matter of Delano's ignorance of the natures and ways of men (and,
hence, of the art of ruling them) is, of course, one of the principal criticisms of
him. This ignorance is detailed in one of the narrator's early descriptions of the
American:

> Captain Delano's surprise [at the actions of the strange ship] might have
> deepened into some uneasiness had he not been a person of a singularly undis-
> trustful good nature, not liable, except on extraordinary and repeated incen-
> tives, and hardly then, to indulge in personal alarms, any way involving the
> imputation of malign evil in man. Whether, in view of what humanity is ca-
> pable, such a trait implies, along with a benevolent heart, more than ordinary
> quickness and accuracy of intellectual perception, may be left to the wise to
> determine (par. 4).

Delano's good nature (that is, his willingness to excuse, overlook, forgive,
and, in general, put the best face on the unexpected actions of real or imagined
inferiors)[20] makes him ill-suited to decipher the true motives behind men's actions. Because he is not by nature suspicious, Delano is unable to combat malignity until it confronts him face-to-face. Only then is he belatedly able to
react; only then do his abilities as a man of action save him from harm. Undoubtedly, if malignity ever failed to identify itself openly when it confronted
him, Delano would succumb to it. For example, Babo's original plan was to
make Benito Cereno "captain of [the] two ships" (par. 407) by killing Delano
during a stealthy, night-time attack on the Bachelor's Delight. Had this plan
not been thwarted by Benito's flight, a peacefully slumbering Amasa Delano
would have been easily overcome by Babo's men. (Given Melville's familiarity
with the Bible,[21] he must have been aware of the irony in the fact that Delano's
biblical namesake, Amasa, met his bloody death at the hands of the treacherous

Zoab as a direct result of his own trusting nature.)[22]

The subject of the relations between white and black men in "Benito Cereno" can be opened more fully by examining the way in which Delano perceives the blacks on board the San Dominick. In Delano's initial encounter with Benito and Babo, the narrator describes the black's face as showing "occasionally, like a shepherd's dog, . . . sorrow and affection . . . equally blended" as he mutely looked up at the Spaniard (par. 21). Later, the narrator relates that, "like most men of a good, blithe heart, Captain Delano took to negroes, not philanthropically, but genially, just as other men to Newfoundland dogs" (par. 253).

There is only one other thing in "Benito Cereno" that is compared to a dog, and that is the previously mentioned Rover—an inanimate object which, as such, is totally obedient to Delano's will. In animating his household boat (by giving it a dog's name and by describing it as a "good dog" with "a white bone in her mouth") and in dehumanizing the negroes (by minimizing or rejecting their exercise of their own wills), Delano is depicted as a "commander" who is both confident that his will is able to predominate and most content when it does so. In fact, Delano is so taken with the apparent loyalty and complete subservience of Babo that he lightly offers to buy him from Benito Cereno (par. 169). (Delano probably believes that such an acquisition would be an admirable complement to Rover.)

Even if one assumes that this offer was only the spontaneous and exuberant expression of what Delano believed to be the highest compliment he could bestow on Babo (that is, a desire to own such a fine slave), one must admit that it raises serious questions about Delano's view of slavery. While it is true that the American is the only character in the work who openly expresses some disapproval of slavery (par. 279), this fact is belied by the captain's other words and actions. For instance, when the blacks' rebellion is finally revealed to him, what does Delano do? Does this democratic man, a representative of a regime founded upon the recognition of man's natural rights, rejoice at or even acquiesce to the blacks' freedom? No! Entirely on his own initiative—even against the advice of Benito Cereno, the blacks' probable "owner"—Delano forcefully undertakes to re-enslave them. His motivation for this action is not entirely clear, but it may be related to the fact that, in addition to being a democrat, he is also a law-abiding commercial man. However, in urging his crew to recapture the San Dominick, Delano does not mention that the blacks have unlawfully broken their bonds or that they have terrorized the whites on board the ship. Rather, Delano tells them that Benito Cereno has given the ship up for lost and that, if they recapture it, great riches will be divided among all of them. Delano does not speak to his crew's reason or to their sense of justice, but to their basest passion: greed. In this sense, it is the Americans' self-interest to re-enslave the blacks (who, after all, are valuable commodities). But beyond the immediate question of the possible gain to be gotten as a consequence of the blacks' return to bondage, there is the matter of Delano's apparent lack of reflection on the whole subject of the justice or injustice of slavery. Evidently convinced that what is conventional is unalterable, he seems to accept slavery's existence much as he accepts the existence of the trades: both are "natural" occurrences to be accepted and used accordingly. There are two major episodes which support this view: Delano's distribution of the supplies and his thoughts on negro inferiority.

When Rover—laden with water, pumpkins, bread, cider, and sugar— returns to the San Dominick the second time, Delano begins the previously mentioned unequal distribution of the provisions (par. 224). It is possible, of course, that the "benevolent" Delano is only conforming to what he believes to be proper conduct on board a slave ship. However, when the incident is viewed in conjunction with the narrator's earlier comments, one can conclude that Delano readily accepts as natural the conventional inferiority of the blacks. When Delano, wrestling with his fourth suspicion about a conspiracy, fears that Benito Cereno might be aligned with the negroes, the narrator remarks:

> The whites, too, by nature, were the shrewder race. A man with some evil design, would he not be likely to speak well of that stupidity which was blind to his depravity, and malign that intelligence from which it might not be hidden? Not unlikely, perhaps. But if the whites had dark secrets concerning Don Benito, could then Don Benito be any way in complicity with the blacks? But they were too stupid. Besides, who ever heard of a white so far a renegade as to apostatize from his very species almost, by leaguing in against it with negroes?[23]

No explicit evidence is given that Delano, an American Protestant from a northern state, has had previous contact with black slaves; his prior associations with blacks seem to have been limited to free men of color. These free men, however, are depicted as being actually or potentially subservient to Delano's will. The reader is told of the black sailor serving under Delano's direct command and the black free man working or playing under his "benign" gaze (par. 253). Prior to his experiences with Babo ("This is an uncommonly intelligent fellow of yours, Don Benito" [par. 297]), Delano probably had no contact with intelligent, (secretly) willful black men. The thought that blacks, like whites, could have both the capability and the desire shrewdly to force their own wills on others is totally outside of Delano's experience and, hence, knowledge. He knows white men to be capable of deceit; consequently, his recurring suspicions center on Benito Cereno. And he is willing to allow for the possibility that mulattoes, particularly those having "regular European face[s]," might be equally dangerous, though he attributes this to the fact that they have white blood (par. 286).

Delano's ready acceptance of the conventional view of blacks, a consequence of his lack of experience with them, plays a major part in deluding him as to the reality on board the San Dominick. He sees the blacks in their accustomed role: subservient to the will of the whites. The few instances of black willfulness or misbehavior—the attack on the cabin-boy, the stomping of the white sailor, the abrupt, menacing silence that suddenly ensues when Delano half-jokingly threatens the jostling blacks—are dismissed as being the consequences of Benito Cereno's inadequacies as a commander and of the miseries suffered because of the calm. These occurrences fail to jar Delano out of his preconceptions about what he believes to be the natural order of things, namely, whites ruling blacks.

This aspect of Delano's character is related to his understanding of the nature of man—an understanding that perhaps stands most clearly revealed in one of his solitary musings about some characteristics of barbarous people:

> His attention had been drawn to a slumbering negress, partly disclosed through the lacework of some rigging, lying, with youthful limbs carelessly disposed, under the lee of the bulwarks, like a doe in the shade of a woodland rock. Sprawling at her lapped breasts was her wide-awake fawn, stark naked, its black little body half lifted from the deck, crosswise with its dam's; its hands, like two paws, clambering upon her; its mouth and noise ineffectually rooting to get at the mark; and meantime giving a vexatious half-grunt, blending with the composed snore of the negress.
>
> The uncommon vigor of the child at length roused the mother. She started up, at a distance facing Captain Delano. But as if not at all concerned at the attitude in which she had been caught, delightedly she caught the child up, with maternal transports, covering it with kisses.
>
> There's naked nature, now; pure tenderness and love, thought Captain Delano, well pleased.
>
> This incident prompted him to remark the other negresses more particularly than before. He was gratified with their manners: like most *uncivilized* women, they seemed at once tender of heart and tough of constitution; equally ready to die for their infants or fight for them. *Unsophisticated* as leopardesses; loving as doves...[24]

This tranquil portrait of the unenlightened "noble savage" in a state of nature is certainly attractive to Delano.[25] The peacefulness of the scene is modified, however, by its animal imagery: "doe," "fawn," "dam," "paws," "rooting," "half-grunt," "leopardesses," and "doves." It is important to note that while roughly one-half of these words represent innocence, the other one-half represent savagery. Melville's use of this double-edged imagery suggests his awareness of a duality in nature that Delano does not seem to perceive. The fawn, doe, and dove all represent innocence; however, they are incapable of savagery (or at least effective savagery) even if their lives or the lives of their offspring are at stake. The leopardess, on the other hand, is not helpless in the face of danger; her savagery probably can match that of the fiercest predator. Among her own kind, though, the leopardess can be as "loving as [a] dove."[26]

Melville's attribution of this dual nature to the "uncivilized [black] women" suggests a questioning of whether human beings possessing this dual or balanced nature can or will survive in "civilization," that is, in the world of white, Christian, Western man. To judge from almost all of the white men portrayed in "Benito Cereno," there is an imbalance between savagery and innocence in their world. Benito Cereno, the physically and spiritually debilitated Spaniard, is forced to masquerade (none too effectively) as a man of power and authority. As we will see, Benito is neither the embodiment of dove-like innocence nor, on the other hand, is he capable of animal savagery. Captain Delano might be said to possess a more nearly balanced nature; however, the predominance of his innocence (in the form of an inability to perceive veiled evil) argues against this view.

One of the few exceptions among the whites is the helmsman, who is described as a "centaur" (that is, one who is half-human and half-beast) and a "grizzly bear" casting "sheep's eyes" (pars. 179, 322). These characterizations, coupled with the brief description of his actions while he is being observed by Delano and several of the blacks, suggest that he may indeed possess a balanced nature. He is not a sheep masquerading as a bear, but the reverse. (It is noteworthy that this disguised bear is one of the three whites killed by the attacking sailors during the retaking of the San Dominick [par. 385].)

The most prominent example of one who might seem to exhibit an appropriately balanced nature in white civilization is black Babo. Neither his savagery nor the artful innocence with which he covers it can be denied. However, as we will see, it is this veil of feigned innocence which lends considerable credence to the argument that Babo's nature is in fact grossly unbalanced. He is too much savagery and too little innocence. Nevertheless, Babo's eventual defeat by Delano should not be taken as overwhelming evidence that his nature is not a substantial asset to a black slave in white civilization. But for Benito's impulsive and desperate leap into Delano's boat, Babo probably would have triumphed over the Americans as well.

Benito Cereno

That Melville attached considerable importance to the character of Benito Cereno can be inferred from several factors. First, of course, is the fact that the work bears his name. Additionally, of the three main characters, the name of this Spanish captain is the only one that Melville has not taken directly from his main source, the real Captain Amasa Delano's narrative.[27] Melville alters the name from Bonito Sereno ("Blessed Serenity") to Benito Cereno ("Pallid Benedictine [monk]"). In one sense, it may be that Melville took ironic delight in the original name's meaning, for this Spaniard was hardly characterized by "blessed serenity."[28] However, the change to a name having a decidedly Catholic cast is particularly revealing in that it serves to emphasize the religious differences of the three main characters: Captain Amasa Delano hails from Duxbury, Massachusetts, a seafaring town of practical, Protestant Americans; Benito Cereno is a member of an old Catholic Spanish aristocracy; and Babo, like almost all the other blacks, is evidently a pagan. It is interesting to note that Benito's and Babo's respective religions are the only ones actually practiced in the tale.[29] (This, of course, causes Delano and his religion to stand out. Thus, it is the representative of modernity, the American, who has the least association with religious practices. It is also this representative who, in confronting his suspicions on board the San Dominick, dismisses them as "superstitions.")

The importance of the linkage of Catholicism with the Spaniard, Benito Cereno, points to another of the major problems treated in the tale, namely, the captivation of a state by a religion. The references to Spain's Charles V in "Benito Cereno" suggest that decay and enervation are related to unfortunate alliances between the political and religious spheres or, perhaps more accurately, conquests of the political sphere by the religious sphere (par. 28). Charles V assumes a position of some prominence due to the fact that he is the only Spaniard among the three actual political rulers mentioned in the tale. (There is substantial textual evidence which supports the suggestion that an 1851 article on Charles V which appeared in *Fraser's Magazine* served as a second source—alongside Delano's *Narrative*—for "Benito Cereno.")[30] The parallels between Emperor Charles V of Spain, who renounced his earthly rule in order to retire to a monastery, and Don Benito Cereno of Chile, who also turned from the world of men to a monastery, are striking. For example, Charles V, after abdicating, decided to reside at a monastery in the Pyrenees.[31] Amasa Delano, in approaching the San Dominick, thinks it a "whitewashed monastery after a thunder-storm, seen perched upon some dun cliff among the Pyrenees" (par. 8). Charles V, afflicted with debilitating physical weakness, was forced to travel to the monastery "in a litter, and often suffering great pain."[32] Benito Cereno likewise was forced to a litter on which he was carried from the Spanish vice-regal courtroom—the symbol of the political world—to the monastery on Mount Agonia (par. 432).

Benito Cereno, the "Pallid Benedictine [monk]," thus could be equated with Charles V, the ruler who so delighted "in conversing with the Benedictines."[33] By directing attention to the earthly demise of Charles V's great empire, Melville may be emphasizing the way in which religious conflict—or, rather, political involvement in religious conflict—can be decidedly destructive of the possibility of earthly happiness.

This point is ironically made in the gruesome disposition of the corpse of Aranda, the slaves' master. After having had Aranda dragged, half-dead, to the main-deck, Babo witnesses the completion of his murder (par. 402). Overruling the other blacks, Babo mysteriously causes the body to be taken below, after which:

> nothing more was seen of it . . . for three days. . . . [On] the fourth day . . . at sunrise, the deponent [Benito Cereno] coming on deck, the negro Babo showed him a skeleton, which had been substituted for the ship's proper figure-head—the image of Christopher Colon, the discoverer of the New World . . . [T]he negro Babo . . . said words to this effect: "Keep faith with

the blacks from here to Senegal, or you shall in spirit, as now in body, follow your leader . . ." (par. 402).

Melville here arranges a chilling parody of the Resurrection of Christ. However, instead of a flesh, blood, and bones Christ arising from interment, Melville produces only the bones, signifying the emaciated state of Catholic Spain.

There is also considerable significance in the replacement of the original figurehead of Christopher Colon with Aranda-Christ's skeleton. It is Christopher ("Christ-bearer") Colon—"the discoverer of the New World"— who symbolizes innovation, courage, acquisitiveness, and, above all, glory.[34] These are precisely the qualities that are considered unimportant or secondary—even undesirable—by the Roman Catholic religion which "captured" Spain. Spain's image of greatness and potential (represented by Christopher Colon) is thus fittingly replaced by one which starkly de-emphasizes the physical things of this world.

Aside from the religious symbolism found in the character of Benito Cereno and his ship, the San Dominick, the reader is confronted by a considerable enigma in attempting to understand Benito the man. For one thing, the narrator does not directly comment on Benito's innermost thoughts and motivations as he does on Delano's. Additionally, Benito's speeches—with two notable exceptions (pars. 417, 421)—are uniformly short and frequently unfinished. Coupled with his real physical dependency on Babo, these things suggest to the reader that the character of Benito Cereno is somehow incomplete.

What is explicitly known about Benito Cereno is that he is a twenty-nine year old member of a well-respected, Spanish seafaring family (par. 121). We also know that, before the mutiny, he captained a slave-transporter; in all probability, he had been so engaged for some time prior to the embarkation of Babo and the other blacks.[35]

We are given a description of Benito's attire which is in stark contrast with his physical condition (par. 51). The contrast is duly noted by Delano during his second suspicion and, in another use of graphic animal imagery, the narrator comments on Delano's thoughts:

> But the Spaniard was a pale invalid. Never mind. For even to the degree of simulating mortal disease, the craft of some tricksters had been known to attain. To think that, under the aspect of infantile weakness, the most savage energies might be couched—those velvets of the Spaniard but the silky paw of his fangs (par. 121).

In reality, of course, Benito Cereno is devoid of "savage energies." Delano, adrift again, is portrayed as being drastically misled by Benito Cereno's appearance. Benito is no centaur or bear casting sheep's eyes; rather, he is a sheep cumbrously masquerading as a bear. His impotence is highlighted by his sword, the empty scabbard of which is later suggestively revealed to have been "artificially stiffened" (par. 430).

In one suspicion (which he never entirely dismisses), Delano, in pondering

Benito's debilitated condition, is said by the narrator to think that:

> [T]he young captain had not got into command at the hawse-hole, but the cabin-window; and if so, why wonder at incompetence, in youth, sickness, and gentility united (par. 54)?

That Melville intended for Benito Cereno to be seen as a man originally unfit or poorly suited to command can be inferred from the selective use that is made of the words "command" and "commander." Only Delano and Babo are every portrayed as actually issuing commands (pars. 317, 402, 409). On those few occasions when Benito Cereno feebly hazards giving an order, he does so only at the behest of Babo (pars, 91, 95, 333). It is highly ironic, then, that Delano believes Benito Cereno to be one of those "paper captains" who "has little of command but the name."[36]

Implicit in this interpretation, of course, is the view that Benito Cereno, unlike Babo and possibly Delano, is not a born leader who rules because of a common recognition of his natural superiority. Evidence for this view may be found in the division of the work itself. The first three-fourths of the narrative is devoted to a presentation of Babo's control of the situation. His "rival" in this matter (which is not a charade—Babo's control is quite real) is Delano, who narrowly succeeds in discovering and crushing the rebellion. It is Delano, a man of action, who conquers Babo, a leader par excellence, and recovers Benito Cereno's "command" for him. The last quarter of the work is primarily devoted to a selective presentation of legal evidence (Benito's deposition) from a court of law. Even here, the word of Benito Cereno is momentarily doubted (par. 394).

The statement of Benito before the vice-regal court at Lima differs from the narrative which precedes it in several ways. In the case of the narrative, we are confronted with a narrator who recounts events which have already occurred — events to which he may or may not have been a witness. Here the reader is, at the very least, two stages removed from the actual events: he is reading an account of events distanced from him both by time and by the selective medium of the narrator. In the case of the deposition, however, the reader is even further removed from the actual events. First, the events described have already occurred and, hence, are not directly verifiable by the reader. Second, the deposition is one man's version of those events. Third, that man's version is transcribed for the court by a notary. Fourth, because that man's version was taken down in Spanish, it was necessary for the narrator to translate it into English. Finally, the document is selectively extracted and presented (not necessarily sequentially) by the narrator.

The deposition, then, is more removed from that reality which it purports to describe than is the narrative. Despite (or because of) the distancing involved in the deposition, the narrator advises that it may serve as the "key" to the narrative. This claim comes after the deposition has dispassionately revealed instances of some of the most horrendous, inhuman, and pitiful actions men have ever committed against their fellow men. On the basis of this document—a statement devoid of the human passions and sentiments which animate the actions of most men—a court of law is presumed to be able to reach a reasoned judgment on the most passion-laden questions men can ever confront, namely, should certain men be enslaved and should certain men live or die? Thus, in order for ordinary men—men like Benito Cereno and the judges of the Lima court—to enter into the philosopher's realm of reason, all elements not properly belonging to that realm (for example, passion and spirit) have to be forcefully dampened and excluded from it. This is a task, however, that is not only exceedingly difficult for ordinary human beings to accomplish, but one that may produce inappropriate solutions for the political community's fundamental problems. In other words, there may be cases in which unadulterated reason cannot (or should not) be achieved by men. There also may be cases which deserve—even demand—more than reason. The matter of the enslavement of human beings goes against reason, but reason (if one is to judge by slavery's longevity) often goes unheeded and, hence, is insufficient to overcome slavery. One thing that is needed is an alliance of reason with a noble passion that cries out against slavery in terms that cannot fail to affect most men. Melville's implication, therefore, would seem to be that the problem of slavery cannot be properly decided by the law; its ultimate resolution lies in the political realm, where the passions, opinions, and prejudices of the citizenry largely dictate what is and is not feasible.

The matter of the deposition's omissions seems to bear on this problem of the proper forum for the resolution of political questions. By means of being quite selective in presenting one man's version of what transpired prior to the point at which the narrative began, Melville may be attempting to emphasize the extremely limited nature of legal proceedings. For instance, there is a real possibility that Benito Cereno may be as selective as the narrator is in telling his story; in short, he (as well as the narrator) may be lying. By the very nature of legal proceedings, the volume and the number of sources of information which the court will accept are limited. From this narrow range of information, however, a court of law frequently makes decisions which have the most profound consequences for the political community—the place where opinions, passions, prejudices, and spiritedness generally have a say equal to, if not greater than, that of reason.

What we do know about the courtroom—and the law it represents—is that it is the origin of Benito Cereno's authority. The court's authority is distinguished from that of Babo only in the sense that it is further removed from its foundation: force. Babo and the other blacks were enslaved by force and their enslavement was maintained by the authority of the law. Babo uses force to discard his bondage and, in turn, to enslave the whites. In a sense, Benito's and Babo's paper agreement constitutes the imposition of law: Babo agrees to sheath his sword in return for the whites' acquiescence to his will (par. 402). In both cases of enslavement, force is the source of one race's rule over the other.

The court is also representative of the world where paper titles (of which Benito's family has several [par. 121]) are dispensed and upheld; it is here that Benito Cereno's version of what transpired on board the San Dominick is finally accepted and here that punishment is meted out to those who transgressed the law. Consequently, it is here that one must consider the question of justice, that is, in which case—that of Babo's revolt or that of the court's punishment—is justice done? An argument can be made that the blacks' savagery is merely retaliatory; that it is the swift punishment of the perpetrators of an enormous wrong—enslavement—that had been and was still being inflicted upon them. In regard to some of the excesses that occurred during the uprising, one could argue that, while not excusable, they are reflections of the possibility that great evils sometimes may require the commission of even greater evils if the initial ones are to be overcome. Thus, the slaves believed that they had to kill Aranda in order to ensure that their liberty would have more permanence (par. 402). Since there is no question that, up until the time of the revolt, the blacks, by being enslaved, had been grievously wronged, and that the whites on board the San Dominick were, to various degrees, the perpetrators of that wrong, the slaves' initial revolt may be seen as the imposition of a form of expedient, absolute justice.

The ultimate return to "legal justice"—the imposition of punishment after a set and ponderous procedure of ascertaining guilt—might be seen as a necessary response to the excesses occurring during the revolt.[37] Alternatively, it could be seen as an abrogation of absolute justice and a reimposition of the unjust rule of the whites. Some support for this latter view can be found in the fact that the only accounts of the revolt given to the court are provided by white men, particularly by Benito Cereno (par. 394).

The reader does not know what Benito's view on the enslavement of black men was prior to the revolt. As previously mentioned, however, he participated in the slave trade by captaining a slave-transporter. Since Benito Cereno had come from a wealthy family (par. 121) and undoubtedly had not been compelled to participate in the slave trade by economic necessity, any moral reservations he may have had about that occupation were insufficient to prevent him from becoming involved in it. This fact alone should suffice to cast doubt on the simplistic view that Benito Cereno "belongs to [the] group of good, harmless men and women . . . ."[38]

At the conclusion of the narrative, the reader sees that Benito Cereno, despite having been liberated from the rebels, continues to suffer from a physical and spiritual collapse so complete that he is unable even to bear the sight of his former master, Babo (pars. 374, 431). After his rescue of Benito, Delano cries, "[Y]ou are saved: what has cast such a shadow upon you?" The Spaniard mournfully replies, "The negro" (par. 427). This response could be interpreted to mean that Benito has finally discerned what Delano has not, namely, that the enslavement of either race is wrong. Both Benito and Babo have now experienced what Delano has not: freedom and enslavement. They have seen both sides and have lived to tell of their experiences. One problem, however, is that neither one of them really does tell. Babo becomes completely mute upon being re-enslaved. While Benito, on the other hand, renders a statement of the events when he is liberated, he expresses neither approval nor disapproval of slavery. Benito's silence—his failure to make a passionate outcry against slavery—may be the result of the horrors he has experienced as a slave of the blacks: "—Oh, my God! rather than pass through what I have, with joy I would have hailed the most terrible gales; but—" (par. 39).

One could also see Benito Cereno's response to Babo as an indication that he is still subjugated, that he remains in awe of the black's will. Benito Cereno has real cause to fear the black, for his experiences have convinced him that the negroes are capable of inflicting great harm in order to win their freedom. The shadow of the negro looms so large over Benito and the other (presumably un-suspecting) whites that Benito withdraws not only from the slave trade, but also from the world; accompanied by the monk Infelez (Unhappy), he enters a mon-astery on Mt. Agonia (Agony), where, after three months of suffering, he dies (par. 432).

Babo

Babo has been pre-emptorily dismissed by one commentator who contends that, "as his name suggests [Babo] is just an animal, a mutinous ba-boon . . . ."[39] While it is true that the name may have connotations of barba-rism, it is also true that Melville deliberately enlarges the role that the real Babo played in the revolt to the point where every act, every atrocity of the rebellion is now directly attributable to the "negro Babo."[40] Benito Cereno's deposition even states that it was by Babo's command that the Ashantee Yan "prepar[ed]" the skeleton of Don Alexandro Aranda "in a way . . . so long as reason is left him, [he] can never divulge" (par. 409).

There does, therefore, seem to be some support for this view. What, then, does the careful reader do with the fact that it is Babo who formulates and or-chestrates the incredible charade in which the whites are made to appear to be still in control and the blacks to be in loose captivity? This charade is accom-plished, furthermore, with a cast of negroes ranging from the rawest savages (the Ashantees) to venerable patriarchs (Dago and the oakum-pickers) and an ex-king (Atufal). Additionally, it requires the willing or unwilling connivance of the whites, some of whom (for example, Don Joaquin and Luys Galgo) are men of intelligence and courage. Finally, the planning and preparation for the complex deception were done within the two or three hour period of time be-tween the San Dominick's entrance into the harbor of St. Maria and Delano's coming on board. The qualities of intellect and leadership required to stage this charade successfully are not those one would associate with "just an animal."

Babo, "that hive of subtlety," is neither a baboon nor an ordinary human being.

It has also been remarked that Babo is "hatred for the happiness of hatred, evil for the sake of evil."[41] Babo's previously discussed veiled savagery lends some support to this view. He could even be seen as Satan incarnate.[42] The question then becomes, Why is he evil? I have already suggested that Babo is inflicting retaliatory evil, which may require the use of an even greater evil than that which it seeks to overcome. This is a considerable part of Babo's role, but, as with Babo himself, there are more subtleties involved.

One way of commencing an examination of Babo is to observe the similarities between the character of Babo and that of Iago in Shakespeare's *Othello*. Both of these characters—white Iago with black Othello and black Babo with white Benito—are exceedingly private individuals who, through their great duplicity, bring important political figures to ruin.[43] Babo, occupying the humble office of a valet, deceitfully overcomes, manipulates, and eventually destroys the supreme political leader of the San Dominick—Benito Cereno, the commander of the ship. Iago, playing the part of a faithful counselor, is ultimately responsible for the destruction of Othello's love for Desdemona, Desdemona herself, Othello's position in Venice, and finally Othello himself. Both of these weavers of evil stubbornly refuse to utter a single word when their crimes are discovered and they are captured:[44]

> [Iago] works like a confidence man; only the quality intrinsic to the one he tempts enables him to succeed. He is a faithful mirror of all around him; he adapts himself to those with whom he speaks. In a sense, we would not know the other characters in the play without Iago. We would see them only as they appear in ordinary life, without penetrating the masks that conceal their real natures. Iago alone lets us know from the outset those weaknesses in others that would otherwise stand unrevealed until the crises of their lives. Iago shows the hidden necessity in men, the things they care about most; he has a diabolic insight.[45]

Like Iago, Babo acts as a mirror, reflecting back both to Delano and to the reader what each wants to see.

It is slavery itself, however, which must bear some of the responsibility for Babo's own acquiescence to and, finally, participation in the brutish treatment of the whites once they are enslaved by the blacks. To understand this, one must ask what it is that enables one group to identify, label, and treat another group as inferior. The answer lies in the former group's recognition of real or imagined dissimilarity between itself and the other group. In order to treat one another as equals, it is necessary that both groups readily be perceived to be alike in certain crucial ways. Thus, sentient men distinguish themselves from sentient animals by acknowledging such things as the latter's lack of reason and speech. Consequently, men neither extend the same rights to brutes as they do to their fellow men nor do they recognize any duties to them.[46]

When the Christian Western world reintroduced slavery, it concentrated on enslaving some men who would always be physically distinguishable from their masters. In so doing, it drastically affected both the character of slavery itself and the consequences which ultimately would follow from that institution for the Christian West. The ease with which one could perceive unlikeness between the black slaves and the white masters is one explanation why many whites could consider the blacks to be inferior and to act on that perception.[47] This same easily perceived unlikeness, undoubtedly augmented by the remembrance of past inhuman actions by the whites, may explain some of the blacks' inhumanity to the whites when the roles of master and slave are reversed. It might even be said that the whites' previous treatment of the blacks as less than men limited their own claims to humane treatment when the blacks became the masters.[48]

Slavery has convinced Babo of the malignity of white men; consequently, he exhibits no qualms about using horrendous means to control them. By forcing everyone on board the San Dominick to appear to be what they are not (that is, black free men to appear to be slaves and white slaves to appear to be free men), Babo hopes to use them in order to advance his own purposes. Babo has only one none-too-realizable desire: to reach Senegal or some other free negro state. Of course, it may be that Babo uses this goal as a means of securing the ready compliance of the other blacks. Some of Babo's actions— his failure to order the San Dominick to flee when Delano's ship is first sighted; his suicidal leap into Delano's boat—suggest that one of his main goals was to punish whites for their parts in or acquiescence to the evil of slavery. Thus, when the ostensible goal of reaching Senegal is denied him by Benito Cereno's flight, Babo abandons the other rebels in order to seek "the centred purpose of his soul" (par. 369): the destruction of Benito Cereno, the principal representative of white malignity toward blacks aboard the San Dominick, in body as well as in spirit.

That Babo ultimately is captured and fails to reach Senegal may have been inevitable. His knowledge as well as his deeds now make him unfit to dwell with other men in a political community. What I have referred to as his dual (and unbalanced) nature is an incongruous combination of the lowest and the highest attributes of man, either of which alone would be sufficient reason to exclude him from that community. After his capture, of course, Babo chooses to exclude himself by remaining mute. Deprived of the opportunity to seek redress through his deeds, Babo refuses to seek it through words.[49] His muteness, therefore, may be the result of a recognition on his part that no amount of persuasive speech could move the white man to act justly toward the black man. Consequently, force may be the blacks' only recourse. (It is interesting to note that Benito Cereno reacts in a similar manner when he is totally subject to the rule of the blacks: his "muteness" is consistent with the conduct of a man who has little reason to expect that words will alter his captor's treatment of him [par. 30].)

There are other facets to the character of Babo which deserve some attention. Of particular interest is the manner in which Babo establishes a degree of order among the blacks and whites on board the San Dominick. He appoints four elderly caulkers who sit picking oakum while overseeing the deck and attempting, with words, to maintain discipline (pars. 18, 405). Additionally, he stations six "raw" Ashantee warriors at an equal height above the deck and sets them to polishing hatchets (pars. 19, 405). The result is a combination of persuasion and force; if the caulkers should prove insufficient (as they eventually did), the warriors could be unleashed.[50] The omnipresent threat of force—which Delano continually feels (pars. 60, 73)—underscores the previous discussion about its being the foundation upon which both the whites and the blacks successively rule one another.[51]

That this arrangement of the oakum-pickers and the hatchet-polishers is not entirely satisfactory is apparent from the disruptions that occur (for example, the knifing of the cabin-boy and the stomping of the sailor). These events are not overlooked by a reproachful Delano (pars. 26, 62–67, 165–68). The problem is that the threat of force is directed only against the whites; the blacks have only the admonishments of the oakum-pickers and a recognition of the desperateness of their situation to deter them. The passions of the moment can and do overcome these restraints, with the inevitable results that Delano witnesses. Of course, the separation of the elements of persuasion and force may be a reflection of the confidence that Babo has in his fellow blacks. If so, the fact that the disruptions were comparatively few in number during Delano's twelve hours or so on board would seem to indicate that this confidence was not entirely misplaced.

However, when one looks at the excesses of the blacks during the revolt and for days afterwards, as well as at the tumult on board the San Dominick when Babo abandons it, it is possible to see that the self-control of many of the blacks is negligible. Of course, one should not wonder at this fact in men who (aside from Atufal) have probably never known self-rule in their lives. The blacks' unsuitability for self-rule only serves to make Babo's failure to provide an effective police force all the more remarkable. This failure recalls Fleece's enforced sermon to the sharks in *Moby Dick*:

> Your woraciousness, fellow-critters, I don't blame ye so much for; dat is natur, and can't be helped; but to gobern dat wicked natur, dat is de pint. You is sharks, sartin; but if you gobern de shark in you, why den you be angel; for all angel is not'ing more dan de shark well goberned . . . .[52]

That order is maintained at all may be due primarily to the fact that Babo is a natural leader. His leadership is so complete that even the ex-king of his own country acquiesces to his will (even though Babo, by his own claim, was a slave in that same land).[53] Atufal, the magnificently proportioned giant garbed in false chains who evokes the awe of the sight-loving Delano, proves to be only the lieutenant of the small-statured, wily Babo.[54] Melville's continual emphasis on the misleading nature of appearance as opposed to reality takes on added import here. This disparity is easily seen in the image of the humble, faithful slave and his "bitter hard" but feeble master. This image assumes ironic pro-

90

portions in a scene where Benito, unbeknownst to Delano, is being menacingly shaved by Babo. According to the narrator, Delano believes he sees the slave "evincing the hand of a master" while calmly making Benito "the creature of his own tasteful hands" (par. 274). Babo, of course, *is* the master and Benito the slave; up until the moment Benito escapes, Babo, the "Nubian sculptor," readily could have "finish[ed] . . . off [the] pale and rigid . . . white statue-head" at any time. As this situation symbolically indicates, Babo holds in his hands the greatest earthly power over everyone on board the San Dominick—that of life and death. In short, Babo is a tyrant. In him, not in Benito, is "lodged a dictatorship beyond which, while at sea, there was no earthly appeal" (par. 29).

The irony in Benito's apparent dictatorship and Babo's actual one is deftly developed in this memorable shaving scene. With few exceptions, up until this point the narrator generally has confined himself to comments about Delano's state of mind; here, however, he seems to interject some of his own views about blacks. The manner in which he does so, however, appears intended to leave the impression that the expressed views are Delano's. The deception is plausible because the narrator's views do not seem to be out of character for the American. The narrator states that:

> There is something in the negro which, in a peculiar way, fits him for avocations about one's person. Most negroes are natural valets and hair- dressers; taking to the comb and brush congenially as to the castinets, and flourishing them apparently with almost equal satisfaction. There is, too, a smooth tact about them in this employment, with a marvelous, noiseless, gliding briskness, not ungraceful in its way, singularly pleasing to behold, and still more so to be the manipulated subject of. And above all is the great gift of good-humor. Not the mere grin or laugh is here meant. Those were unsuitable. But a certain easy cheerfulness, harmonious in every glance and gesture; as though God had set the whole negro to some pleasant tune.
>
> When to this is added the docility arising from the unaspiring contentment of a limited mind, and that susceptibility of blind attachment sometimes inhering in indisputable inferiors, one readily perceives why those hypochondriacs, Johnson and Byron—it may be, something like the hypochondriac Benito Cereno—took to their hearts, almost to the exclusion of the entire white race, their serving men, the negroes, Barber and Fletcher. But if there be that in the negro which exempts him from the inflicted sourness of the morbid or cynical mind, how, in his most prepossessing aspects, must he appear to a benevolent one . . . (pars. 252–53)?

When viewed from the perspective of what is really happening in the shaving scene—Babo is completely in control and is secretly terrorizing Benito—the irony of the narrator's comments is almost overwhelming. Babo is very far from being an "indisputable inferior"; contrary to the narrator's statement, Babo is proof that whatever is "in the negro," it is not something which "exempts him from the inflicted sourness of the morbid or cynical mind."

Melville's portrait of Babo is a study in contrasts: master and slave, feared tyrant and worshipping subject, evil-doer and savior. At the very least, Babo's possession of tyrannical power suggests the possibility that such power eventually may (have to) be used against the whites who would re-enslave the blacks. This dire prospect brings to mind Yoomy's speech in *Mardi*, which contains forebodings of retaliatory evil:

> Pray, heaven! . . . they may yet find a way to loose their bonds without one drop of blood. But hear me, Oro! were there no other way, and should their masters not relent, all honest hearts must cheer this tribe of Hamo on; though they cut their chains with blades thrice edged, and gory to the haft! 'Tis right to fight for freedom, whoever be the thrall.[55]

Conclusion

The interaction of Babo, Benito Cereno, and Amasa Delano is imbued by Melville with a sense of fatalism. Each character has an opportunity to avoid the course of action he ultimately follows; each one brusquely rejects any other alternative. Benito Cereno could have prevented the uprisings altogether by insisting that the slaves wear fetters, as would seem to have been "customary." Instead, he serenely accepts his friend's word that the one hundred and sixty blacks (who outnumber the whites by nearly four to one) are tractable (par. 402). Babo could have accepted the counsel of his former king, Atufal, and immediately sailed away from St. Maria after the American ship was sighted in the harbor (par. 405). In so doing, he would have avoided contact with Delano and the Bachelor's Delight, and he might have succeeded in reaching Senegal. Delano could have heeded the worried advice of his mate and refrained from offering his personal assistance to the San Dominick (par. 7).

Melville seems to have intended to leave the reader with the foreboding that the clash between whites and blacks, masters and slaves (or apparent masters and slaves) is unavoidable. The image of an inevitable linkage—one that is in some ways mutually supportive as well as potentially destructive—is vividly apparent in the leave-taking scene at the San Dominick's gangway:

> And so, still presenting himself as a crutch, and walking between the two captains, he [Babo] advanced with them towards the gangway; while still, as if full of kindly contrition, Don Benito would not let go the hand of Captain Delano, but retained it in his, across the black's body.[56]

The relations between the races on board the San Dominick all occur within the enveloping embrace of slavery. It is in the role of masters that members of each race are the most inhuman to each other. Thus, on the part of the blacks, we are told of horrifying actions taken against the subdued whites: trussed, wounded Spaniards are hurled alive into the sea; noblemen are hacked to death in their beds; one white man is presumably cannibalized. The conduct of the whites, once they are again the masters, is distinguishable only by degree: after having inflicted the most hideous wounds on the blacks with long-edged sealing spears, the whites shackle them to the ship's deck, where they evidently languish, for no mention is made of medical treatment; while shackled, several of the blacks are brutally murdered by vengeful whites.[57] The cause of this inhuman treatment of fellow human beings is perhaps best summed up in a statement Captain Delano makes in the wake of the earlier shaving scene: "Ah, this slavery breeds ugly passions in man" (par. 279).

As for the rebellion itself, its end may seem to have been foreordained when Delano, after first Benito Cereno and then Babo leap into the boat, appears to imitate the San Dominick's stern-piece:[58]

> At this juncture, the left hand of Captain Delano, on one side, again clutched the half-reclined Don Benito, heedless that he was in a speechless faint, while his right foot, on the other side, ground the prostrate negro; and his right arm pressed for added speed on the after[-]oar, his eye bent forward, encouraging his men to their utmost (par. 367).

However, there are several discrepancies between the scene in the boat and that depicted on the stern-piece. The most obvious one is that, up until the penultimate moment, Delano is unable to distinguish the conqueror from the conquered, for he pins both Benito Cereno and Babo to the boat's bottom. He is convinced that both master and slave are allied against him. Additionally, the stern-piece's victorious figure is described as being "dark"; both Delano and Benito are members of the "pale" white race. The suggestion that Delano's victory may be illusory (like his perceptions on board the San Dominick) is fortified when one considers the "satyr." According to the *Oxford English Dictionary*, satyrs are "one of a class of woodland gods or demons, in form *partly human and partly bestial*, supposed to be companions of Bacchus" (emphasis added).

I have already discussed how Melville uses animal imagery to emphasize the duality of man's nature. In this portrait of a victorious satyr, he adds an ironic element. Consider the image of one of these supposedly lustful, playful followers of Bacchus triumphing over a formidable opponent in a physical conflict. Then turn to the narrator's description of the negro as one having "the great gift of good-humor . . . a certain easy cheerfulness, harmonious in every glance and gesture; as though God had set the whole negro to some pleasant tune" (par. 252). According to the stern-piece and the reality aboard the San Dominick, the carefree satyr and the cheerful negro are not what they seem to be. The "masked . . . dark satyr" is Babo, who, unmasked (and perhaps knowing to whom the ultimate victory belongs), later "met, unabashed, the gaze of the whites" after being beheaded (par. 432).

Negroes for Sale.

A Cargo of very fine stout Men and Women, in good order and fit for immediate service, just imported from the Windward Coast of Africa, in the Ship Two Brothers.——

Conditions are one half Cash or Produce, the other half payable the first of January next, giving Bond and Security if required.

The Sale to be opened at 10 o'Clock each Day, in Mr. Bourdeaux's Yard, at No. 48, on the Bay.
May 19, 1784.   JOHN MITCHELL.

Thirty Seasoned Negroes

To be Sold for Credit, at Private Sale.

AMONGST which is a Carpenter, none of whom are known to be dishonest.

Also, to be sold for Cash, a regular bred young Negroe Man-Cook, born in this Country, who served several Years under an exceeding good French Cook abroad, and his Wife a middle aged Washer-Woman, (both very honest) and their two Children. *Likewise,* a young Man a Carpenter.

For Terms apply to the Printer.

Chapter XVIII of Amasa Delano's *Narrative of Voyages and Travels**

**Particulars of the Capture of the Spanish Ship Tryal,
at the island of St. Maria;
with the Documents relating to that affair.**

In introducing the account of the capture of the Spanish ship Tryal, I shall first give an extract from the journal of the ship Perseverance, taken on board that ship at the time, by the officer who had the care of the log book.

"Wednesday, February 20th, commenced with light airs from the north east, and thick foggy weather. At six A. M. observed a sail opening round the south head of St. Maria, coming into the bay. It proved to be a ship. The captain took the whale boat and crew, and went on board her. As the wind was very light, so that a vessel would not have much more than steerage way at the time; observed that the ship acted very awkwardly. At ten A. M. the boat returned. Mr. Luther informed that Captain Delano had remained on board her, and that she was a Spaniard from Buenos Ayres, four months and twenty six days out of port, with slaves on board; and that the ship was in great want of water, had buried many

---

*Amasa Delano, *A Narrative of Voyages and Travels, in the Northern and Southern Hemispheres: Comprising Three Voyages Round the World, Together with a Voyage of Survey and Discovery in the Pacific Ocean and Oriental Islands* (Boston: E. G. House, 1817).

white men and slaves on her passage, and that captain Delano had sent for a large boat load of water, some fresh fish, sugar, bread, pumpkins, and bottled cider, all of which articles were immediately sent. At twelve o'clock (Meridian) calm. At two P.M. the large boat returned from the Spaniards, had left our water casks on board her. At four P. M. a breeze sprung up from the southern quarter, which brought the Spanish ship into the roads. She anchored about two cables length to the south east of our ship. Immediately after she anchored, our captain with his boat was shoving off from along side the Spanish ship; when to his great surprise the Spanish captain leaped into the boat, and called out in Spanish, that the slaves on board had risen and murdered many of the people; and that he did not then command her; on which manoeuvre, several of the Spaniards who remained on board jumped overboard, and swam for our boat, and were picked up by our people. The Spaniards, who remained on board, hurried up the rigging, as high aloft as they could possibly get, and called out repeatedly for help—that they should be murdered by the slaves. Our captain came immediately on board, and brought the Spanish captain and the men who were picked up in the water; but before the boat arrived, we observed that the slaves had cut the Spanish ship adrift. On learning this, our captain hailed, and ordered the ports to be got up, and the guns cleared; but unfortunately, we could not bring but one of our guns to bear on the ship. We fired five or six shot with it, but could not bring her too. We soon observed her making sail, and standing directly out of the bay. We dispatched two boats well manned, and well armed after her, who, after much trouble, boarded the ship and retook her. But unfortunately in the business, Mr. Rufus Low, our chief officer, who commanded the party, was desperately wounded in the breast, by being stabbed with a pike, by one of the slaves. We likewise had one man badly wounded and two or three slightly. To continue the misfortune, the chief officer of the Spanish ship, who was compelled by the slaves to steer her out of the bay, received two very bad wounds, one in the side, and one through the thigh, both from musket balls. One Spaniard, a gentleman passenger on board, was likewise killed by a musket ball. We have not rightly ascertained what number of slaves were killed; but we believe seven, and a great number wounded. Our people brought the ship in, and came to nearly where she first anchored, at about two o'clock in the morning of the 21st. At six A. M. the two captains went on board the Spanish ship; took with them irons from our ship, and doubled ironed all the remaining men of the slaves who were living. Left Mr. Brown, our second officer, in charge of the ship, the gunner with him as mate, and eight other hands; together with the survivors of the Spanish crew. The captain, and chief officer, were removed to our ship, the latter for the benefit of having his wounds better attended to with us, than he could have had them on board his own ship. At nine A. M. the two captains returned, having put every thing aright, as they supposed, on board the Spanish ship.

The Spanish captain then informed us that he was compelled by the slaves to say, that he was from Buenos Ayres, bound to Lima: that he was not from Buenos Ayres, but sailed on the 20th of December last from Valparaiso for Lima, with upwards of seventy slaves on board; that on the 26th of December, the slaves rose upon the ship, and took possession of her, and put to death eighteen white men, and threw overboard at different periods after, seven more; that the slaves had commanded him to go to Senegal; that he had kept to sea until his water was expended, and had made this port to get it; and also with a view to save his own and the remainder of his people's lives if possible, by run[n]ing away from his ship with his boat.'

I shall here add some remarks of my own, to what is stated above from the ship's journal, with a view of giving the reader a correct understanding of the peculiar situation under which we were placed at the time this affair happened. We were in a worse situation to effect any important enterprize than I had been in during the voyage. We had been from home a year and a half, and had not made enough to amount to twenty dollars for each of my people, who were all on shares, and our future prospects were not very flattering. To make our situation worse, I had found after leaving New Holland, on mustering my people, that I had seventeen men, most of whom had been convicts at Botany bay. They had secreted themselves on board without my knowledge. This was a larger number than had been inveigled away from me at the same place, by people who had been convicts, and were then employed at places that we visited. The men whom we lost were all of them extraordinarily good men. This exchange materially altered the quality of the crew. Three of the Botany-bay-men were outlawed convicts; they had been shot at many times, and several times wounded. After making this bad exchange, my crew were refractory; the convicts were ever unfaithful, and took all the advantage that opportunity gave them. But sometimes exercising very strict discipline, and giving them good wholesome floggings; and at other times treating them with the best I had, or could get, according as their deeds deserved, I managed them without much difficulty during the passage across the South Pacific Ocean; and all the time I had been on the coast of Chili. I had lately been at the islands of St. Ambrose and St. Felix, and left there fifteen of my best men, with the view of procuring seals; and left that place in company with my consort the Pilgrim. We appointed Massa Fuero as our place of rendezvous, and if we did not meet there, again to rendezvous at St. Maria. I proceeded to the first place appointed; the Pilgrim had not arrived. I then determined to take a look at Juan Fernandez, and see if we could find any seals, as some persons had informed me they were to be found on some part of the island. I accordingly visited that place, as has been stated; from thence I proceeded to St. Maria; and arrived the 13th of February at that place, where we commonly find visitors. We found the ship Mars of Nantucket, commanded by Captain Jonathan Barney. The day we arrived, three of my Botany bay men run from the boat when on shore. The next day, (the 14th) I was informed by Captain Barney, that some of my convict men had planned to run away with one of my boats, and go over to the main. This information he obtained through the medium of his people. I examined into the affair, and was satisfied as to the truth of it; set five more of the above description of men on shore, making eight in all I had gotten clear of in two days. Captain Barney sailed about the 17th, and left me quite alone. I continued in that unpleasant situation till the 20th, never at any time after my arrival at this place, daring to let my whale boat be in the water fifteen minutes unless I was in her myself, from a fear that some of my people would run away with her. I always hoisted her in on deck the moment I came along side, by which means I had the advantage of them; for should they run away with any other boat belonging to the ship, I could overtake them with the whale boat, which they very well knew. They were also well satisfied of the reasons why that boat was always kept on board, except when in my immediate use. During this time, I had no fear from them, except of their running away. Under these disadvantages the Spanish ship Tryal made her appearance on the morning of the 20th, as has been stated; and I had in the course of the day the satisfaction of seeing the great utility of good discipline. In every part of the business of the Tryal, not one disaffected word was spoken by the men, but all flew to obey the commands they received; and to their credit it should be recorded, that no men ever behaved better than they, under such circumstances. When it is considered that we had but two boats, one a whale boat, and the other built by ourselves, while on the coast of New Holland, which was very little larger than the whale boat; both of them were clinker built, one of cedar, and the other not much stouter; with only twenty men to board and carry a ship, containing so many slaves, made desperate by their situation; for they were certain, if taken, to suffer death; and when arriving along side of the ship, they might have staved the bottom of the boats, by heaving into them a ballast stone or log of wood of twenty pounds: when all these things are taken into view, the reader may conceive of the hazardous nature of the enterprise, and the skill and the intrepidity which were requisite to carry it into execution.

On the afternoon of the 19th, before night, I sent the boatswain with the large boat and seine to try if he could catch some fish; he returned at night with but few, observing that the morning would be better, if he went early. I then wished him to go as early as he thought proper, and he accordingly went at four o'clock. At sunrise, or about that time, the officer who commanded the deck, came down to me while I was in my cot, with information that a sail was just opening round the south point, or head of the island. I immediately rose, went on deck, and observed that she was too near the land, on account of a reef that lay off the head; and at the same time remarked to my people, that she must be a stranger, and I did not well understand what she was about. Some of them observed that they did not know who she was, or what she was doing; but that they were accustomed to see vessels shew their colours, when coming into a port. I ordered the whale boat to be hoisted out and manned, which was accordingly done. Presuming the vessel was from sea, and had been many days out, without perhaps fresh provisions, we put the fish which had been caught the night before into the boat, to be presented if necessary. Every thing being soon ready, as I thought the strange ship was in danger, we made all the haste in our power to get on board, that we might prevent her getting on the reefs; but before we came near her, the wind headed her off, and she was doing well. I went along side, and saw the decks were filled with slaves. As soon as I got on deck, the captain, mate, people and slaves, crowded around me to relate their stories, and to make known their grievances; which could not but impress me with feelings of pity for their sufferings. They told me they had no water, as is related in their different accounts and depositions. After promising to relieve all the wants they had mentioned, I ordered the fish to be put on board, and sent the whale boat to our ship, with orders that the large boat, as soon as she returned from fishing, should take a set of gang casks to the watering place, fill them, and bring it for their relief as soon as possible. I also ordered the small boat to take what fish the large one had caught, and what soft bread they had baked, some pumpkins, some sugar, and bottled cider, and return to me without delay. The boat left me on board the Spanish ship, went to our own, and executed the orders; and returned to me again about eleven o'clock. At noon the large boat came with the water, which I was obliged to serve out to them myself, to keep them [from] drinking so much as to do themselves injury. I gave them at first one gill each, an hour after, half a pint, and the third hour, a pint. Afterward, I permited them to drink as they pleased. They all looked up to me as a benefactor; and as I was deceived in them, I did them every possible kindness. Had it been otherwise there is no doubt I should have fallen a victim to their power. It was to my great advantage, that, on this occasion, the temperament of my mind was unusually pleasant. The apparent sufferings of those about me had softened my feelings into sympathy; or, doubtless my interference with some of their transactions would have cost me my life. The Spanish captain had evidently lost much of his authority over the slaves, whom he appeared to fear, and whom he was unwilling in any case to oppose. An instance of this occured in the conduct of the four cabin boys, spoken of by the captain. They were eating with the slave boys on the main deck, when, (as I was afterwards informed) the Spanish boys, feeling some hopes of release, and not having prudence sufficient to keep silent, some words dropped respecting their expectations, which were understood by the slave boys. One of them gave a stroke with a knife on the head of one of the Spanish boys, which penetrated to the bone, in a cut four inches in length. I saw this and inquired what it meant. The captain replied, that it was merely the sport of the boys, who had fallen out. I told him it appeared to me to be rather serious sport, as the wound had caused the boy to lose about a quart of blood. Several similar instances of unruly conduct, which, agreeably to my manner of thinking, demanded immediate resistance and punishment, were thus easily winked at, and passed over. I felt willing however to make some allowance even for conduct so gross, when I considered them to have been broken down with fatigue and long suffering.

The act of the negro, who kept constantly at the elbows of Don Bonito and myself, I should, at any other time, have immediately resented; and although it excited my wonder, that his commander should allow this extraordinary liberty, I did not remonstrate against it, until it became troublesome to myself. I wished to have some private conversation with the captain alone, and the negro as usual following us into the cabin, I requested the captain to send him on deck, as the business about which we were to talk could not be conveniently communicated in presence of a third person. I spoke in Spanish, and the negro understood me. The captain assured me, that his remaining with us would be of no disservice; that he had made him his confidant and companion since he had lost so many of his officers and men. He had introduced him to me before, as captain of the slaves, and told me he kept them in good order. I was alone with them, or rather on board by myself, for three or four hours, during the absence of my boat, at which time the ship drifted out with the current three leagues from my own, when the breeze sprung up from the south east. It was nearly four o'clock in the afternoon. We ran the ship as near to the Perseverance as we could without either ship's swinging afoul the other. After the Spanish ship was anchored, I invited the captain to go on board my ship and take tea or coffee with me. His answer was short and seemingly reserved; and his air very different from that with which he had received my assistance. As I was at a loss to account for this change in his demeanour, and knew he had seen nothing in my conduct to justify it, and as I felt certain that he treated me with intentional neglect; in return I became less sociable, and said little to him. After I had ordered my boat to be hauled up and manned, and as I was going to the side of the vessel, in order to get into her, Don Bonito came to me, gave my hand a hearty squeeze, and, as I thought, seemed to feel the weight of the cool treatment with which I had retaliated. I had committed a mistake in attributing his apparent coldness to neglect; and as soon as the discovery was made, I was happy to rectify it, by a prompt renewal of friendly intercourse. He continued to hold my hand fast till I stepped off the gunwale down the side, when he let it go, and stood making me compliments. When I had seated myself in the boat, and ordered her to be shoved off, the people having their oars up on end, she fell off at a sufficient distance to leave room for the oars to drop. After they were down, the Spanish captain, to my great astonishment, leaped from the gunwale of the ship into the middle of our boat. As soon as he had recovered a little, he called out in so alarming a manner, that I could not understand him; and the Spanish sailors were then seen jumping overboard and making for our boat. These proceedings excited the wonder of us all. The officer whom I had with me anxiously inquired into their meaning. I smiled and told him, that I neither knew, nor cared; but it seemed the captain was trying to impress his people with a belief that we intended to run away with him. At this moment one of my Portuguese sailors in the boat, spoke to me, and gave me to understand what Don Bonito said. I desired the captain to come aft and sit down by my side, and in a calm deliberate manner relate the whole affair[.] In the mean time the boat was employed in picking up the men who had jumped from the ship. They had picked up three, (leaving one in the water till after the boat had put the Spanish captain and myself on board my ship,) when my officer observed the cable was cut, and the ship was swinging. I hailed the Perseverance, ordering the ports got up, and the guns run out as soon as possible. We pulled as fast as we could on board; and then despatched the boat for the man who was left in the water, whom we succeeded to save alive.

We soon had our guns ready; but the Spanish ship had dropped so far astern of the Perseverance, that we could bring but one gun to bear on her, which was the after one. This was fired six times, without any other effect than cutting away the fore top-mast stay, and some other small ropes which were no hindrance to her going away. She was soon out of reach of our shot, steering out of the bay. We then had some other calculations to make. Our ship was moored with two bower anchors, which were all the cables or anchors of that description we had. To slip and leave them would be to break our policy of insurance by a deviation, against which I would here caution the masters of all vessels. It should always be borne in mind, that to do any thing which will destroy the guaranty of their policies, how great soever may be the inducement, and how generous soever the motive, is not justifiable; for should any accident subsequently occur, whereby a loss might accrue to the underwriters, they will be found ready enough, and sometimes too ready, to avail themselves of the opportunity to be released from responsibility; and the damage must necessarily be sustained by the owners. This is perfectly right. The law has wisely restrained the powers of the insured, that the insurer should not be subject to imposition, or abuse. All bad consequences may be avoided by one who has a knowledge of his duty, and is disposed faithfully to obey its dictates.

At length, without much loss of time, I came to a determination to pursue, and take the ship with my two boats. On inquiring of the captain what fire arms they had on board the Tryal, he answered, they had none which they could use; that he had put the few they had out of order, so that they could make no defence with them; and furthermore, that they did not understand their use, if they were in order. He observed at the same time, that if I attempted to take her with boats we should all be killed; for the negros were such bravos and so desperate, that there would be no such thing as conquering them. I saw the man in the situation that I have seen others, frightened at his own shadow. This was probably owing to his having been effectually conquered and his spirits broken.

After the boats were armed, I ordered the men to get into them, and they obeyed with cheerfulness. I was going myself, but Don Bonito took hold of my hand and forbade me, saying, you have saved my life, and now you are going to throw away your own. Some of my confidential officers asked me if it would be prudent for me to go, and leave the Perseverance in such an unguarded state; and also, if any thing should happen to me, what would be the consequence to the voyage. Every man on board, they observed, would willingly go, if it were my pleasure. I gave their remonstrances a moment's consideration, and felt their weight. I then ordered into the boats my chief officer, Mr. Low, who commanded the party; and under him, Mr. Brown, my second officer, my brother William, Mr. George Russell, son to major Benjamin Russell of Boston, and Mr. Nathaniel Luther, midshipmen; William Clark, boatswain; Charles Spence, gunner; and thirteen seamen. By way of encouragement, I told them that Don Bonito considered the ship and what was in her as lost; that the value was more than one hundred thousand dollars; that if we would take her, it should be all our own; and that if we should afterwards be disposed to give him up one half, it would be considered as a present. I likewise reminded them of the suffering condition of the poor Spaniards remaining on board, whom I then saw with my spy-glass as high aloft as they could get on the top-gallant-masts, and knowing that death must be their fate if they came down. I told them, never to see my face again, if they did not take her; and these were all of them pretty powerful stimulants. I wished God to prosper them in the discharge of their arduous duty, and they shoved off. They pulled after and came up with the Tryal, took their station upon each quarter, and commenced a brisk fire of musketry, directing it as much at the man at the helm as they could, as that was likewise a place of resort for the negroes. At length they drove the chief mate from it, who had been compelled to steer the ship. He ran up the mizen rigging as high as the cross jack yard, and called out in Spanish, "Don't board." This induced our people to believe that he favoured the cause of the negroes; they fired at him, and two balls took effect; one of them went through his side, but did not go deep enough to be mortal; and the other went through one of his thighs. This brought him down on deck again. They found the ship made such head way, that the boats could hardly keep up with her, as the breeze was growing stronger. They then called to the Spaniards, who were still as high aloft as they could get, to come down on the yards, and cut away the robings and earings of the topsails, and let them fall from the yards, so that they might not hold any wind. They accordingly did so. About the same time, the Spaniard who was steering the ship, was killed; (he is sometimes called *passenger* and sometimes *clerk*, in the different depositions,) so that both these circumstances combined, rendered her unmanageable by such people as were left on board. She came round to the wind, and both boats boarded, one on each bow, when she was carried by hard fighting. The negroes defended themselves with desperate courage; and after our people had boarded them, they found they had barricadoed the deck by making a breast work of the water casks which we had left on board, and sacks of matta, abreast the mainmast, from one side of the ship to the other, to the height of six feet; behind which they defended themselves with all the means in their power to the last; and our people had to force their way over this breast work before they could compel them to surrender. The other parts of the transaction have some of them been, and the remainder will be hereafter stated.

On going on board the next morning with hand-cuffs, leg-irons, and shackled bolts, to secure the hands and feet of the negroes, the sight which presented itself to our view was truly horrid. They had got all the men who were living made fast, hands and feet, to the ring bolts in the deck; some of them had parts of their bowels hanging out, and some with half their backs and thighs shaved off. This was done with our boarding lances, which were always kept exceedingly sharp, and as bright as a gentleman's sword. Whilst putting them in irons, I had to exercise as much authority over the Spanish captain and his crew, as I had to use over my own men on any other occasion, to prevent them from cutting to pieces and killing these poor unfortunate beings. I observed one of the Spanish sailors had found a razor in the pocket of an old jacket of his, which one of the slaves had on; he opened it, and made a cut upon the negro's head. He seemed to aim at his throat, and it bled shockingly. Seeing several more about to engage in the same kind of barbarity, I commanded them not to hurt another of them, on pain of being brought to the gang-way and flogged. The captain also, I noticed, had a dirk, which he had secreted at the time the negroes were massacreing the Spaniards. I did not observe, however, that he intended to use it, until one of my people gave me a twitch by the elbow, to draw my attention to what was passing, when I saw him in the act of stabbing one of the slaves. I immediately caught hold of him, took away his dirk, and threatened him with the consequences of my displeasure, if he attempted to hurt one of them. Thus I was obliged to be continually vigilant, to prevent them from using violence towards these wretched creatures.

After we had put every thing in order on board the Spanish ship, and swept for and obtained her anchors, which the negroes had cut her from, we sailed on the 23d, both ships in company, for Conception, where we anchored on the 26th. After the common forms were passed, we delivered the ship, and all that was on board her, to the captain, whom we had befriended. We delivered him also a bag of doubloons, containing, I presume, nearly a thousand; several bags of dollars, containing a like number; and several baskets of watches, some gold, and some silver: all of which had been brought on board the Perseverance for safe keeping. We detained no part of this treasure to reward us for the services we had rendered:—all that we received was faithfully returned.

After our arrival at Conception, I was mortified and very much hurt at the treatment which I received from Don Bonito Sereno; but had this been the only time that I ever was treated with ingratitude, injustice, or want of compassion, I would not complain. I will only name one act of his towards me at this place. He went to the prison and took the depositions of five of my Botany bay convicts, who had left us at St. Maria, and were now in prison here. This was done by him with a view to injure my character, so that he might not be obliged to make us any compensation for what we had done for him. I never made any demand of, nor claimed in any way whatever, more than that they should give me justice; and did not ask to be my own judge, but to refer it to government. Amongst those who swore against me were the three outlawed convicts, who have been before mentioned. I had been the means, undoubtedly, of saving every one of their lives, and had supplied them with clothes. They swore every thing against me they could to effect my ruin. Amongst other atrocities, they swore I was a pirate, and made several statements that would operate equally to my disadvantage had they been believed; all of which were brought before the viceroy of Lima against me. When we met at that place, the viceroy was too great and too good a man to be misled by these false representations. He told Don Bonito, that my conduct towards him proved the injustice of these depositions, taking his own official declaration at Conception for the proof of it; that he had been informed by Don Jose Calminaries, who was commandant of the marine, and was at that time, and after the affair of the Tryal, on the coast of Chili; that Calminaries had informed him how both Don Bonito and myself had conducted, and he was satisfied that no man had behaved better, under all circumstances, than the American captain had done to Don Bonito, and that he never had seen or heard of any man treating another with so much dishonesty and ingratitude as he had treated the American. The viceroy had previously issued an order, on his own authority, to Don Bonito, to deliver to me eight thousand dollars as part payment for services rendered him. This order was not given till his Excellency had consulted all the tribunals holding jurisdiction over similar cases, except the twelve royal judges. These judges exercise a supreme authority over all the courts in Peru, and reserve to themselves the right of giving a final decision in all questions of law. Whenever either party is dissatisfied with the decision of the inferior courts in this kingdom, they have a right of appeal to the twelve judges. Don Bonito had attempted an appeal from the viceroy's order to the royal judges. The viceroy sent for me, and acquainted me of Don Bonito's attempt; at the same time recommending to me to accede to it, as the royal judges well understood the nature of the business, and would do much better for me than his order would. He observed at the same time, that they were men of too great characters to be biassed or swayed from doing justice by any party; they holding their appointments immediately from his majesty. He said, if I requested it, Don Bonito should be holden to his order. I then represented, that I had been in Lima nearly two months, waiting for different tribunals, to satisfy his Excellency what was safe for him, and best to be done for me, short of a course of law, which I was neither able nor willing to enter into; that I had then nearly thirty men on different islands, and on board my tender, which was then somewhere amongst the islands on the coast of Chili; that they had no method that I knew of to help themselves, or receive succor, except from me; and that if I was to defer the time any longer it amounted to a certainty, that they must suffer. I therefore must pray that his Excellency's order might be put in force.

Don Bonito, who was owner of the ship and part of the cargo, had been quibbling and using all his endeavors to delay the time of payment, provided the appeal was not allowed, when his Excellency told him to get out of his sight, that he would pay the money himself, and put him (Don Bonito) into a dungeon, where he should not see sun, moon, or stars; and was about giving the order, when a very respectable company of merchants waited on him and pleaded for Don Bonito; praying that his Excellency would favour him on account of his family, who were very rich and respectable. The viceroy remarked that Don Bonito's character had been such as to disgrace any family, that had any pretensions to respectability; but that he should grant their prayer, provided there was no more reason for complaint. The last transaction brought me the money in two hours; by which time I was extremely distressed, enough, I believe, to have punished me for a great many of my bad deeds.

When I take a retrospective view of my life, I cannot find in my soul, that I ever have done any thing to deserve such misery and ingratitude as I have suffered at different periods, and in general, from the very persons to whom I have rendered the greatest services.

The following Documents were officially translated, and are inserted without alteration, from the original papers. This I thought to be the most correct course, as it would give the reader a better view of the subject than any other method that could be adopted. My deposition and that of Mr. Luther, were communicated through a bad linguist, who could not speak the English language so well as I could the Spanish, Mr. Luther not having any knowledge of the Spanish language. The Spanish captain's deposition, together with Mr. Luther's and my own, were translated into English again, as now inserted; having thus undergone two translations. These circumstances, will, we hope, be a sufficient apology for any thing which may appear to the reader not to be perfectly consistent, one declaration with another; and for any impropriety of expression.

OFFICIAL DOCUMENTS.

STAMP.	A FAITHFUL TRANSLATION OF THE DEPOSITIONS OF DON BENITO CERENO, OF DON AMASA DELANO, AND OF DON NATHANIEL LUTHER, TOGETHER WITH THE DOCUMENTS OF THE COMMENCEMENT OF THE PROCESS, UNDER THE KING'S SEAL.

I DON JOSE DE ABOS, and Padilla, his Majesty's Notary for the Royal Revenue, and Register of this Province, and Notary Public of the Holy

105

Crusade of this Bishoprick, &c.

Do certify and declare, as much as requisite in law, that, in the criminal cause, which by an order of the Royal Justice, Doctor DON JUAN MARTINEZ DE ROZAS, deputy assessor general of this province, conducted against the Senegal Negroes, that the ship Tryal was carrying from the port of Valparaiso, to that of Callao of Lima, in the month of December last. There is at the beginning of the prosecution, a decree in continuation of the declaration of her captain, Don Benito Cereno, and on the back of the twenty-sixth leaf, that of the captain of the American ship, the Perseverance, Amasa Delano; and that of the supercargo of this ship, Nathaniel Luther, midshipman, of the United States, on the thirtieth leaf; as also the Sentence of the aforesaid cause, on the back of the 72d leaf; and the confirmation of the Royal Audience, of this District, on the 78th and 79th leaves; and an official order of the Tribunal with which the cause and every thing else therein continued, is remitted back; which proceedings with a representation made by the said American captain, Amasa Delano, to this Intendency, against the Spanish captain of the ship Tryal, Don Benito Cereno, and answers thereto—are in the following manner—

Decree of the Commencement of the Process.

In the port of Talcahuane, the twenty-fourth of the month of February, one thousand eight hundred and five, Doctor Don Juan Martinez de Rozas, Counsellor of the Royal Audience of this Kingdom, Deputy Assessor, and learned in the law, of this Intendency, having the deputation thereof on account of the absence of his Lordship, the Governor Intendent—Said, that whereas the ship Tryal, has just cast anchor in the road of this port, and her captain, Don Benito Cereno, has made the declaration of the twentieth of December, he sailed from the port of Valparaiso, bound to that of Callao; having his ship loaded with produce and merchandize of the country, with sixty-three negroes of all sexes and ages, and besides nine sucking infants; that the twenty-sixth, in the night, revolted, killed eighteen of his men, and made themselves master of the ship—that afterwards they killed seven men more, and obliged him to carry them to the coast of Africa, at Senegal, of which they were natives; that Tuesday the nineteenth, he put into the island of Santa Maria, for the purpose of taking in water, and he found in its harbour the American ship, the Perseverance, commanded by captain Amasa Delano, who being informed of the revolt of the negroes on board the ship Tryal, killed five or six of them in the engagement, and finally overcame them; that the ship being recovered, he supplied him with hands, and brought him to the port.—Wherefore, for examining the truth of these facts, and inflict on the guilty of such heinous crimes, the penalties provided by law. He therefore orders that this decree commencing the process, should be extended, that agreeably to its tenor, the witnesses, that should be able to give an account of them, be examined—thus ordered by his honour, which I attest.—Doctor ROZAS

Before me, JOSE DE ABOS, and Padilla, his Majesty's Notary of Royal Revenue and Registers.

Declaration of first Witness, DON BENITO CERENO.

The same day and month and year, his Honour ordered the captain of the ship Tryal, Don Benito Cereno, to appear, of whom he received before me, the oath, which he took by God, our Lord, and a Sign of the Cross, under which he promised to tell the truth of whatever he should know and should be asked —and being interrogated agreeably to the tenor of the act, commencing the process, he said, that the twentieth of December last, he set sail with his ship from the port of Valparaiso, bound to that of Callao; loaded with the produce of the country, and seventy-two negroes of both sexes, and of all ages, belonging to Don Alexandro Aranda, inhabitant of the city of Mendosa; that the crew of the ship consisted of thirty-six men, besides the persons who went [as] passengers; that the negroes were of the following ages,—twenty from twelve to sixteen years, one from about eighteen to nineteen years, named Jose, and this was the man that waited upon his master Don Alexandro, who speaks well the Spanish, having had him four or five years; a mulatto, named Francisco, native of the province of Buenos Ayres, aged about thirty-five years; a smart negro, named Joaquin, who had been for many years among the Spaniards, aged twenty six years, and a caulker by trade; twelve full grown negroes, aged from twenty-five to fifty years, all raw and born on the coast of Senegal—whose names are as follow,—the first was named Babo, and he was killed,—the second who is his son, is named Muri,—the third, Matiluqui,—the fourth, Yola,—the fifth, Yau,—the sixth Atufal, who was killed,—the seventh, Diamelo, also killed,— the eighth, Lecbe, likewise killed,—the ninth, Natu, in the same manner killed, and that he does not recollect the names of the others; but that he will take due account of them all, and remit to the court; and twenty-eight women of all ages;—that all the negroes slept upon deck, as is customary in this navigation; and none wore fetters, because the owner, Aranda told him that they were all tractable; that the twenty-seventh of December, at three o'clock in the morning, all the Spaniards being asleep except the two officers on the watch, who were the boatswain Juan Robles, and the carpenter Juan Balltista Gayete, and the helmsman and his boy; the negroes revolted suddenly, wounded dangerously the boatswain and the carpenter, and successively killed eighteen men of those who were sleeping upon deck,—some with sticks and daggers, and others by throwing them alive overboard, after tying them; that of the Spaniards who were upon deck, they left about seven, as he thinks, alive and tied, to manoeuvre the ship; and three or four more who hid themselves, remained also alive, although in the act of revolt, they made themselves masters of the hatchway, six or seven wounded, went through it to the cock-pit without any hindrance on their part; that in the act of revolt, the mate and another person, whose name he does not recollect, attempted to come up through the hatchway, but having been wounded at the onset, they were obliged to return to the cabin; that the deponent resolved at break of day to come up the companion-way, where the negro Babo was, being the ring leader, and another who assisted him, and having spoken to them, exhorted them to cease committing such atrocities—asking them at the same time what they wanted and intended to do—offering himself to obey their commands; that notwithstanding this, they threw, in his presence, three men, alive and tied, overboard; that they told the deponent to come up, and that they would not kill him—which having done, they asked him whether there were in these seas any negro countries, where they might be carried, and he answered them, no; that they afterwards told him to carry them to *Senegal*, or to the neighbouring islands of St. Nicolas—and he answered them, that this was impossible, on account of the great distance, the bad condition of the vessel, the want of provisions, sails and water; that they replied to him, he must carry them in any way; that they would do and conform themselves to every thing the deponent should require as to eating and drinking, that after a long conference, being absolutely compelled to please them, for they threatened him to kill them all, if they were not at all events carried to Senegal. He told them that what was most wanting for the voyage was water; that they would go near the coast to take it, and thence they would proceed on their course—that the negroes agreed to it; and the deponent steered towards the intermediate ports, hoping to meet some Spanish or foreign vessel that would save them; that within ten or eleven days they saw the land, and continued their course by it in the vicinity of Nasca; that the deponent observed that the negroes were now restless, and mutinous, because he did not effect the taking in of water, they having required with threats that it should be done, without fail the following day; he told them they saw plainly that the coast was steep, and the rivers designated in the maps were not to be found, with other reasons suitable to the circumstances; that the best way would be to go to the island of Santa Maria, where they might water and victual easily, it being a desert island, as the foreigners did; that the deponent did not go to Pisco, that was near, nor make any other port of the coast, because the negroes had intimated to him several times, that they would kill them all the very moment they should perceive any city, town, or settlement, on the shores to which they should be carried; that having determined to go to the island of Santa Maria, as the deponent had planned, for the purpose of trying whether in the passage or in the island itself, they could find any vessel that should favour them, or whether he could escape from it in a boat to the neighbouring coast of Arruco. To adopt the necessary means he immediately changed his course, steering for the island; that the negroes held daily conferences, in which they discussed what was necessary for their design of returning to Senegal, whether they were to kill all the Spaniards, and particularly the deponent; that eight days after parting from the coast of Nasca, the deponent being on the watch a little after day-break, and soon after the negroes had their meeting, the negro Mure came to the place where the deponent was, and told him, that his comrades had determined to kill his master, Don Alexandro Aranda, because they said they could not otherwise obtain their liberty, and that he should call the mate, who was sleeping, before they executed it, for fear, as he understood, that he should not be killed with the rest; that the deponent prayed and told him all that was necessary in such a circumstance to dissuade him from his design, but all was useless, for the negro Mure answered him, that the thing could not be prevented, and that they should all run the risk of being killed if they should attempt to dissuade or obstruct them in the act; that in this conflict the deponent called the mate, and immediately the negro Mure ordered the negro Matinqui, and another named Lecbe, who died in the island of Santa Maria, to go and commit this murder; that the two negroes went down to the birth of Don Alexandro, and stabbed him in his bed; that yet half alive and agonizing, they dragged him on deck and threw him overboard; that the clerk, Don Lorenzo Bargas, was sleeping in the opposite birth, and awaking at the cries of Aranda, surprised by them, and at the sight of the negroes, who had bloody daggers in their hands, he threw himself into the sea through a window which was near him, and was miserably drowned, without being in the power of the deponent to assist, or take him up, though he immediately put out his boat; that a short time after killing Aranda, they got upon deck his german-cousin, Don Francisco Masa, and his other clerk, called Don Hermenegildo, a native of Spain, and a relation of the said Aranda, besides the boatswain, Juan Robles, the boatswain's mate, Manuel Viseaya, and two or three others of the sailors, all of whom were wounded, and having stabbed them again, they threw them alive into the sea, although they made no resistance, nor begged for any thing else but mercy; that the boatswain, Juan Robles, who knew how to swim, kept himself the longest above water, making acts of contrition, and in the last words he uttered, charged this deponent to cause mass to be said for his soul, to our Lady of Succour; that having finished this slaughter, the negro Mure told him that they had now done all, and that he might pursue his destination, warning him that they would kill all the Spaniards, if they saw them speak, or plot any thing against them—a threat which they repeated almost every day; that before this occurrence last mentioned, they had tied the cook to throw him overboard for I know not what thing they heard him speak, and finally they spared his life at the request of the deponent; that a few days after, the deponent endeavoured not to omit any means to preserve their lives—spoke to them peace and tranquillity, and agreed to draw up a paper, signed by the deponent, and the sailors who could write, as also by the negroes, Babo and Atufal, who could do it in their language, though they were new, in which he obliged himself to carry them to Senegal, and they not to kill any more, and to return to them the ship with the cargo, with which they were for that satisfied and quieted; that omitting other events which daily happened, and which can only serve to recal their past misfortunes and conflicts, after forty-two days navigation, reckoned from the time they sailed from Nasca, during which they navigated under a scanty allowance of water, they at last arrived at the island of Santa Maria, on Tuesday the nine-teenth instant, at about five o'clock in the afternoon, at which hour they cast anchor very near the American ship Perseverance, which lay in the same port, commanded by the *generous captain Amasa Delano*, but at seven o'clock in the morning they had already descried the port, and the negroes became uneasy as soon as they saw the ship, and the deponent, to appease and quiet them, pro-posed to them to say and do all that he will declare to have said to the American captain, with which they were tranquilized warning him that if he varied in the least, or uttered any word that should give the least intimation of the past oc-currences, they would instantly kill him and all his companions; that about eight o'clock in the morning, captain Amasa Delano came in his boat, on board the Tryal, and all gladly received him; that the deponent, acting then the part of an owner and a free captain of the ship, told them that he came from Buenos Ayres, bound to Lima, with that parcel of negroes; that at the cape many had died, that also, all the sea officers and the greatest part of the crew had died, there remained to him no other sailors than these few who were in sight, and that for want of them the sails had been torn to pieces; that the heavy storms off the cape had obliged them to throw overboard the greatest part of the cargo, and the water pipes; that consequently he had no more water; that he had thought of putting into the port of Conception, but that the north wind had prevented him, as also the want of water, for he had only enough for that day, concluded by asking of him supplies;—that the *generous captain Amasa Delano* immediately offered them sails, pipes, and whatever he wanted, to pursue his voyage to Lima, without entering any other port, leaving it to his pleasure to refund him for these supplies at Callao, or pay him for them if he thought best; that he immediately ordered his boat for the purpose of bringing him water, sugar, and bread, as they did; that Amasa Delano remained on board the Tryal all the day, till he left the ship anchored at five o'clock in the afternoon, depo-nent speaking to him always of his pretended misfortunes, under the fore- men-tioned principles, without having had it in his power to tell a single word, nor giving him the least hint, that he might know the truth, and state of things; because the negro Mure, who is a man of capacity and talents, performing the office of an officious servant, with all the appearance of submission of the hum-ble slave, did not leave the deponent one moment, in order to observe his actions and words; for he understands well the Spanish, and besides there were ther-eabout some others who were constantly on the watch and understood it also; that a moment in which Amasa Delano left the deponent, Mure asked him, how do we come on? and the deponent answered them, well; he gives us all the sup-plies we want, but he asked him afterwards how many men he had, and the deponent told him that he had thirty men; but that twenty of them were on the island, and there were in the vessel only those whom he saw there in the two boats; and then the negro told him, well, you will be the captain of this ship to night and his also, for three negroes are sufficient to take it; that as soon as they

had cast anchor, at five of the clock, as has been stated, the American captain took leave, to return to his vessel, and the deponent accompanied him as far as the gunwale, where he staid under pretence of taking leave, until he should have got into his boat; but on shoving off, the deponent jumped from the gunwale into the boat and fell into it, without knowing how, and without sustaining, fortunately, any harm; but he immediately hallooed to the Spaniards in the ship, "Overboard, those that can swim, the rest to the rigging." That he instantly told the captain, by means of the Portuguese interpreter, that they were revolted negroes, who had killed all his people; that the said captain soon understood the affair, and recovered from his surprise, which the leap of the deponent occassioned, and told him, "Be not afraid, be not afraid, set down and be easy," and ordered his sailors to row towards his ship, and before coming up to her, he hailed, to get a cannon ready and run it out of the port hole, which they did very quick, and fired with it a few shots at the negroes; that in the mean while the boat was sent to pick up two men who had thrown themselves overboard, which they effected; that the negroes cut the cables, and endeavoured to sail away; that Amasa Delano, seeing them sailing away, and the cannon could not subdue them, ordered his people to get muskets, pikes, and sabres ready, and all his men offered themselves willingly to board them with the boats; that captain Amasa Delano wanted to go in person, and was going to embark the first, but the deponent prevented him, and after many entreaties he finally remained, saying, though that circumstance would procure him much honour, he would stay to please him, and keep him company in his affliction, and would send a brother of his, on whom he said he placed as much reliance as on himself; his brother, the mates, and eighteen men, whom he had in his vessel, embarked in the two boats, and made their way towards the Tryal, which was already under sail; that they rowed considerably in pursuing the ship, and kept up a musketry fire; but that they could not overtake them, until they hallooed to the sailors on the rigging, to unbend or take away the sails, which they accordingly did, letting them fall on the deck; that they were then able to lay themselves alongside, keeping up constantly a musketry fire, whilst some got up the sides on deck, with pikes and sabres, and the others remained in the stern of the boat, keeping up also a fire, until they got up finally by the same side, and engaged the negroes, who defended themselves to the last with their weapons, rushing upon the points of the pikes with an extraordinary fury; that the Americans killed five or six negroes, and these were Babo, Atufal, Dick, Natu, Qiamolo, and does not recollect any other; that they wounded several others, and at last conquered and made them prisoners; that at ten o'clock at night, the first mate with three men, came to inform the captain that the ship had been taken, and came also for the purpose of being cured of a dangerous wound, made by a point of a dagger, which he had received in his breast; that two other Americans had been slightly wounded; the captain left nine men to take care of the ship as far as this port; he accompanied her with his own until both ships, the Tryal and Perseverance,

111

cast anchor between nine and eleven o'clock in the forenoon of this day; that the deponent has not seen the twenty negroes, from twelve to sixteen years of age, have any share in the execution of the murders; nor does he believe they have had, on account of their age, although all were knowing to the insurrection; that the negro Jose, eighteen years old, and in the service of Don Alexandro, was the one who communicated the information to the negro Mure and his comrades, of the state of things before the revolt; and this is known, because in the preceding nights he used to come to sleep from below, where they were, and had secret conversations with Mure, in which he was seen several times by the mate; and one night he drove him away twice; that this same negro Jose, was the one who advised the other negroes to kill his master, Don Alexandro; and that this is known, because the negroes have said it; that on the first revolt, the negro Jose was upon deck with the other revolted negroes, but it is not known whether he materially participated in the murders; that the mulatto Francisco was of the band of revolters, and one of their number; that the negro Joaquin was also one of the worst of them, for that on the day the ship was taken, he assisted in the defence of her with a hatchet in one hand and a dagger in the other, as the sailors told him; that in sight of the deponent, he stabbed Don Francisco Masa, when he was carrying him to throw him overboard alive, he being the one who held him fast; that the twelve or thirteen negroes, from twenty-five to fifty years of age, were with the former, the principal revolters, and committed the murders and atrocities before related; that five or six of them were killed, as has been said, in the attack on the ship, and the following remained alive and are prisoners,—to wit—Mure, who acted as captain and commander of them, and on all the insurrections and posterior events, Matinqui, Alathano, Yau, Luis, Mapenda, Yola, Yambaio, being eight in number, and with Jose, Joaquin, and Francisco, who are also alive, making the member of eleven of the remaining insurgents; that the negresses of age, were knowing to the revolt, and influenced the death of their master; who also used their influence to kill the deponent; that in the act of murder, and before that of the engagement of the ship, they began to sing, and were singing a very melancholy song during the action, to excite the courage of the negroes; that the statement he has just given of the negroes who are alive, has been made by the officers of the ship; that of the thirty-six men of the crew and passengers, which the deponent had knowledge of, twelve only including the mate remained alive, besides four cabin boys, who were not included in that number; that they broke an arm of one of those cabin boys, named Francisco Raneds, and gave him three or four stabs, which are already healed; that in the engagement of the ship, the second clerk, Don Jose Morairi, was killed by a musket ball fired at him through accident, for having incautiously presented himself on the gunwale; that at the time of the attack of the ship, Don Joaquin Arambaolaza was on one of the yards flying from the negroes, and at the approach of the boats, he hallooed by order of the negroes, not to board, on which account the Americans thought he was also one of the revolters, and fired two balls at him, one passed through one of his thighs, and the other in the chest of his body, of which he is now confined, though the American captain, who has him on board, says he will recover; that in order to be able to proceed from the coast of Nasca, to the island of Santa Maria, he saw himself obliged to lighten the ship, by throwing more than one third of the cargo overboard, for he could not have made that voyage otherwise; that what he has said is the most substantial of what occurs to him on this unfortunate event, and the truth, under the oath that he has taken;—which declaration he affirmed and ratified, after hearing it read to him. He said that he was twenty-nine years of age;—and signed with his honour—which I certify.

BENITO CERENO.

DOCTOR ROZAS
Before me.—PADILLA.

RATIFICATION.

In the port of Talcahuano, the first day of the month of March, in the year one thousand eight hundred and five,—the same Honourable Judge of this cause caused to appear in his presence the captain of the ship Tryal, Don Benito Cereno, of whom he received an oath, before me, which he took conformably to law, under which he promised to tell the truth of what he should know, and of what he should be asked, and having read to him the foregoing declaration, and being asked if it is the same he has given and whether he has to add or to take off any thing,—he said, that it is the same he has given, that he affirms and ratifies it; and has only to add, that the new negroes were thirteen, and the females comprehended twenty-seven, without including the infants, and that one of them died from hunger or thi[r]st, and two young negroes of those from twelve to sixteen, together with an infant. And he signed it with his honour—which I certify.

BENITO CERENO.

DOCTOR ROZAS.
Before me.—PADILLA.

Declaration of DOM AMASA DELANO.

The same day, month and year, his Honour, ordered the captain of the American ship Perseverance to appear, whose oath his Honour received, which he took by placing his right hand on the Evangelists, under which he promised to tell the truth of what he should know and be asked—and being interrogated according to the decree, beginning this process, through the medium of the

113

interpreter Carlos Elli, who likewise swore to exercise well and lawfully his office, that the nineteenth or twentieth of the month, as he believes, agreeably to the calculation he keeps from the eastward, being at the island of Santa Maria, at anchor, he descried at seven o'clock in the morning, a ship coming round the point; that he asked his crew what ship that was; they replied that they did not know her; that taking his spy-glass he perceived she bore no colours; that he took his barge, and his net for fishing, and went on board of her, that when he got on deck he embraced the Spanish captain, who told him that he had been four months and twenty six days from Buenoes Ayres; that many of his people had died of the scurvy, and that he was in great want of supplies —particularly pipes for water, duck for sails, and refreshment for his crew; that the deponent offered to give and supply him with every thing he asked and wanted; that the Spanish captain did nothing else, because the ringleader of the negroes was constantly at their elbows, observing what was said. That immediately he sent his barge to his own ship to bring, (as they accordingly did) water, peas, bread, sugar, and fish. That he also sent for his long boat to bring a load of water, and having brought it, he returned to his own ship; that in parting he asked the Spanish captain to come on board his ship to take coffee, tea, and other refreshments; but he answered him with coldness and indifference; that he could not go then, but that he would in two or three days. That at the same time he visited him, the ship Tryal cast anchor in the port, about four o'clock in the afternoon,—that he told his people belonging to his boat to embark in order to return to his ship, that the deponent also left the deck to get into his barge,—that on getting into the barge, the Spanish captain took him by the hand and immediately gave a jump on board his boat,—that he then told him that the negroes of the Tryal had taken her, and had murdered twenty-five men, which the deponent was informed of through the medium of an interpreter, who was with him, and a Portuguese; that two or three other Spaniards threw themselves into the water, who were picked up by his boats; that he immediately went to his ship, and before reaching her, called to the mate to prepare and load the guns; that having got on board, he fired at them with his cannon, and this same deponent pointed six shots at the time the negroes of the Tryal were cutting away the cables and setting sail; that the Spanish captain told him that the ship was already going away, and that she could not be taken; that the deponent replied that he would take her; then the Spanish captain told him that if he took her, one half of her value would be his, and the other half would remain to the real owners; that thereupon he ordered the people belonging to his crew, to embark in the two boats, armed with knives, pistols, sabres, and pikes, to pursue her, and board her; that the two boats were firing at her near an hour with musketry, and at the end boarded and captured her; and that before sending his boats, he told his crew, in order to encourage them, that the Spanish captain offered to give them the half of the value of the Tryal if they took her. That having taken the ship, they came to anchor at about two o'clock in the morning very near the

114

deponent's, leaving in her about twenty of his men; that his first mate received a very dangerous wound in his breast made with a pike, of which he lies very ill; that three other sailors were also wounded with clubs, though not dangerously; that five or six of the negroes were killed in boarding; that at six o'clock in the morning, he went with the Spanish captain on board the Tryal, to carry manacles and fetters from his ship, ordering them to be put on the negroes who remained alive, he dressed the wounded, and [accompanied] the Tryal to the anchoring ground; and in it he delivered her up manned from his crew; for until that moment he remained in possession of her; that what he has said is what he knows, and the truth, under the oath he has taken, which he affirmed and ratified after the said declaration had been read to him,—saying he was forty-two years of age,—the interpreter did not sign it because he said he did not know how—the captain signed it with his honour—which I certify.

AMASA DELANO.

DOCTOR ROZAS.
Before me.—PADILLA.

RATIFICATION.

The said day, month and year, his Honour ordered the captain of the American ship, Don Amasa Delano to appear, of whom his Honour received an oath, which he took by placing his hand on the Evangelists, under which he promised to tell the truth of what he should know, and be asked, and having read to him the foregoing declaration, through the medium of the interpreter, Ambrosio Fernandez, who likewise took an oath to exercise well and faithfully his office,—he said that he affirms and ratifies the same; that he has nothing to add or diminish, and he signed it, with his Honour, and likewise the Interpreter.

AMASA DELANO.

AMBROSIO FERNANDEZ.

DOCTOR ROZAS.
Before me.—PADILLA.

Declaration of DON NATHANIEL LUTHER, *Midshipman.*

The same day, month and year, his Honour ordered Don Nathaniel Luther, first midshipman of the American ship Perseverance, and acting as clerk to the captain, to appear, of whom he received an oath, and which he took by placing his right hand on the Evangelists, under which he promised to tell the truth of what he should know and be asked, and being interrogated agreeably to the decree commencing this process, through the medium of the Interpreter Carlos Elli, he said that the deponent himself was one that boarded, and helped to take the ship Tryal in the boats; that he knows that his captain, Amasa Delano, has deposed on every thing that happened in this affair; that in order to avoid delay he requests that his declaration should be read to him, and he will tell whether it is [con]formable to the happening of the events; that if anything should be omitted he will observe it, and add to it, doing the same if he erred in any part thereof; and his Honour having acquiesced in this proposal, the Declaration made this day by captain Amasa Delano, was read to him through the medium of the Interpreter, and said, that the deponent went with his captain, Amasa Delano, to the ship Tryal, as soon as she appeared at the point of the island, which was about seven o'clock in the morning, and remained with him on board of her, until she cast anchor; that the deponent was one of those who boarded the ship Tryal in the boats, and by this he knows that the narration which the captain has made in the deposition which has been read to him, is certain and exact in all its parts; and he has only three things to add: the first, that whilst his captain remained on board the Tryal, a negro stood constantly at his elbow, and by the side of the deponent, the second, that the deponent was in the boat, when the Spanish captain jumped into it, and when the Portuguese declared that the negroes had revolted; the third, that the number of killed was six, five negroes and a Spanish sailor; that what he has said is the truth, under the oath which he has taken; which he affirmed and ratified, after his Declaration had been read to him; he said he was twenty one years of age, and signed it with his Honour, but the Interpreter did not sign it, because he said he did not know how—which I certify,

NATHANIEL LUTHER.

DOCTOR ROZAS.
Before me.—PADILLA.

RATIFICATION.

The aforesaid day, month and year, his Honour, ordered Don Nathaniel Luther, first midshipman of the American ship Perseverance, and acting as clerk to the captain, to whom he administ[e]red an oath, which he took by placing his hand on the Evangelists, under the sanctity of which he promised to tell the truth of what he should know and be asked; and the foregoing Declaration having been read to him, which he thoroughly understood, through the medium of the Interpreter, Ambrosio Fernandez, to whom an oath was likewise administred, to exercise well and faithfully his office, he says that he affirms and ratifies the same, that he has nothing to add or diminish, and he signed it with his Honour, and the Interpreter, which I certify.

NATHANIEL LUTHER.

AMBROSIO FERNANDEZ.

DOCTOR ROZAS.

Before me.—PADILLA.

SENTENCE.

In this city of Conception, the second day of the month of March, of one thousand eight hundred and five, his Honour Doctor Don Juan Martinez de Rozas, Deputy Assessor and learned in the law, of this intendency, having the execution thereof on account of the absence of his Honour, the principal having seen the proceedings, which he has conducted officially against the negroes of the ship Tryal, in consequence of the insurrection and atrocities which they have committed on board of her.—He declared, that the insurrection and revolt of said negroes, being sufficiently substantiated, with premeditated intent, the twenty seventh of December last, at three o'clock in the morning; that taking by surprise the sleeping crew, they killed eighteen men, some with sticks, and daggers, and others by throwing them alive overboard; that a few days afterward with the same deliberate intent, they stabbed their master Don Alexandro Aranda, and threw Don Franciso Masa, his german cousin, Hermenegildo, his relation, and the other wounded persons who were confined in the berths, overboard alive; that in the island of Santa Maria, they defended themselves with arms, against the Americans, who attempted to subdue them, causing the death of Don Jose Moraira the second clerk, as they had done that of the first, Don Lorenzo Bargas; the whole being considered, and the consequent guilts resulting from those [heinous] and atrocious actions as an example to others, he ought and did condemn the negroes, Mure, Martinqui, Alazase, Yola, Joaquin, Luis, Yau, Mapenda, and Yambaio, to the common penalty of death, which shall be executed, by taking them out and dragging them from the prison, at the tail of a beast of burden, as far as the gibbet, where they shall be hung until they are dead, and to the forfeiture of all their property, if they should have any, to be applied to the Royal Treasury; that the heads of the five first be cut off after they are dead, and be fixed on a pole, in the square of the port of Talcahuano, and the corpses of all be burnt to ashes. The negresses and young negroes of the same gang shall be present at the execution, if they should be in that city at the time thereof; that he ought and did condemn likewise, the negro Jose, servant to said Don Alexandro, and Yambaio, Francisco, Rodriguez, to ten years confinement in the place of Valdivia, to work chained, on allowance and without pay, in the work of the King, and also to attend the execution of the other criminals; and judging definitively by this sentence thus pronounced and ordered by his Honour, and that the same should be executed notwithstanding the appeal,

117

for which he declared there was no cause, but that an account of it should be previously sent to the Royal Audience of this district, for the execution thereof with the costs.

DOCTOR ROZAS.

Before me.—JOSE DE ABOS PADILLA.

His Majesty's Notary of the Royal Revenue and Registers.

CONFIRMATION OF THE SENTENCE.

SANTIAGO, *March the twenty first, of one thousand eight hundred and five.*

Having duly considered the whole, we suppose the sentence pronounced by the Deputy Assessor of the City of Conception, to whom we remit the same for its execution and fulfilment, with the official resolution, taking first an authenticated copy of the proceedings, to give an account thereof to his Majesty: and in regard to the request of the acting Notary, to the process upon the pay of his charges, he will exercise his right when and where he shall judge best.—

There are four flourishes.

Their Honours, the President, Regent, and Auditors of his Royal Audience passed the foregoing decree, and those on the Margin set their flourishes, the day of this date, the twenty first of March, one thousand eight hundred and five;—which I certify,

ROMAN.

NOTIFICATION.

The twenty third of said month, I acquainted his Honour, the King's Attorney of the foregoing decree,—which I certify,

ROMAN.

OFFICIAL RESOLUTION.

The Tribunal has resolved to manifest by this official resolve and pleasure for the exactitude, zeal and promptness which you have discovered in the cause against the revolted negroes of the ship Tryal, which process it remits to you, with the approbation of the sentence for the execution thereof, forewarning you that before its completion, you may agree with the most Illustrious Bishop, on the subject of furnishing the spiritual aids to those miserable beings, affording the same to them with all possible dispatch.—At the same time this Royal Audience has thought fit in case you should have an opportunity of speaking with the Bostonian captain, Amasa Delano, to charge you to inform him, that they will give an account to his Majesty, of the generous and benevolent conduct which he displayed in the punctual assistance that he afforded the Spanish captain of the aforesaid ship, for the suitable manifestation, publication and noticety of such a memorable event.

God preserve you many years.

SANTIAGO, *March the twenty second, of one thousand eight hundred and five.*

JOSÉ DE SANTIAGO CONCHA.

DOCTOR DON JUAN MARTINEZ DE ROZAS,

Deputy assessor, and learned in the law, of the Intendency of Conception.

I the unde[r]signed, sworn Interpreter of languages, do certify that the foregoing translation from the Spanish original, is true.

FRANCIS SALES.

Boston, April 15th, 1808.

N.B. It is proper here to state, that the difference of two days, in the dates of the process at Talquahauno, that of the Spaniards being the 24th of February and ours the 26th, was because they dated theirs the day we anchored in the lower harbour, which was one day before we got up abreast of the port at which time we dated ours; and our coming by the way of the Cape of Good Hope, made our reckoning of time one day different from theirs.

It is also necessary to remark, that the statement in page 332, respecting Mr. Luther being supercargo, and United States midshipman, is a mistake of the linguist. He was with me, the same as Mr. George Russell, and my brother William, midshipmen of the ship Perseverance.

On my return to America in 1807, I was gratified in receiving a polite letter from the Marquis DE CASE YRUSO, through the medium of JUAN STOUGHTON Esq. expressing the satisfaction of his majesty, the king of Spain, on account of our conduct in capturing the Spanish ship Tryal at the island St. Maria, accompanied with a gold medal, having his majesty's likeness on one side, and on the other the inscription, REWARD OF MERIT. The correspondence relating to that subject, I shall insert for the satisfaction of the reader. I had been assured by the president of Chili, when I was in that country, and likewise by the viceroy of Lima, that all my conduct, and the treatment I had received, should be faithfully represented to his majesty Charles IV, who most probably would do something more for me. I had reason to expect, through the medium of so many powerful friends as I had procured at different times and places, and on different occasions, that I should most likely have received something essentially to my advantage. This probably would have been the case had it not been for the unhappy catastrophe which soon after took place in Spain, by the dethronement of Charles IV, and the distracted state of the Spanish government, which followed that event.

Philadelphia, 8th September, 1806.

Sir,

HIS Catholic Majesty the king of Spain, my master, having been informed by the audience of Chili of your noble and generous conduct in rescuing, off the island St. Maria, the Spanish merchant ship Tryal, captain Don Benito Cereno, with the cargo of slaves, who had mutinized, and cruelly massacred the greater part of the Spaniards on board; and by humanely supplying them afterwards with water and provisions, which they were in need of, has desired me to express to you, sir, the high sense he entertains of the spirited, humane, and successful effort of yo[u]rself and the brave crew of the Perseverance, under your command, in saving the lives of his subjects thus exposed, and in token whereof, his majesty has directed me to present to you the golden medal, with his likeness, which will be handed to you by his consul in Boston. At the same time permit me, sir, to assure you I feel particular satisfaction in being the organ of the grateful sentiments of my sovereign, on an occurrence which reflects so much honour on your character.

I have the honour to be, sir,

Your obedient servant,

(Signed)   MARQUIS DE CASE YRUSO.
Captain AMASA DELANO, *of the American*
Ship Perseverance, Boston.

Boston, August, 1807

Sir,

WITH sentiments of gratitude I acknowledge the receipt of your Excellency's much esteemed favour of September 8th, conveying to me the pleasing information of his Catholic Majesty having been informed of the conduct of myself and the crew of the Perseverance under my command. It is peculiarly gratifying to me, to receive such honours from your Excellency's sovereign, as entertaining a sense of my spirit and honour, and successful efforts of myself and crew in saving the lives of his subjects; and still more so by receiving the token of his royal favour in the present of the golden medal bearing his likeness. The services rendered off the island St. Maria were from pure motives of humanity. They shall ever be rendered his Catholic Majesty's subjects when wanted, and it is in my power to grant. Permit me, sir, to thank your Excellency for the satisfaction that you feel in being the organ of the grateful sentiments of your sovereign on this occasion, and believe me, it shall ever be my duty publicly to acknowledge the receipt of such high considerations from such a source.

I have the honour to be

Your Excellency's most obedient,

And devoted humble servant,

(Signed)   AMASA DELANO.
His Excellency the Marquis DE CASE YRUSO.

Consular Office, 30th *July,* 1807.

Sir,

Under date of September last, was forwarded me the enclosed letter from his Excellency the Marquis DE CASE YRUSO, his Catholic Majesty's minister plenipotentiary to the United States of America, which explains to you the purport of the commission with which I was then charged, and until now have anxiously waited for the pleasing opportunity of carrying into effect his Excellency's orders, to present to you at the same time the gold medal therein mentioned.

It will be a pleasing circumstance to that gentleman, to be informed of your safe arrival, and my punctuality in the discharge of that duty so justly owed to the best of sovereigns, under whose benignity and patronage I have the honour to subscribe myself, with great consideration, and much respect, sir,

Your obedient humble servant,

(Signed)   JUAN STOUGHTON,

121

Consul of his Catholic majesty,

Residing at Boston.

AMASA DELANO, *E*SQ.

BOSTON, AUGUST 8TH, *1807.*

SIR,

I Feel particular satisfaction in acknowledging the receipt of your esteemed favour, bearing date the 30th ult. covering a letter from the Marquis DE CASE YRUSO, his Catholic Majesty's minister plenipotentiary to the United States of America, together with the gold medal bearing his Catholic Majesty's likeness.

Permit me, sir, to return my most sincere thanks for the honours I have received through your medium, as well as for the generous, friendly treatment you have shown on the occasion. I shall ever consider it one of the first honours publicly to acknowledge them as long as I live.

These services rendered his Catholic Majesty's subjects off the island St. Maria, with the men under my command, were from pure motives of humanity. The like services we will ever render, if wanted, should it be in our power.

With due respect, permit me, sir, to subscribe myself,

Your most obedient, and

Very humble servant,

(Signed)   AMASA DELANO.

To Don JUAN STOUGHTON *E*SQ. HIS *C*ATHOLIC *M*AJESTY'S *C*ONSUL, RESIDING IN *B*OSTON.

Textual Variations

While the text adopted in this volume is that of the 1856 edition of *The Piazza Tales*, there are numerous differences between it and the earlier 1855 version which appeared serially in *Putnam's Monthly Magazine*. The following tabulation presents these differences—both substantive and trivial—between the two texts. (The numerals in the left-hand margin refer to the paragraph numbers of the 1856 text.)

The Piazza Tales
(Dix & Edwards, 1856)

	The Piazza Tales (Dix & Edwards, 1856)	**Putnam's Monthly (1855)**
1	lay at anchor with	lay at anchor, with
3	a gray surtout.	a gray mantle.
4	undistrustful goodnature	undistrustful good nature
4	and repeated incentives,	and repeated excitement,
4	involving the imputation	involving an imputation
5	too near the land; a sunken reef	too near the land, for her own safety's sake, owing to a sunken reef
5	hemisphered on the rim	crescented on the rim
5	and, apparently,	and apparently,
5	ship entering the harbor	ship, entering the harbor
6	stranger was watched the more	stranger was watched, the more
6	manoeuvres	maneuvers
9	merchantman of the first class,	merchantman of the first class;
14	As, at last, the boat	As at last the boat

14	like a wen—	like a wen;
15	outnumbering the former	out-numbering the former
15	Off Cape Horn they had	Off Cape Horn, they had
16	took in all faces,	took in all the faces,
17	Both house and ship—the one	Both house and ship, the one
17	the last moment: but	the last moment; but
18	some such influence, as	some such influence as
22	the Spaniard returned for	the Spaniard returned, for
22	for the present but grave	for the present, but grave
22	mood of ill-health.	mood of ill health.
23	Captain Delano, returning	Captain Delano returning
23	his basket of fish	his baskets of fish
24	sought, with good hopes, to cheer	sought with good hopes to cheer
24	their condition, he could	their condition he could
25	induced by hardships,	induced by the hardships
25	that day, or evening	that day or evening
25	lungs half gone—hoarsely	lungs half gone, hoarsely
25	pleasing body-servant	pleasing body servant
26	inefficiency of the whites it was	inefficiency of the whites, it was
27	as if forced to black	as if, forced to black
28	his faithful personal attendant.	his personal attendant.
30	Thus, the Spaniard,	Thus the Spaniard,
30	seemed the involuntary	seemed as the involuntary
30	If so, then here was	If so, then in Don Benito was
31	In a well-appointed vessel,	In a well appointed vessel,
31	But the Spaniard, perhaps, thought	But the Spaniard perhaps thought
31	But probably	But more probably
32	breaches, not only of discipline but of decency, were observed.	breaches not only of discipline but of decency were observed.
32	as a fourth-mate	as a fourth mate
33	the whole story.	the whole story?
34	when, with a sort of eagerness, Don Benito	when with a sort of eagerness, Don Benito
36	general cargo, hardware, Paraguay tea	general cargo, Paraguay tea
41	"But be patient, Senor,"	"But be patient, Senor,"
43	ship, for successive days and nights, was	ship for successive days and nights was
43	every remaining officer on board.	every officer on board.
43	the already rent sails, having	the already rent sails having
43	to the beggars' rags	to the beggar's rags
43	captain, at the earliest opportunity, had made	captain at the earliest opportunity, had made

124

43	southernmost civilized port	southermost civilized port
43	and, at intervals, giving	and at intervals giving
45	Again his mind wandered;	Again his mind wandered:
50	cried Captain Delano.	cried Capt. Delano.
51	white small-clothes	white small clothes
51	knot in his sash—the last	knot in his sash; the last
51	in his attire curiously	in his attire, curiously
54	sickness, and gentility united?	sickness, and aristocracy united?
54	united?	united? Such was his democratic conclusion.
55	Captain Delano, having	Captain Delano having
60	As, during the telling	As during the telling
60	since, with an untimely	since with an untimely
61	late fidgety panic.	late fidgeting panic.
62	standing with his host,	standing with Don Benito,
62	together on the hatches,	together on the hatchets,
62	seized a knife, and, though	seized a knife, and though
63	the pale Don Benito	the pale Benito
65	then, relapsing into	then relapsing into
66	this hapless man	this helpless man
69	keep some, at least, of your host	keep some at least of your host
73	where, in spots, it had been	where in spots it had been
75	but none of the slaves,	but not of the slaves,
76	'I am owner of all	"I am owner of all
77	his knees shook; his	his knees shook: his
78	Delano, after a pause, said:	Delano, after a pause, said,
78	so afflicts you, at the	so afflicts you at the
81	'Died of the fever. Oh,	"Died of the fever.—Oh,
83	Captain Delano, lowly,	Captain Delano lowly,
83	to lose, at sea, a dear	to lose at sea a dear
84	against some spectre,	against some specter,
85	when you, for months, were	when you for months were
86	proclaimed ten o'clock, through	proclaimed ten o'clock through
93	will you ask my pardon, now?"	will you ask my pardon now?"
95	eyeing his countryman,	eying his countryman,
96	"say but the one word, *pardon*,	"say but the one word *pardon*,
108	"he, has a royal spirit	"he has a royal spirit
114	for the first, that	for the first time that
114	from Don Benito's neck, hung	from Don Benito's neck hung
114	muttered syllables, divining	muttered syllables divining
116	seemed some way	seemed in some way
116	still sourly digesting	still slowly digesting
116	the good sailor, himself of	the good sailor himself, of

117	by his servant somewhat	by his servant, somewhat
117	over from his guest;	over from Captain Delano;
121	the silky paw	the velvet paw
123	once more towards his host—	once more towards Don Benito—
123	towards him—he was	towards him—Captain Delano was
123	by the thinness, incident to	by the thinness incident to
135	men have you, Senor?"	men have you on board, Senor?"
142	repeated his question:	repeated his question:—
144	Captain Delano—"but nay,"	Captain Delano, "but nay,"
148	sailor, before mentioned, was seen	sailor before mentioned was seen
148	signs, of some Freemason sort, had	signs of some Freemason sort had
149	the late questionings, and	the late questionings and
150	it was a moment or two	I was a moment or two
153	Spanish sailors, prowling	Spanish sailors prowling
154	dead cabin-passengers?	dead cabin passengers?
154	ah—if, now, that was,	ah—if now that was,
154	that, in my uneasiness, my senses	that in my uneasiness my senses
155	the strange questions	the point of the strange questions
157	the ship, now helplessly	the ship now helplessly
157	And yet, when he	And yet when he
158	was, for the time, at least,	was, for the time at least,
159	If Don Benito's story was, throughout, an invention,	If Don Benito's story was through-out an invention,
159	mistrusting his veracity,	mistrusting the Spanish captain's veracity,

160   But those questions of the Spaniard. There, indeed, one might pause. Did they not seem put with much the same object with which the burglar or assassin, by day-time, reconnoitres the walls of a house? But, with ill purposes, to solicit such information openly of the chief person endangered, and so, in effect, setting him on his guard; how unlikely a procedure was that? Absurd, then, to suppose that those questions had been prompted by evil designs. Thus, the same conduct, which, in this instance, had raised the alarm,

126

served to dispel it. In short, scarce any suspicion or uneasiness, however apparently reasonable at the time, which was not now, with equal apparent reason, dismissed.

161 At last he began to laugh at his former forebodings; and laugh at the strange ship for, in its aspect, someway

161 old knitting women,

161 and almost at the dark Spaniard himself,

162 or putting idle questions

162 command from him, Captain

162 —a plan not more convenient for the San Dominick

162 his servant, would, probably,

165 sailors, violently pushed him aside, which the sailor

165 resenting, they dashed him to the deck, despite the earnest

167 since, when left to himself, he could

168 His glance called away

168 congratulating his host upon

169 "I should like to have your man here, myself—

170 faithful slave, appreciated

172 he refrained; as a ship-master

173 that one or two of them returned

173 assuming a good-humored,

174 a large block, a circle of blacks

176 a haggardness combined with a

176 and then again recalling Don Benito's confessed ill opinion of his crew, insensibly he was operated upon by

In short, scarce an uneasiness entered the honest sailor's mind but, by a subsequent spontaneous act of good sense, it was ejected. At last he began to laugh at these forebodings; and laugh at the strange ship for, in its aspect someway old knitting-women, and, in a human way, he almost began to laugh at the dark Spaniard himself,

or putting random questions command from Captain —a plan which would prove no wiser for the San Dominick his servant, would probably, sailors, flew out against him with horrible curses, which the sailor resenting, the two blacks dashed him to the deck and jumped upon him, despite the earnest since when left to himself he could

His glance thus called away congratulating Don Benito upon "I should like to have your man here myself— faithful slave appreciated he refrained, as a ship-master

that some of them returned assuming a good humored, a large block, with a circle of blacks a haggardness to be combined with a and then, however illogically, uniting in his mind his own private suspicions of the crew with the confessed ill-opinion on the part of their Captain, he was

127

		insensibly operated upon by
176	general notions which,	general notions, which,
176	abashment from virtue, invariably	abashment from virtue, as invariably
176	concerning the voyage—questions	concerning the voyage, questions
179	in with the old sailor; but, as	in with the old sailor, but as
182	at her lapped breasts, was her	at her lapped breasts was her
183	at a distance facing Captain Delano.	at distance facing Captain Delano.
185	with their manners: like most	with their manners; like most
185	these, perhaps, are some of the very	these perhaps are some of the very
185	women whom Ledyard saw in Africa,	women whom Mungo Park saw in Africa,
187	into the mizzen-chains, he clambered	into the mizzen-chains he clambered
187	starboard quarter-gallery—one of	starboard quarter-gallery; one of
187	previously mentioned-retreats cut	previously mentioned; retreats cut
187	ghostly cats paw	ghostly cats-paw
187	fanning his cheek; as his glance	fanning his cheek, as his glance
187	round, dead-lights—all closed	round, dead-lights, all closed
187	eyes of the coffined—and the state-	eyes of the coffined, and the state-
187	a sarcophagus lid; and to a purple-black tarred-over, panel, threshold,	a sarcophagus lid, to a purple-black, tarred-over panel, threshold,
188	upon the ribbon grass,	upon the ribboned grass,
190	which she had been built.	which probably she had been built.
191	but immediately as if alarmed	but immediately, as if alarmed
193	there maturing his plot,	there maturing some plot,
194	For intricacy, such a knot	For intricacy such a knot
194	an American ship, nor indeed any	an American ship, or indeed any
194	making Gordian knots	making gordian knots
200	English—the first heard in the ship—something to this effect: "Undo	English,—the first heard in the ship,—something to this effect— "Undo
202	playing his odd tricks.	playing his old tricks.
202	and, turning his back,	and turning his back,
202	a detective custom-house officer	a detective Custom House officer
203	but, as one feeling incipient	but as one feeling incipient
204	with unforeseen efficacy soon	with unforeseen efficiency, soon
205	paddle along the water-side	paddle along the waterside

128

205	from the old hulk—I,	from the old hulk;—I,
205	horrible Spaniard? Too nonsensical	horrible Spaniard?—Too nonsensical
207	dark-lantern in had,	dark-lantern in hand,
210	than sixty minutes, drifting.	than sixty minutes drifting.
211	and at last—his eye	and at last, his eye
211	and, by-and-by, recognizing	and by and by recognising
211	the main-chains—something	the main chains, something
215	curious points recurred:	curious points recurred.
216	to their master, of all the	to their master of all the
217	now nearing boat—what then?	now nearing boat,—what then?
219	Don Benito, with his servant, now	Don Benito with his servant now
220	While the visitor's attention	While Captain Delano's attention
222	surprised, on the	surprised on the
222	who, upon a legitimate occasion,	who upon a legitimate occasion
223	name of his captain, entreated	name of Don Benito, entreated
223	he had proposed—dole out	he had proposed: dole out
223	as he was for it, the Spaniard	as he was for fresh water, Don Benito
224	would have given the whites alone,	would have given the Spaniards alone,
224	which disinterestedness not a little	which disinterestedness, on his part, not a little
226	peculiar good-humor	peculiar good humor
226	who, from recent indications, counted	who from recent indications counted
226	to the sealer, with orders	to the sealer with orders
226	if, against present expectation, the	if against present expectation the
226	no concern; for as there	no concern, for as there
226	pilot, come the wind soon or late.	pilot, should the wind come soon or late
227	the servant, as it happened, having	the servant as it happened having
228	matters some. Did you sail	matters some.—Did you sail
230	Boats and men. Those must	Boats and men.—Those must
234	answered Captain Delano, with almost	answered Captain Delano with almost
238	starting, as from dreams	starting, somewhat as from dreams
243	picturesque disarray of odd	picturesque disarray, of odd
245	poor friars' girdles.	poor friar's girdles.
245	a rude barber's crotch	a rude barber's crutch

129

245	some grotesque engine of torment.	some grotesque, middle-age engine of torment.
246	windows or port-holes,	windows or port holes,
251	drawing opposite one of the settees,	drawing opposite it one of the settees,
252	great gift of good-humor.	great gift of good humor.
253	When to this is added	When to all this is added
253	it may be, something like the hypochondriac Benito Cereno—	it may be something like the hypochondriac, Benito Cereno—
253	he was on chatty and half-gamesome	he was on chatty, and half-gamesome
254	Hitherto, the circumstances	Hitherto the circumstances
258	nor, for the present, did	nor for the present did
259	nervously shuddered; his	nervously shuddered, his
259	is not always free.	is not free.
260	blood red field	blood-red field
261	he added, with a smile,	he added with a smile,
261	towards the black—	towards the black,—
262	"now, master,"	"now master,"
264	master. See, Don	master.—See, Don
264	that; master can hear, and, between times, master	that, master can hear, and between times master
266	hand, however it was,	hand; however it was,
266	under the throat: immediately	under the throat; immediately
266	"See, master—you	"See, master,—you
270	seemed, by its expression, to hint,	seemed by its expression to hint,
270	exceedingly long; now	exceedingly long, now
270	their general good conduct. These particulars were not given consecutively, the servant, at convenient times, using his razor, and so between the intervals of shaving, the story and panegyric went on with more than usual huskiness.	their general good conduct. These particulars were not given consecutively, the servant now and then using his razor, and so, between the intervals of shaving, the story and panegyric went on with more than usual huskiness.
273	scissors, and brush;	scissors and brush;
276	as he had prophesied,	as he had prochecied,
277	to the main-mast,	to the mainmast,
279	Ah this slavery	Ah, this slavery
279	ugly passions in man.—	ugly passions in man—
284	ushered them on,	ushered them in,
285	was European—classically so.	was European; classically so.
286	voice he has, too?	voice he has, too?"

288	"But tell me,	"But, tell me,
290	For it were strange, indeed,	For it were strange indeed
305	his manner became	this manner became
309	the cabin windows	the cabin-windows
320	there sponsible post	the responsible post
323	The man assented with an	"Si, Senor," assented the man with an
323	eyed the sailor intently.	eyed the sailor askance.
326	while the servant was engaged	while his servant was engaged
327	toward the seated Spaniard, he heard	toward the Spaniard, on the transom, he heard
329	for the brisk confidence	for the buoyant confidence
329	a sudden indefinite association	a sudden involuntary association
331	apparent good breeding	apparent good-breeding
334	ex-king indeed.	ex-king denied.
336	Again conversation became constrained.	Conversation now became constrained.
340	as he blithely re-entered:	as he blithely reentered;
346	at his guest, as if impatient	at his guest; as if impatient
347	the fair wind at its height.	the fair wind at its hight.
351	the smaller details	the practical details
355	stood unharmed in the light.	stood unarmed in the light.
355	ship lying peacefully at anchor,	ship lying peacefully at her anchor,
355	as charmed eye and ear	as his charmed eye and ear
355	black, clenched jaw and hand	black, the clenched jaw and hand
355	that, by harboring them	that, by indulging them
355	betrayed an atheist doubt	betrayed an almost atheist doubt
357	withdrawing his foot,	revoking his foot,
363	The bowsmen pushed	The bowsman pushed
363	at the same time calling towards	at the same time, calling towards
363	three sailors,	three Spanish sailors,
364	the unaccountable Spaniard, answered	the unaccountable Benito Cereno, answered
364	as if Don Benito had taken it	as if the Spaniard had taken it
364	the three white sailors were	the three Spanish sailors were
368	the towing sailors,	the towing Spanish sailors,
370	illuminating, in unanticipated clearness, his host's whole mysterious demeanor,	illuminating in unanticipated clearness Benito Cereno's whole mysterious demeanor,
371	now with scales dropped	now with the scales dropped
375	now dusky moors of ocean—	now dusky expanse of ocean—
377	what fire-arms they had	what fire arms they had
377	crushed by misery the American	crushed by misery, the American

131

378	ordered his men into them.	ordered twenty-five men into them.
379	have you saved my life, Senor,	have you saved my life, senor,
380	a privateer's-man—to head the party.	a privateer's-man and, as his enemies whispered, a pirate—to head the party.
380	considered his ship good as lost;	considered his ship as good as lost;
380	were worth more than a thousand	were worth upwards of ten thousand
382	But, ere long, perceiving	But ere long perceiving
382	proved, in the end, favorable	proved in the end favorable
385	in the dress of sailors, and	in the dress of sailors and
386	swinging into view	swinging, into view
387	Sealing-spears and cutlasses	Scaling-spears and cutlasses
388	they sprang inboard, where,	they sprang inboard; where,
388	would have had respite.	would have had a respite.
389	long-edged sealing-spears, resembling	long-edged scaling-spears— resembling
390	the ships sailed in company	the two ships sailed in company
392	will, it is hoped, shed	will it is hoped, shed
396	against the negroes of the ship	against the Senegal negroes of the ship
396	was made:	was made.
398	of whom he received the oath,	of whom he received, before Don José de Abos and Padilla, Notary Public of the Holy Crusade, the oath,
398	the country beside thirty cases of hardware and one hundred and sixty	the country and one hundred and sixty
400	named Francesco, the cabin steward,	named Francisco, the cabin steward,
400	Atufal, who being supposed to have been	Atufal, who, being supposed to have been
401	[The catalogue over, the deposition goes on]	[After the catalogue, the deposition goes on as follows:]
402	that during the act of revolt,	that in the act of revolt,
402	but being quickly wounded, were obliged	but having been wounded at the onset, they were obliged
402	that notwithstanding this, they threw,	that, notwithstanding this, they threw,
402	and he answered them, No;	and he answered them. No;
402	they threatened to kill all the whites	they threatened him to kill all the whites

132

402	they might water easily, it being a solitary island,	they might water and victual easily, it being a desert island,
402	on the passage or near the island itself,	in the passage or in the island itself,
402	coast of Arruco, to adopt the necessary	coast of Arruco; to adopt the necessary
402	and that to keep the seamen	and that, to keep the seamen
402	moreover the negro Babo proposed	moreover, the negro Babo proposed
402	that awakening at his cries,	that, awakening at his cries,
402	that a short time after killing Aranda,	that, a short time after killing Aranda,
402	the negro Babo, for purposes	the negro Babo for purposes
402	figure-head—the image of Christopher	figure-head, the image of Christopher
402	upon discovering his face,	upon his covering his face,
402	way of Don Alexandro, if he saw them	way of Don Alexandro if he saw them
402	which knowing it would yet be wanted for towing the water casks,	which, knowing it would yet be wanted for lowering the water casks,
404	Raneds, to the deponent in the act	Raneds, to the deponent, in the act
405	he told them; that, among other	he told them, that, among other
405	Atufal, his right hand man,	Atufal, his right-hand man,
405	deponent was to tell; charging them	deponent was to tell, charging them
406	After the fictitious story, etc.	After the fictitious, strange story, etc.,
407	had been obtained the negro Babo	had been obtained, the negro Babo
407	Captain took leave, to return to his	Captain took leave to return to his
408	From this portion is the following;]	From this portion is the following:]
409	negro José was the one who,	negro José, was the one who,
409	the mulatto steward, Francesco,	the mulatto steward, Francisco,
409	design, forbade Francesco;	design, forbade Francisco;
409	hatchet in each hand, with one of which	hatchet in each hand, which one of which
409	Don Francisco Masa, when, by the negro	Don Francisco Masa when, by the negro
409	throw him overboard, alive, beside	throw him overboard, alive; beside

133

409	death of their master, Don Alexandro;	death of their masters, Don Alexandro;
409	men of the crew, exclusive of the passengers (all of whom are now dead),	men of the crew exclusive of the passengers, (all of whom are now dead),
410	The following are extracted;]	The following are extracted:]
411	and, furthermore, owing to the devices	and furthermore owing to the devices
411	true state of affairs, as well as owing	true state of affairs; as well as owing
411	remark some expression in his countenance,	remark a certain unconscious hopeful expression in his countenance,
411	arising from a cause similar	arising from some cause similar
411	killed by a musket ball fired through mistake from the boats before boarding;	killed by a musket-ball fired through mistake from the American boats before boarding;
411	having in his fright run up	having in his fright ran up
411	awaiting the disposition of the	awaiting the decision of the
411	Barlo a dagger, secreted at the time	Barlo, a dagger secreted at the time
413	If the Deposition have served as the key	If the deposition of Benito Cereno has served as the key
413	which precede it,	which preceded it,
415	which the sufferer a little recovered	which Don Benito a little recovered
416	again it was repeated, how hard	again, it was repeated how hard
417	"Ah, my dear friend," Don Benito once	"Ah, my dear Don Amasa," Don Benito once
418	"you have saved my life, Don Benito,	"you saved my life, Don Benito,
420	Providence, I know: but the temper	Providence, I know; but the temper
420	added to my good-nature, compassion,	added to my good nature, compassion,
420	my interferences might have ended	my interferences with the blacks might have ended
420	Besides, those feelings I spoke of	Besides that, those feelings I spoke of
421	clutch for a monster, not only an	clutch for a villain, not only an
422	"You generalize, Don Benito;	"I think I understand you; you generalize, Don Benito;
424	fan your cheek, do they not	fan your cheek, Don Benito, do

		they not
425	me to my tomb, Senor," was the	me to my tomb, senor," was the
426	"You are saved," cried Captain Delano,	"You are saved, Don Benito," cried Captain Delano,
426	"you are saved: what has cast	"you are saved; what has cast
430	The dress, so precise and costly,	The dress so precise and costly,
431	During the passage, Don Benito	During the passage Don Benito
431	rested the legal identity of Babo.	rested the legal identity of Babo. And yet the Spaniard would, upon occasion, verbally refer to the negro, as has been shown; but look on him he would not, or could not.
432	the recovered bones of Aranda: and	the recovered bones of Aranda; and

Concordance to the Text of "Benito Cereno"
(by paragraph number)

abbot
    25   like some hypochondriac abbot he moved slowly about,

Abraham
    355   shining out like the mild light from Abraham's tent,

Acapulco
    9   sometimes superseded Acapulco treasure-ships,

Akim
    400   Yambaio, Akim; four of whom were killed;

Ammon
    194   Gordian knots for the temple of Ammon.

ancient
    12   forecastle seemed some ancient turret,
    190   Of an ancient style,

angels
>407 to have come from God and his angels,

animal
>151 his previous grin of mere animal humor

Aranda, Don Alexandro
>76 who belonged to my late friend, Alexandro Aranda."
>85 Poor Alexandro Aranda!
>373 "'Tis he, Aranda! my murdered, unburied friend!"
>398 mostly belonging to Don Alexandro Aranda, gentleman,
>399 *certain recovered documents of Aranda's*
>400 his master, Don Alexandro,
>402 his friend Aranda
>402 Don Alexandro Aranda, both because he and his companions
>402 death of Don Alexandro,
>402 death of Don Alexandro was intended
>402 should be killed with Don Alexandro and the rest;
>402 of Don Alexandro, prayed and conjured,
>402 berth of Don Alexandro; that, yet half alive
>402 opposite Don Alexandro's;
>402 short time after killing Aranda, they brought upon deck
>402 three young clerks of Aranda,
>402 the remains of Don Alexandro, frequently asked
>402 go the way of Don Alexandro, if he saw them
>409 and in the personal service of Don Alexandro,
>409 stabbed his master, Don Alexandro, after he had been dragged
>409 Don Alexandro Aranda, and others of the cabin-passengers;
>409 skeleton of Don Alexandro, in a way the negroes
>409 at the death of their master, Don Alexandro
>432 the recovered bones of Aranda:

Arruco
>402 the neighboring coast of Arruco,

atheist
>355 have betrayed an atheist doubt of the ever-watchful
>Providence above.

atrocities
>402 cease committing such atrocities, asking them,

attendant/attendance
>84 into the ready arms of his attendant,

111   Captain Delano turned curiously upon the attendant,
125   still supported by his attendant,
147   with his attendant, withdrew to the opposite bulwarks,
167   might have attached to the attendant,
294   he relished not superfluous attendance.
302   only his constant attendant and companion,

Atufal

87   "How like a mute Atufal moves,"
93   "Atufal, will you ask my pardon, now?"
110   "those slits in Atufal's ears once held wedges of gold;
112   "What, pray, was Atufal's offence, Don Benito?"
113   "proud Atufal must first ask master's pardon.
201   the chained negro, Atufal, standing quietly there.
216   Atufal, the black; as if a child should lead a bull of
        the Nile
314   unexpected figure of Atufal, monumentally fixed
315   Atufal's presence, singularly attesting docility
327   at whose porch Atufal still stood—
329   indefinite association in his mind of Babo with Atufal.
353   Atufal, the pretended rebel, but punctual shadow,
355   he passed Atufal, and stood unharmed in the light.
385   Atufal, the black, and the Spaniard at the helm
400   a powerful negro named Atufal,
402   and Atufal, who assisted him,
402   that the negroes Babo and Atufal held daily conferences,
405   the negro Babo and the negro Atufal conferred;
405   that the negro Atufal was for sailing away,
405   the device of presenting Atufal, his right hand man,
409   that Atufal was his lieutenant in all;
409   but Atufal, with his own hand, committed no murder;
409   that Atufal was shot, being killed in the fight with the boats,

Babo

26   witnessed the steady good conduct of Babo.
27   But the good conduct of Babo, hardly more than the ill-behavior
48   "But it is Babo here to whom, under God, I owe
49   Babo is nothing;
49   what Babo has done was but duty."
110   but poor Babo here, in his own land,
110   a black man's slave was Babo, who now is the white's."
150   I have trust in Babo."
151   Here Babo, changing his previous grin of mere animal humor

170 "Master wouldn't part with Babo for a thousand doubloons,"
224 which Babo insisted upon setting aside for his master.
239 while Babo here lathers and strops."
266 —here's Babo's first blood."
278 made him serve Babo so;
278 cutting Babo with the razor, because, only by accident,
278 Babo had given master one little scratch;
284 the insignificance of the small bare-headed Babo,
291 glancing at Babo—"not to speak of negroes,
302 he had made Babo (whose original office, it now appeared,
317 turning, he saw Babo, now for the time acting,
329 indefinite association in his mind of Babo with Atufal.
370 He smote Babo's hand down, but his own heart
400 which negro's name was Babo;
402 where the negro Babo was, being the ringleader,
402 the negro Babo asked him whether there were in those seas
402 the negro Babo afterwards told him to carry them
402 the negro Babo replied to him he must carry them
402 the negro Babo agreed to it;
402 the negro Babo having required, with threats,
402 the negro Babo had intimated to him several times,
402 the negroes Babo and Atufal held daily conferences,
402 the negro Babo came to the place where the deponent was,
402 the negro Babo proposed to the deponent to call the mate Raneds,
402 the negro Babo answered him that the thing
402 immediately the negro Babo commanded the Ashantee Martinqui
402 the negro Babo stopped them, bidding the murder
402 the negro Babo, for purposes hereafter to appear,
402 the negro Babo ordered to be thrown alive into the sea,
402 the negro Babo where they were, and, if still on board,
402 the negro Babo answered nothing till the fourth day,
402 the negro Babo showed him a skeleton, which had been
402 the negro Babo asked him whose skeleton that was,
402 the negro Babo, coming close, said words to this effect:
402 the negro Babo took by succession each Spaniard forward,
402 the negro Babo repeated the words in the first place said
402 the negro Babo harangued them, saying that he had now
      done all;
402 the negro Babo spared his life, at the request of the deponent;
402 the negro Babo, for himself and all the blacks,
402 the negro Babo commanded all the boats to be destroyed
405 the negro Babo pacified them, assuring them that no fear need
405 the negro Babo and the negro Atufal conferred;

140

409 Yan was bad as Lecbe;
411 inflicting a bad wound, but of which the boy is now healing;

Baldivia
43 had made for Baldivia, the southernmost civilized port

Barbados
286 a Barbadoes planter;

barbarous
19 hatchets together, like cymbals, with a barbarous din.

Barber
253 the negroes, Barber and Fletcher.

Barcelona
178 an old Barcelona tar, in ragged red breeches

Bargas, Lorenzo
402 Lorenzo Bargas, and Hermenegildo Gandix, all of Cadiz;
402 and Lorenzo Bargas, with Ponce the servant, beside

Bartholomew
411 wrenched from the hand of Bartholomew Barlo a dagger,
432 looked towards St. Bartholomew's church,

bats
227 social circle of bats, sheltering in some friendly cave;

bear
179 a grizzly bear, instead of growling and biting,

Benito Cereno (see Cereno, Benito)

benevolent/benign
4 along with a benevolent heart, more than ordinary quickness
33 renewing the expression of his benevolent interest,
162 On some benevolent plea withdrawing the command from him,
226 oblivious of any but benevolent thoughts, Captain Delano,
253 must he appear to be a benevolent one?
355 as he saw the benign aspect of nature, taking her innocent

black
8 Black Friars pacing the cloisters.

15	clamorous throng of whites and blacks,
18	heads like black, doddered willow tops,
19	the cross-legged figures of six other blacks;
21	black of small stature, in whose rude face,
25	both for the Spaniards and blacks, alike evidently reduced
26	noisy indocility of the blacks in general,
27	as if, forced to black bread themselves,
28	either a white, mulatto or black, he hardly had patience
32	their countrymen, the blacks;
37	the black with one arm still encircled his master,
43	carrying off numbers of the whites and blacks.
46	no fetters would be needed with his blacks;
49	sighed the black, bowing his face,
51	black upholding the white,
51	forward of the main-mast, wholly occupied by the blacks.
62	Three black boys, with two Spanish boys,
62	one of the black boys, enraged at a word
67	advantageous to keep all your blacks employed,
71	shepherds to your flock of black sheep?"
76	except the main company of blacks,
78	at the outset of the voyage accompanied his blacks?"
86	the moving figure of a gigantic black,
88	The black mounted the steps of the poop,
94	The black was silent.
97	the black, slowly raising both arms,
99	Deliberately as he had come, the black obeyed.
110	a black man's slave was Babo, who now is the white's."
116	lordship over the black;
124	Spaniard's black-letter text, it was best, for awhile,
149	your black here seems high in your trust;
156	the black wizards of Ashantee would strike up
159	ejaculations of the indiscriminate multitude, white and black,
161	odd-looking blacks, particularly those old scissors-grinders,
162	either sulking in black vapors,
164	observed by the blacks.
165	two blacks, to all appearances accidentally incommoded
167	the black withdrew his support, slipping aside a little,
170	murmured the black, overhearing the offer,
173	he made his way through the blacks,
173	sparsely mixed in with the blacks, like stray white pawns,
174	a circle of blacks squatted round him
175	His hand, black with continually thrusting it into the tar-pot
178	sleepy-looking blacks performing the inferior function

143

180	spoke pleasantly to the blacks to make way for him;
182	its black little body half lifted from the deck
193	could then Don Benito be any way in complicity with the blacks?
193	Some blacks were about him obligingly dipping the strands
216	Don Benito's treatment of Atufal, the black;
216	all the ship's underlings, mostly blacks;
218	sought to restrain the blacks,
220	he bade the blacks stand back;
220	Instantly the blacks paused, just where they were,
221	whites and blacks singing at the tackle.
223	no better than the youngest black;
224	given alike to whites and blacks;
227	family groups of the blacks, mostly women
245	black with age, and uncomfortable to look at
245	cumbrous washstand, of black mahogany,
253	If on a voyage he chanced to have a black sailor
255	in the black's informally taking from the flag-locker
259	that in the black he saw a headsman,
261	turning towards the black—
266	the black barber drew back his steel,
270	to the blacks, for their general good conduct.
290	effect of pouring vitriolic acid into black broth;
296	the black was still true to his master;
299	while destroying less than half of the blacks.
302	the black's remaining with them could be of no disservice;
314	those sculptured porters of black marble
320	a subordinate black, and between them, at the tiller-head,
323	the two blacks eyed the sailor intently.
355	with the chained figure of the black,
360	across the black's body.
364	while, seemingly to aid the black, the three white sailors
366	the black seemed of purpose to have leaped there
368	to see what the black was about;
370	the black, in leaping into the boat, had intended to stab.
371	Both the black's hands were held,
371	Like delirious black dervishes,
371	helplessly mixed in, on deck, with the blacks.
375	the blacks thickly clustering round the bowsprit,
382	sought to decoy the blacks into entirely disarming themselves
385	Atufal, the black, and the Spaniard at the helm
388	through shoals of black-fish.
388	Exhausted, the blacks now fought in despair.
388	wolf-like, from their black mouths.

144

398   and one hundred and sixty blacks, of both sexes,
402   "Keep faith with the blacks from here to Senegal,
402   for himself and all the blacks,
411   the blacks remark some expression in his countenance
431   As for the black—whose brain, not body, had schemed
432   the black met his voiceless end.

blood/bleeding
62   a gash from which blood flowed.
260   a closed castle in a blood red field
264   I never yet have drawn blood,
266   just then the razor drew blood,
266   here's Babo's first blood."
268   can't even bear the sight of barber's blood;
268   meant to spill all my blood
277   Captain Delano perceived that the cheek was bleeding
284   full-blooded African entertains for the adulterated one.
290   if a little of our blood mixed with the African's,
402   negroes with their bloody hatchets in their hands,

boat
7   Captain Delano ordered his whale-boat to be dropped,
7   into his boat, and so pulled away.
7   ere the boat came up, the wind, light though it was,
10   As the whale-boat drew more and more nigh,
14   the boat was hooked from the bow
23   as the whale-boat could carry,
24   after the boat's pushing off, to the vexation of all,
163   perceived his whale-boat in the distance.
165   anxiously watching the coming boat,
172   to while away the time till his boat should arrive,
186   looked to see how his boat was getting on;
187   a leisurely observation of the coming boat,
188   again looking off toward his boat;
193   again he gazed off for his boat.
203   Once more he looked off for his boat.
204   distant sight of that well-known boat—
204   that boat, Rover by name,
204   that household boat evoked a thousand trustful associations,
207   glancing towards the boat; there's Rover;
211   a vexation arising from the delay of his boat;
215   till the boat should arrive, he tried to occupy
217   glancing towards his now nearing boat—what then?

218   the boat touched the side,
221   Captain Delano would have sprung for his boat,
225   as on the first visit of the boat,
226   dispatched the boat back to the sealer,
227   observing the departing boat—
227   regrets that the San Dominick had no boats;
227   old hulk of the long-boat,
228   "Had you three or four boats now, Don Benito,"
228   Did you sail from port without boats, Don Benito?"
230   Boats and men.
349   The whale-boat was seen darting over the interval.
351   His boat was ready to receive him;
355   as he saw his household boat, with familiar faces in it,
356   the boat was being hooked along to the gangway.
357   in the first act of descent into the boat,
361   looking over into the boat, whose crew turned up their
362   with a hasty farewell, he descended into his boat,
363   ordered the boat shoved off.
363   The bowsmen pushed the boat a sufficient distance
363   that none in the boat could understand him.
364   The dismayed officer of the boat eagerly asked
366   the assailant dashed down into the bottom of the boat,
368   the officer of the boat, who had at last succeeded
369   snakishly writhing up from the boat's bottom,
370   in leaping into the boat, had intended to stab.
375   The boat was immediately dispatched back
376   to pursue with whale-boat and yawl seemed more promising.
378   The boats were got ready and armed.
381   the boats came up on the ship's quarters,
381   Another struck the whale-boat's bow,
383   the boats alternately falling behind, and pulling up,
384   could not be done by boats while she was sailing
386   the prow slowly swinging into view of the boats,
387   and, one on each bow, the boats boarded.
387   Huddled upon the long-boat amidships,
402   he could escape from it in a boat to the neighboring coast
402   Babo commanded all the boats to be destroyed
402   but the long-boat, which was unseaworthy,
405   Captain Amasa Delano coming in his boat, and all
407   until Amasa Delano should have been seated in his boat;
407   sprang from the gunwale into the boat, and fell into it,
409   the Ashantees fought in the engagement with the boats,
409   being killed in the fight with the boats, ere boarding;

146

409
    during the action,
411   fired through mistake from the boats before boarding
411   calling to the boats—"don't board,"
411   as upon the approach of the boats, Don Joaquin, with a hatchet
411   the haste in which the boats departed for the attack,
417   nerved me to that leap into your boat,
431   yielded to the superior muscular strength of his captor,
    in the boat.

body/bodily
25   induced by hardships bodily and mental,
25   repute of making the most pleasing body-servant in the world;
29   their delivery was delegated to his body-servant,
55   supplied in their immediate bodily needs,
85   associates goblins with the deserted body of man,
86   a chain, thrice wound round his body;
182   its black little body half lifted from the deck,
259   the contrasting sootiness of the negro's body.
360   across the black's body.
402   the body was carried below, forward;
402   or you shall in spirit, as now in body, follow your leader,"
402   they should, soul and body, go the way of Don Alexandro,
412   and broken in body and mind;
431   —whose brain, not body, had schemed and led the revolt,
432   The body was burned to ashes;

bones
432   the recovered bones of Aranda;

brave
88   like a brave prisoner, brought up to receive sentence,

brethren
48   of pacifying his more ignorant bretheren
411   is in the custody of brethren of the Hospital de Sacerdotes,

Buenos Ayres
36   sailed from Buenos Ayres bound to Lima,
53   sailing from Buenos Ayres, he had avowed himself a native
400   native of the province of Buenos Ayres,
405   that he came from Buenos Ayres, bound to Lima,

147

Byron
253   hypochondriacs, Johnson and Byron—

cadaverous
60   rendered distressing by his cadaverous aspect,
346   with a sort of cadaverous sullenness,

Cadiz
402   Lorenzo Bargas, and Hermenegildo Gandix, all of Cadiz;

Caffre
173   and escorted as by a Caffre guard of honor,

Callao
398   from the port of Valparaiso, bound to that of Callao;

camel
227   warped as a camel's skeleton in the desert,

Canary
293   the San Dominick's last bottle of Canary.
299   his servant pushing the Canary over towards him.
305   slowly pushed over the Canary.

Canton
129   "Canton."

Cape Horn
15   Off Cape Horn they had narrowly escaped shipwreck;
36   Off Cape Horn we had heavy gales.
43   in storms off the Cape, the scurvy broke out,
232   were these gales immediately off the pitch of Cape Horn?"
233   "Cape Horn?—
233   who spoke of Cape Horn?"
234   spoke of Cape Horn," he emphatically repeated.
265   two months and more getting from Cape Horn to St. Maria,
270   the passage from Cape Horn to St. Maria had been so
     exceedingly long;
402   the necessity involved of rounding Cape Horn,
405   that off Cape Horn, and in a subsequent fever, many negroes

Castile/Castilian
12   with the arms of Castile and Leon,

148

60   Don Benito, with Castilian bows, solemnly insisted
121   a sort of Castilian Rothschild, with a noble brother

Cereno, Benito
25   had Benito Cereno been a man of greater energy,
27   withdraw the half-lunatic Don Benito from his cloudy languor.
27   Don Benito's unfriendly indifference towards himself.
28   it was Don Benito's reserve which displeased him;
29   pilot-fish within easy call continually hovering round
       Don Benito.
31   whether Don Benito's manner was designed or not,
33   accosted Don Benito, renewing the expression of his benevolent
33   Would Don Benito favor him with the whole story[?]
34   Don Benito faltered;
34   Don Benito invited him back, regretting his momentary absence
42   Don Benito reviving, went on;
44   huskily continued Don Benito, painfully turning
50   "Don Benito, I envy you such a friend; slave I cannot
       call him."
53   the toilette of Don Benito might not, in fashion at least,
54   Eying Don Benito's small, yellow hands,
55   see Don Benito and his people supplied in their
       immediate bodily needs,
58   When Don Benito returned, the American was pained
60   Don Benito, with Castilian bows, solemnly insisted
63   the pale Don Benito duly muttered,
67   "I should think, Don Benito," he now said,
68   "Doubtless, doubtless," muttered Don Benito.
71   Don Benito, or have you appointed them shepherds
73   seems a curious business they are at, Don Benito?
75   "A prudent idea, Don Benito.
76   impatiently returned Don Benito,
78   "And may I ask, Don Benito, whether—
83   I conjecture, Don Benito, what it is
83   Were your friend's remains now on board this ship, Don Benito,
88   stood in muteness before Don Benito,
89   Don Benito had started, a resentful shadow swept over
       his face;
92   Thus reminded, Don Benito, nervously averting his glance,
96   "Answer," said Don Benito, still averting his glance,
98   "Go," said Don Benito, with inkept and unknown emotion.
100   "Excuse me, Don Benito," said Captain Delano,
109   bitterly returned Don Benito,

149

112	"What, pray, was Atufal's offense, Don Benito?"
114	a slender silken cord from Don Benito's neck, hung a key
114	"So, Don Benito—padlock and key—significant symbols, truly."
115	Biting his lip, Don Benito faltered.
119	From something in Don Benito's manner just then,
121	Benito Cereno—
121	Don Benito Cereno—a sounding name.
121	The alleged Don Benito was in early manhood,
123	He was a true off-shoot of a true hidalgo Cereno.
124	not to betray to Don Benito that he had at all mistrusted
124	did he allow Don Benito to become aware
127	"Oh, but a day or two, Don Benito."
139	"All on board, Don Benito," replied the Captain,
147	Captain Delano again glanced at Don Benito,
149	glance in the direction of Don Benito,
149	"Ha, Don Benito, your black here seems high in your trust;
152	demeanor of Don Benito Cereno.
157	a ghostly dread of Don Benito.
159	Don Benito's story had corroborated not only the wailing
159	If Don Benito's story was, throughout, an invention,
162	more convenient for the San Dominick than for Don Benito;
163	the idea of Don Benito's darkly pre-ordaining Captain Delano's fate,
163	lightly arranging Don Benito's.
164	Their shouts attracted the attention of Don Benito,
166	"Don Benito," said Captain Delano quickly,
167	Don Benito restored, the black withdrew his support,
169	"Tell me, Don Benito," he added, with a smile—
170	But Don Benito, apparently hardly yet completely restored,
172	something that Don Benito had said touching their ill conduct,
173	in the absence of Don Benito, with less of panic than before.
176	recalling Don Benito's confessed ill opinion of his crew,
179	referring to several particulars in Don Benito's narrative,
180	with regained confidence in Benito Cereno.
186	to see if Don Benito had returned; but he had not.
193	that Don Benito's plea of indisposition, in withdrawing below,
193	that Don Benito had, beforehand,
193	had dark secrets concerning Don Benito,
193	could then Don Benito be any way in complicity with the blacks?
206	and there was met by Don Benito's servant,
206	and say that he (Don Benito) would soon have the happiness
210	to see Don Benito approaching,
216	an act winked at by Don Benito.

216	Second, the tyranny in Don Benito's treatment of Atufal,
217	Why, Don Benito is a very capricious commander.
219	Don Benito, with his servant, now appeared;
219	on Don Benito's account, kind as this offer was,
219	Don Benito, with the true jealousy of weakness,
220	unmindful of Don Benito,
220	a rapid cry came from Don Benito.
222	Captain Delano glanced towards Don Benito.
223	poor Don Benito, whose condition, if not rank, demanded
224	and in chief Don Benito; but the latter objected;
230	Those must have been hard gales, Don Benito."
232	"Tell me, Don Benito," continued his companion
234	"You yourself, Don Benito, spoke of Cape Horn,"
240	"yes, Don Benito, unless you had rather not,
247	"You sleep here, Don Benito?"
249	and private closet all together, Don Benito,"
251	Don Benito signified his readiness,
253	something like the hypochondriac Benito Cereno—
258	did Don Benito appear disposed to renew any.
259	Don Benito nervously shuddered; his usual ghastliness
261	"why, Don Benito, this is the flag of Spain you use here.
263	Again Don Benito faintly shuddered.
265	"but the more I think of your voyage, Don Benito,
265	Why, Don Benito, had almost any other gentleman told me
266	back to Captain Delano, and face to Don Benito,
267	than was now presented by Don Benito.
269	and to Don Benito had said—
270	Don Benito resumed, rehearsing to Captain Delano,
271	to the very tremor of Don Benito's limbs,
271	the theatrical aspect of Don Benito in his harlequin ensign,
273	Don Benito bore all, much less uneasily, at least,
275	at the same time congratulating Don Benito.
279	this poor friend of his, that Don Benito, by his sullen manner,
281	Don Benito leaning on his servant as if nothing had happened.
283	He accosted Don Benito, and they slowly walked together.
286	"Don Benito," whispered he,
289	a sort of sluggishly responded Don Benito,
295	Don Benito waving Captain Delano to his place,
296	The negro placed a rug under Don Benito's feet,
297	an uncommonly intelligent fellow of yours, Don Benito,"
299	the guest again reverted to parts of Don Benito's story,
300	imagining that Don Benito for a few minutes could dispense
300	Don Benito, without being prompted, would perceive

301 "Don Benito, pardon me, but there is an interference
304 Don Benito, in fact, appeared to submit to hearing
306 Don Benito sighed heavily, as if for breath.
308 amid all Don Benito's distress,
310 "I told you so, Don Benito, look!"
311 Don Benito seemed to have even less welcome for the breeze
315 that lax as Don Benito's general authority might be, still,
326 to report affairs to Don Benito in the cabin;
330 "Don Benito," said he, "I give you joy;
331 Don Benito recoiled, as if at some bland satirical touch,
334 Ah, Don Benito," smiling, "for all the license you permit
335 Again Don Benito shrank;
336 Don Benito returned words few and reserved.
340 "Better and better, [Don Benito,"] he cried
340 We are getting on famously, Don Benito.
340 What say you, Don Benito, will you?"
345 "I cannot go," decisively and repulsively repeated Don Benito.
351 communicating to Don Benito the smaller details
351 Don Benito, as if he began to feel the weight
357 saw Don Benito advancing—an unwonted energy in his air,
360 Don Benito would not let go the hand of Captain Delano,
361 but still Don Benito would not let go his hand.
362 followed by the continual adieus of Don Benito,
363 Don Benito sprang over the bulwarks,
364 but it seemed as if Don Benito had taken it into his head
364 and seizing Don Benito by the throat he added,
367 again clutched the half-reclined Don Benito,
370 With infinite pity he withdrew his hold from Don Benito.
370 Not Captain Delano, but Don Benito, the black,
371 not as if frantically concerned for Don Benito,
373 Don Benito, covering his face, wailed out:
374 assisted the now almost helpless Don Benito up the side;
374 but Don Benito, wan as he was, refused to move,
377 Upon inquiring of Don Benito what firearms they had on board
377 Don Benito entreated the American not to give chase,
378 He was going himself when Don Benito grasped his arm.
394 the deposition of Benito Cereno; the first taken in the case.
397 *Declaration of the first witness*, DON BENITO CERENO.
398 Don Benito Cereno, to appear; which he did in his litter,
412 BENITO CERENO.
418 "you have saved my life, Don Benito, more than I yours;
421 "Wide, indeed," said Don Benito, sadly;
422 "You generalize, Don Benito; and mournfully enough.

431 Don Benito did not visit him.

432 dismissed by the court, Benito Cereno, borne on the bier,

chain

25 chained to one dull round of command,

86 from which depended a chain, thrice wound round his body;

96 and your chains shall be off."

101 I have put him in chains; I—"

187 into the mizzen-chains

190 his eye fell on the corroded main-chains

191 something moved nigh the chains.

191 Groves of rigging were about the chains;

201 Turning, he saw the chained negro, Atufal,

211 the Spanish sailor who had seemed to beckon from the main-
chains—

355 with the chained figure of the black

405 device of presenting Atufal, his right hand man, as chained,

405 though in a moment the chains could be dropped;

chapel

249 sail-loft, chapel, armory, and private closet

charity/charitable

27 But this the American in charity ascribed

28 he might not, after all, have exercised charity enough.

176 Captain Delano at the time, charitable man as he was.

420 good-nature, compassion, and charity, happily interweaving

Charles V.

28 supposed to have been his imperial countryman's,
Charles V.,

charm/becharmed

117 lost its original charm of simple-hearted attachment.

189 Trying to break one charm,

189 he was but becharmed anew.

355 as charmed eye and ear took in all these,

419 "God charmed your life, but you saved mine.

Chesterfieldian

284 as at once Christian and Chesterfieldian.

Chili

43 the southernmost civilized port of Chili and South America;

153

51   The Spaniard wore a loose Chili jacket of dark velvet;
53   he had avowed himself a native and resident of Chili,
390 the ships sailed in company for Conception, in Chili,
413 he shall not return home to Chili, but betake himself

Christian
284 as at once Christian and Chesterfieldian.

Christopher Colon
402 the image of Christopher Colon, the discoverer of the New World;

church
400 having sung in the Valparaiso churches,
432 looked towards St. Bartholomew's church,

civilized (also see uncivilized)
43   southernmost civilized port of Chili and South America;

command/commander/commanding
1   commanding a large sealer and general trader,
20   whosoever it might be that commanded the ship.
25   chained to one dull round of command,
30   more or less adopted by all commanders of large ships,
66   I know no sadder sight than a commander
66   who has little of command but the name.
103 At my command, every two hours he stands before me."
158 or her commander, either for himself or those under him,
162 On some benevolent plea withdrawing the command from him,
217 Why, Don Benito is a very capricious commander.
219 as if aware that he lacked energy as a commander,
222 on the darting supposition that such a commander,
222 could lose all self-command,
333 according to my command; which is, that if at a given hour
380 strongly objected against their commander's going.
402 to obey their commands;
402 the negro Babo commanded the Ashantee Martinqui
402 the negro Babo commanded all the boats to be destroyed
405 commanded by the generous Captain Amasa Delano;
408 *according to command of the court,*
409 without being commanded to do so by the negro Babo,
409 by Babo's command, willingly prepared the skeleton of Don Alexandro,
409 the Spaniards slain by command of the negro Babo;

154

crucifix
    245   a small, meagre crucifix attached to the bulk-head.

Dago
    400   a smart negro, named Dago, who had been for many years

dark/darkly
    8   in the hazy distance, throngs of dark cowls;
    8   other dark moving figures were dimly descried,
    12   a dark satyr in a mask, holding his foot on the prostrate neck
    13   dark festoons of sea-grass slimily swept to and fro
    51   The Spaniard wore a loose Chili jacket of dark velvet;
    153   was passing near a dark hatchway,
    158   until a dark deed had been done.
    161   and almost at the dark Spaniard himself,
    163   Don Benito's darkly pre-ordaining Captain Delano's fate,
    176   a haggardness combined with a dark eye,
    193   But if the whites had dark secrets concerning Don Benito,
    207   dark-lantern in [hand,] was dodging round some old
    227   perched above in the dark dome, on the elevated seats,
    346   as reproaching him for his dark spleen;
    354   to rush from darkness to light was the involuntary choice.

Delano, Amasa
    1   Captain Amasa Delano, of Duxbury, in Massachusetts,
    4   To Captain Delano's surprise, the stranger, viewed
    4   Captain Delano's surprise might have deepened
    5   Captain Delano continued to watch her—
    7   Captain Delano ordered his whale-boat to be dropped,
    8   almost led Captain Delano to think that nothing less
    16   While Captain Delano was thus made the mark of all eager tongues,
    18   in Captain Delano's mind, heightened whatever, upon a staid scrutiny,
    23   Captain Delano, returning to the gangway,
    24   Captain Delano sought, with good hopes,
    25   Still, Captain Delano was not without the idea,
    26   Captain Delano witnessed the steady good conduct of Babo.
    27   Still, Captain Delano was not a little concerned
    28   But ere long Captain Delano bethought him that, indulgent as he was
    31   the more Captain Delano noted its pervading reserve,
    32   These Captain Delano could not but ascribe, in the main,

33   that did he (Captain Delano) but know the particulars
34   Captain Delano, almost equally disconcerted,
41   again turning to Captain Delano,
50   "Faithful fellow!" cried Captain Delano.
51   Captain Delano could not but bethink him of the beauty
55   Captain Delano, having heard out his story,
60   Captain Delano had once or twice started at the occasional
60   it may be, that Captain Delano, with apparent complaisance,
60   stepped good Captain Delano between them,
63   In amazement, Captain Delano inquired what this meant.
64   "Pretty serious sport, truly," rejoined Captain Delano.
66   It is, thought Captain Delano, that this hapless man
69   "But," continued Captain Delano, again glancing upon
71   continued Captain Delano, pointing to the oakum-pickers,
73   continued Captain Delano, rather uneasily eying
78   to confirm his surmise, Captain Delano, after a pause, said:
83   "Pardon me," said Captain Delano, lowly,
84   with a silent appeal toward Captain Delano,
86   when Captain Delano's attention was caught by the moving
90   thought Captain Delano, surveying, not without a mixture
100 "Excuse me, Don Benito," said Captain Delano,
108 "Upon my conscience, then," exclaimed Captain Delano,
111 Captain Delano turned curiously upon the attendant,
112 asked Captain Delano; "if it was not something very serious,
114 His attention thus directed, Captain Delano now noticed
116 Though the remark of Captain Delano,
116 Captain Delano shifted the subject;
116 Captain Delano likewise became less talkative,
113 kept his eye fixed on Captain Delano,
119 Captain Delano gave a slight start.
121 wholly a stranger to Captain Delano's mind,
122 Captain Delano's good-nature regained its meridian.
124 Captain Delano thought he might extremely regret it,
133 Captain Delano, fidgeting a little, answered—
136 Captain Delano slightly started, but answered—
141 for the soul of him captain Delano could not but look
144 "Yes, for aught I know," returned Captain Delano—
147 Captain Delano again glanced at Don Benito,
148 and ere Captain Delano could cast a cool thought
148 and Captain Delano thought he observed a lurking significance
152 Captain Delano, unwilling to appear uncivil even to incivility
154 thought Captain Delano. It was no lamp—
158 have reference not so much to him (Captain Delano)

157

158	Not that Captain Delano had entirely credited such things.
159	which Captain Delano saw.
162	Captain Delano would yet have to send her to Conception,
163	Don Benito's darkly pre-ordaining Captain Delano's fate,
163	and Captain Delano's lightly arranging Don Benito's.
164	approaching Captain Delano, expressed satisfaction
165	Captain Delano responded;
166	"Don Benito," said Captain Delano quickly,
167	Captain Delano would have supported him,
168	Captain Delano could not avoid again congratulating his host
173	Captain Delano resolved forthwith to accost one of them.
173	Captain Delano, assuming a good-humored, off-handed air,
176	this reflection occurred to Captain Delano
177	thought Captain Delano, be sure that man there
179	Upon Captain Delano's approach, the man at once
180	Captain Delano, after glancing round for a more
183	at a distance facing Captain Delano.
184	thought Captain Delano, well pleased.
185	Ah! thought Captain Delano, these, perhaps, are some
192	previous misgivings of Captain Delano's about to be verified?
193	the mad idea now darted into Captain Delano's mind,
193	Captain Delano, who had now regained the deck,
194	Captain Delano crossed over to him, and stood in silence
195	Captain Delano addressed the knotter:—
200	While Captain Delano stood watching him,
201	Captain Delano stood mute;
201	Presently, there was a slight stir behind Captain Delano.
202	now approached Captain Delano.
203	thought Captain Delano, with a qualmish sort of emotion;
204	often pressed the beach of Captain Delano's home,
205	"What, I, Amasa Delano—Jack of the Beach,
205	I, Amasa; the same that, duck-satchel in hand,
205	Who would murder Amasa Delano?
206	present his compliments to his good guest, Don Amasa,
207	again thought Captain Delano, walking the poop.
210	Captain Delano, despite present prospects,
217	thought Captain Delano, glancing towards his now nearing boat—
219	Of him Captain Delano sought permission
219	So, at least, Captain Delano inferred.
220	accidentally jostled Captain Delano, where he stood
221	Captain Delano would have sprung for his boat,
222	Captain Delano glanced towards Don Benito.
223	Captain Delano was handed a number of jars and cups

158

223	Captain Delano presented a fair pitcher of the fluid;
224	Captain Delano would have given the whites alone,
226	Captain Delano, who, from recent indications,
226	he (Captain Delano) would remain on board
228	Don Benito," said Captain Delano,
234	answered Captain Delano, with almost equal astonishment
238	then turning upon Captain Delano, he said
239	"Then if master means to talk more to Don Amasa,"
239	"why not let Don Amasa sit by master in the cuddy,
239	and master can talk, and Don Amasa can listen,
240	"Yes," said Captain Delano, not unpleased with this
247	Captain Delano said, "You sleep here, Don Benito?"
249	added Captain Delano, looking round.
253	Captain Delano's nature was not only benign,
253	Captain Delano took to negroes, not philanthropically,
258	somewhat novel to Captain Delano, he sat curiously eying them,
259	at least to Captain Delano, nor, as he saw the two
261	"The castle and the lion," exclaimed Captain Delano—
264	See, Don Amasa, master always shakes when I shave him.
264	"And now, Don Amasa, please go on with your talk about the gale,
265	"Ah yes, these gales," said Captain Delano;
266	back to Captain Delano, and face to Don Benito,
268	Poor fellow, thought Captain Delano, so nervous
268	Surely, Amasa Delano, you have been beside yourself this day.
268	Tell it not when you get home, sappy Amasa.
269	"But answer Don Amasa, please, master, while I wipe
270	rehearsing to Captain Delano, that not only were the calms
271	To Captain Delano's imagination, now again not wholly at rest,
271	Captain Delano speedily banished it.
275	Captain Delano playfully complimented him upon his
276	Captain Delano, thinking that his presence was undesired
277	Advancing, Captain Delano perceived that the cheek
279	It is possible, thought Captain Delano;
282	But a sort of love-quarrel, after all, thought Captain Delano.
284	Captain Delano imputed his jealous watchfulness
285	Captain Delano observed with interest that
288	said Captain Delano, pausing, while with a final genuflexion
293	Some of Captain Delano's fresh fish and pumpkins,
295	Don Benito waving Captain Delano to his place,
296	stood behind, not his master's chair, but Captain Delano's.
297	whispered Captain Delano across the table.
300	Presently Captain Delano, intending to say something
301	Captain Delano, with a slight backward gesture

303	Captain Delano could hardly avoid some little tinge
307	said Captain Delano; "there is more air there."
310	"There," exclaimed Captain Delano, "I told you so,
312	Poor fellow, thought Captain Delano,
313	since he (Captain Delano) would with pleasure
314	Captain Delano started at the unexpected figure of Atufal,
316	with a free step Captain Delano advanced
317	suddenly Captain Delano heard a voice faithfully repeating
318	Good fellows, thought Captain Delano,
322	exclaimed Captain Delano—"well, no more sheep's-eyes now;—
326	Captain Delano, giving his last orders to the sailors,
327	Captain Delano, taking the nighest entrance—
328	thought Captain Delano; "what a vexatious coincidence."
332	He is like one flayed alive, thought Captain Delano;
336	In vain Captain Delano called attention to the now
338	Meantime Captain Delano had again repaired to the deck,
348	Captain Delano's pride began to be roused.
348	Captain Delano once more went to the deck.
351	Captain Delano had intended communicating to Don Benito
351	Well, thought Captain Delano, if he has little breeding,
351	and grasping Captain Delano's hand, stood tremulous;
351	Captain Delano bowed and withdrew.
353	yet acquiescent farewell to Captain Delano forever.
356	a sort of saddened satisfaction stole over Captain Delano,
357	With instinctive good feeling, Captain Delano,
359	self-reproachfully thought Captain Delano;
360	Don Benito would not let go the hand of Captain Delano,
361	the now embarrassed Captain Delano lifted his foot,
361	Adieu, my dear, dear Don Amasa. Go—go!"
362	Captain Delano would now have lingered;
363	Captain Delano, making a last salute,
363	falling at the feet of Captain Delano;
364	To which, Captain Delano, turning a disdainful smile
366	Captain Delano had flung the Spaniard aside,
366	dagger presented at Captain Delano's heart,
367	the left hand of Captain Delano, on one side,
368	suddenly called to Captain Delano, to see
369	Captain Delano saw the freed hand of the servant aiming
370	across the long-benighted mind of Captain Delano,
370	Not Captain Delano, but Don Benito, the black,
371	Captain Delano, now with scales dropped from his eyes,
372	Meantime Captain Delano hailed his own vessel,
374	Captain Delano bound the negro, who made no resistance,

160

161

dictatorship
>   29   dictatorship beyond which, while at sea, there was no
>   earthly appeal.

disorder/disorderly
>   51   at variance with the unsightly disorder around;
>   168   the spectacle of disorder to the more pleasing one before him,
>   218   hung over the bulwarks in disorderly raptures.

distrust/distrustful
>   124   the circumstance which had provoked that distrust
>   156   even into the least distrustful heart, some ugly misgivings
>   obtruded.
>   352   all his former distrusts swept through him.
>   420   enabled me to get the better of momentary distrust,

divining/divined
>   78   Thinking he divined the cause of such unusual emotion,
>   114   divining the key's purpose, he smiled and said:—

docility
>   253   When to this is added the docility
>   315   Atufal's presence, singularly attesting docility

Don Jose
>   395   I, DON JOSE DE ABOS AND PADILLA

doubt/doubtless
>   32   some individuals, doubtless, as little troublesome as crates
>   33   The best account would, doubtless, be given by the captain.
>   65   "Doubtless,
>   65   doubtless, Senor."
>   68   "Doubtless,
>   68   doubtless," muttered Don Benito.
>   181   No doubt, when he saw me coming, he dreaded lest I,
>   291   "Doubtless,
>   291   doubtless, Senor, but"—glancing at Babo—
>   420   Had it been otherwise, doubtless, as you hint,

doves
>   185   Unsophisticated as leopardesses; loving as doves.

159 one making up his tale for evil purposes, as he goes.

160 those questions had been prompted by evil designs.

193 A man with some evil design, would he not

eye/eyeing/eying

5 a Lima intriguante's one sinister eye

21 and rather young man to a stranger's eye,

32 suffering host repeatedly challenged his eye.

37 keeping his eye fixed on his face, as if to watch

44 to your inexperienced eyes appearing unruly,

54 Eying Don Benito's small, yellow hands,

83 but that honest eye, that honest hand—

95 with bitter upbraiding eyeing his countryman,

118 kept his eye fixed on Captain Delano,

141 dropped his eyes to the deck;

147 but the latter's eyes were averted;

148 the young sailor's eye was again fixed on the whisperers,

151 not ungratefully eyed his master.

167 as quite wiped away, in the visitor's eyes, any blemish

173 standing with eye directed forward towards that handful

173 He rubbed his eyes, and looked again;

173 and his eye curiously surveying the white faces,

174 squatted round him inquisitively eying the process.

176 a haggardness combined with a dark eye, averted as in trouble

179 should simper and cast sheep's eyes.

181 so earnestly eying me here awhile since.

187 all closed like coppered eyes of the coffined—

188 but found his eye falling upon the ribbon grass,

190 as his eye fell on the corroded main-chains.

191 He rubbed his eyes, and looked hard.

211 his eye falling continually, as from a stage-box into the pit,

258 he sat curiously eying them, so that no conversation took place,

284 eyed askance the graceful steward.

299 plague before the Spaniard's eyes,

299 With starting eyes he stared before him at vacancy.

301 At last catching his host's eye,

308 He only rested his eye on his master's,

322 "well, no more sheep's-eyes now;—

323 the two blacks eyed the sailor intently.

336 with lack-lustre eye, Don Benito returned words few

351 with half-averted eyes, he silently reseated himself

355 as charmed eye and ear took in all these,

358 casting an earnest glance into his eyes,

164

361 whose crew turned up thier curious eyes.
362 but catching the meekly admonitory eye of the servant,
367 his eye bent forward, encouraging his men to their utmost.
371 now with scales dropped from his eyes, saw the negroes,
405 that that dagger would be alert as his eye;

Ezekiel

10 and she launched, from Ezekiel's Valley of Dry Bones.

faithful/faith

28 reserve shown towards all but his faithful personal attendant
50 "Faithful fellow!" cried Captain Delano.
170 strange vanity of a faithful slave appreciated by his master,
172 indisposed to countenance cowardice or unfaithfulness in seamen.
317 Captain Delano heard a voice faithfully repeating his orders.
328 "Confound the faithful fellow," thought Captain Delano;
402 "Keep faith with the blacks from here to Senegal,

family

25 In armies, navies, cities, or families, in nature herself,
32 the sealer's comfortable family of a crew,
43 whole families of the Africans, and a yet larger number,
121 most enterprising and extensive mercantile families

fidelity

51 such a spectacle of fidelity on the one hand
179 with more than common fidelity, in his task.
242 the servant's anxious fidelity had something to do
276 But neither sweet waters, nor shampooing, nor fidelity,
308 to refresh his spirit by the silent sight of fidelity.
364 as if with desperate fidelity to befriend his master

Fletcher

253 the negroes, Barber and Fletcher.

fool

112 take a fool's advice, and, in view of his general docility,
221 bidding him, in substance, not be a fool.

fortune

83 It was once my hard fortune to lose,

fox

193 reconnoitering from a port-hole like a fox from the mouth of its den

Francesco
- 289   "Francesco is a good man,"
- 294   As they entered, Francesco, with two or three colored aids,
- 294   Francesco making a smiling congé, and the Spaniard,
- 308   And Francesco coming in on tiptoes, handed the negro
- 400   a mulatto, named Francesco, the cabin steward,
- 409   that the mulatto steward, Francesco, was of the first band
- 409   Babo, having another design, forbade Francesco;

free/freed
- 253   watching some free man of color at his work or play.
- 259   the best regulated mind is not always free.
- 316   with a free step Captain Delano advanced to the forward edge
- 369   Captain Delano saw the freed hand of the servant
- 391   signs of regaining health with free-will;
- 405   and a free captain of the ship, told Captain Amasa Delano,

Freemason
- 148   signs, of some Freemason sort, had that instant been interchanged.

friar
- 8   as of Black Friars pacing the cloisters.
- 52   something like a begging friar of St. Francis.
- 245   like a heap of poor friars' girdles.

friend/befriend/friendly/unfriendly
- 25   and a brother captain to counsel and befriend,
- 27   Don Benito's unfriendly indifference towards himself.
- 32   but the friendly remonstrances of such with their ruder
- 32   the unfriendly arm of the mate.
- 50   I envy you such a friend; slave I cannot call him."
- 76   who belonged to my late friend, Alexandro Aranda."
- 78   the friend, whose loss so afflicts you, at the outset
- 83   a dear friend, my own brother, then supercargo.
- 83   Were your friend's remains now on board this ship,
- 85   could you here see your friend—who, on former voyages,
- 221   with gestures friendly and familiar, almost jocose,
- 279   his Spanish spite against this poor friend of his,
- 299   he had had so many friends and officers round him,
- 339   I will cheer up my poor friend, this time, thought he.
- 340   The Bachelor's Delight, my good friend.
- 361   and God guard you better than me, my best friend."

166

364   with desperate fidelity to befriend his master to the last;
373   "'Tis he, Aranda! my murdered, unburied friend!"
402   because the owner, his friend Aranda, told him that they were
402   who was the friend, from youth, of Don Alexandro,
406   *and also recounting the friendly offers of Captain Delano,*
417   "Ah, my dear friend," Don Benito once said,
417   you, my best friend, with all who might be with you,
419   "Nay, my friend," rejoined the Spaniard,
424   Warm friends,
424   steadfast friends are the trades."

frock
148   his voluminous, unconfined frock, or shirt, or coarse woolen,
153   placing his hand in the bosom of his frock, as if hiding something.

Galgo, Luys
412   that Luys Galgo, a sailor about sixty years of age,

Gandix, Hermenegildo
402   and Hermenegildo Gandix, all of Cadiz;
402   Don Joaquin and Hermenegildo Gandix, the negro Babo,
411   and one by Hermenegildo Gandix, to convey hints to him
411   Hermenegildo Gandix, who before had been forced to live among
411   like Hermenegildo Gandix, the third clerk,

Gayete, Juan Bautista
402   and the carpenter, Juan Bautista Gayete,

generous/generosity
56   Such generosity was not without its effect,
405   commanded by the generous Captain Amasa Delano;
407

    the day,
407   the generous Captain Amasa Delano, the deponent at first
407   followed the generous Captain Amasa Delano as far as the gunwale,
408   *the "generous Captain Amasa Delano."*
409   poisoning a dish for the generous Captain Amasa Delano;
411   owing to the generosity and piety of Amasa Delano

gentility
54   in youth, sickness, and gentility united?

Ghetto
51   especially in the belittered Ghetto, forward of the main-mast,

173   object of this deliberate visit to their Ghetto,

Ghofan
400   the fourth, Ghofan; and six full-grown negroes,

ghost/ghostly
85   as ghosts with an abandoned house.
157   to feel a ghostly dread of Don Benito.
187   as this ghostly cats paw came fanning his cheek;
386   One extended arm of the ghost seemed beckoning the whites
430   not, indeed, a sword, but the ghost of one.

god (see also: Prince, Providence, Lord)
31   thought it was with captains as with gods:
39   —"Oh, my God! rather than pass through what I have,
48   "But it is Babo here to whom, under God, I owe
252   as though God had set the whole negro to some pleasant tune.
361   "go, and God guard you better than me, my best friend."
398   which he took by God, our Lord, and a sign of the Cross;
407   to have come from God and his angels,
407   he knows not how, God guarding him;
417   And as God lives, Don Amasa, I know not whether desire
419   "God charmed your life, but you saved mine.
419   but you had the Prince of Heaven's safe-conduct

Gola, Martinez
411   struck down Martinez Gola, who, having found a razor

gold
110   "those slits in Atufal's ears once held wedges of gold;
286   this usher-of-the-golden-rod of yours;
380   her cargo, including some gold and silver,

good
4   a person of a singularly undistrustful [good nature],
24   Captain Delano sought, with good hopes,
25   the less good-natured qualities of the negroes,
25   as good order than misery
26   the steady good conduct of Babo.
27   But the good conduct of Babo
60   Gingerly enough stepped good Captain Delano between them,
116   But the good sailor, himself of a quite contrary disposition,
122   Captain Delano's good-nature regained its meridian.

168

150   the servant looked up with a good-natured grin,
162   was now good-naturedly explained away by the thought
162   a worthy person and good navigator—
162   under the good nursing of his servant,
163   the good seaman presently perceived his whale-boat
173   assuming a good-humored, off-handed air,
202   and with a good-natured, knowing wink, he informed him
206   present his compliments to his good guest, Don Amasa,
207   good dog; a white bone in her mouth.
210   since, with a good wind, ten minutes' sailing would retrace
213   and so, exerting his good-nature to the utmost,
217   are as good folks as any in Duxbury, Massachusetts.
217   Ah good! At last "Rover" has come.
220   with good-natured authority he bade the blacks stand back;
226   the peculiar good-humor at present prevailing,
251   as if waiting his master's good pleasure.
252   And above all is the great gift of good-humor.
253   like most men of a good, blithe heart, Captain Delano
265   with a good wind, have sailed in a few days.
268   this day's experience shall be a good lesson.
270   to the blacks, for their general good conduct.
288   always proved a good, worthy fellow?" said Captain Delano,
289   "Francesco is a good man," a sort of sluggishly responded
318   Good fellows, thought Captain Delano, a little training
318   I must have a good hand there.
322   Good hand, I trust?
331   of apparent good breeding as to present no handle for retort.
335   as the good sailor thought, from a genuine twinge
340   The Bachelor's Delight, my good friend.
348   that even the forbearing good-nature of his guest
351   But the good augury hence drawn was suddenly dashed,
353   Hitherto, credulous good-nature had been too ready
356   after good actions one's conscience is never ungrateful,
357   With instinctive good feeling, Captain Delano,
380   considered his ship good as lost
400   the cabin steward, of a good person and voice,
402   that the mate, who was a good navigator, should be killed
402   a cutter in good condition, which knowing it would yet
420   added to my good-nature, compassion, and charity,

Gordian
194   making Gordian knots for the temple of Ammon.

gratitude
- 56 With gratitude he seemed overcome.
- 408 *"eternal gratitude" to the "generous Captain Amasa Delano."*
- 411 to attest his gratitude, when he should have landed in Peru,

guilt/guilty
- 142 still with a guilty shuffle, repeated his question:
- 175 so innocence and guilt, when, through casual association

Guinea
- 46 not thrust below, as in the Guinea-men—

Guy-Fawkish
- 217 Guy-Fawkish twang to it.

harmony
- 252 harmonious in every glance and gesture; as though God

heart
- 4 such a trait implies, along with a benevolent heart,
- 77 his air was heart-broken;
- 83 and that warm heart; all, all—like scraps to the dogs—
- 117 original charm of simple-hearted attachment.
- 156 into the least distrustful heart, some ugly misgivings
- 158 On heart-broken pretense of entreating a cup of cold water,
- 185 they seemed at once tender of heart and tough of constitution;
- 206 Light of heart and foot, he stepped aft,
- 234 even as he ever seemed eating his own heart,
- 253 took to their hearts, almost to the exclusion of the entire
- 253 like most men, of a good, blithe heart, Captain Delano
- 278 only the sour heart that sour sickness breeds made him
- 286 the king of kind hearts and polite fellows.
- 340 all its vast weight seems lifted from the captain's heart.
- 366 with dagger presented at Captain Delano's heart,
- 369 at the heart of his master, his countenance lividly vindictive,
- 370 but his own heart smote him harder.
- 417 at those very times my heart was frozen;

Heaven
- 419 but you had the Prince of Heaven's safe-conduct through all ambuscades."

Highlanders
- 389 made by the poled scythes of the Highlanders.

170

honest
56	he met the honest glance of his visitor.
83	but that honest eye,
83	that honest hand—both of which had so often met mine—
121	would a gentleman, nay, any honest boor, act the part
269	things were running through the honest seaman's mind,

Hospital de Sacerdotes
411	custody of the brethren of the Hospital de Sacerdotes,
412	to the Hospital de Sacerdotes.

host
32	the San Dominick's suffering host repeatedly challenged his eye.
59	the host invited his guest to accompany him there,
60	acquiesced in his host's invitation.
62	while standing with his host, looking forward upon the decks
69	"I see you keep some, at least, of your host employed."
119	as it was little flattering to the host.
121	act the part now acted by his host?
123	Glancing over once more towards his host—
168	Captain Delano could not avoid again congratulating his host
242	his host's capriciousness, this being shaved with such uncommon
295	Without companions, host and guest sat down,
300	intending to say something to his host concerning
301	At last catching his host's eye, Captain Delano,
307	But the host sat silent and motionless.
313	he urged his host to remain quietly where he was,
342	Come, all day you have been my host;
351	but his host still tarried below.
364	Meantime, the whole host of negroes, as if inflamed
370	his host's whole mysterious demeanor, with every enigmatic

human
158	fiends in human form had got into lonely dwellings,
159	by the very expression and play of every human feature,
372	death for the figure-head, in a human skeleton;
423	"because they are not human."
424	do they not come with a human-like healing to you?

Hurta, Roderigo
402	the boatswain's mates, Manuel Viscaya and Roderigo Hurta,

171

imagined/imagination

    268   I should have imagined he meant to spill all my blood,

    271   To Captain Delano's imagination, now again not

Indian

      5   from the Indian loop-hole of her dusk *saya-y-manta.*

    191   like an Indian from behind a hemlock, a Spanish sailor,

    291   the Spanish and Indian intermixtures in our provinces.

    381   Indian-like, they hurtled their hatchets.

Infelez

    389   attended by the monk Infelez;

    412   with the monk Infelez, to the Hospital de Sacerdotes.

inferior/inferiority

    178   performing the inferior function of holding the outer parts

    253   attachment sometimes inhering in indisputable inferiors,

    284   Babo, who, as if not unconscious of inferiority,

innocence/innocent

    175   so innocence and guilt, when, through casual association

    355   taking her innocent repose

    421   not only an innocent man, but the most pitiable of all men.

inquisitor

    245   and uncomfortable to look at as inquisitor's racks,

invalid

     29   So that to have beheld this undemonstrative invalid gliding about,

     43   the surviving mariners, most of whom were become invalids,

     53   image of an invalid courtier tottering about London streets

     56   generosity was not without its effect, even upon the invalid.

     60   and in the ears of an invalid.

    121   But the Spaniard was a pale invalid.

    162   the poor invalid scarcely knew what he was about;

    168   would be invaluable to one in the invalid's situation.

    222   into which the agitated invalid had fallen,

Jack

    177   this old Jack here on the windlass.

    205   —Jack of the Beach, as they called me when a lad—

    205   I, little Jack of the Beach, that used to go berrying

    205   Fie, fie, Jack of the Beach!

king/kingdom

109	"he says he was king in his own land."
173	His progress thus proclaimed as by mounted kings-at-arms,
261	It's well it's only I, and not the King, that sees this,"
267	no assassination in that timid King's presence,
286	has features more regular than King George's of England;
286	a king, indeed—
286	the king of kind hearts and polite fellows.
334	treating the poor fellow like an ex-king indeed.
391	the many religious institutions of the city of Kings
398	Councilor of the royal Audience of this Kingdom,
411	and formerly of the king's navy, was one of those

knot/knotter

51	a slender sword, silver mounted, hung from a knot in his sash—
193	which he was working into a large knot.
194	and stood in silence surveying the knot;
194	such a knot he had never seen in an American ship,
194	making Gordian knots for the temple of Ammon.
194	The knot seemed a combination of
194	double-bowline-knot,
194	treble-crown-knot,
194	back-handed-well-knot,
194	knot-in-and-
194	out-knot,
194	and jamming-knot.
195	puzzled to comprehend the meaning of such a knot,
195	Captain Delano addressed the knotter:—
196	"What are you knotting there, my man?"
197	"The knot," was the brief reply, without looking up.
199	the knot being now nearly completed.
200	suddenly the old man threw the knot towards him,
201	For a moment, knot in hand,
201	and knot in head, Captain Delano stood mute;
202	the old knotter was simple-witted, but harmless;
202	The negro concluded by begging the knot,
202	he tossed the knot overboard.

Lascars

17	a nondescript crew such as Lascars or Manilla men,

leader

13	*"Sequid vuestro jefe,"*

London
    53   tottering about London streets in the time of the plague.

Lord/lordship
    116   the Spaniard's singularly evidenced lordship over the black;
    398   which he took by God, our Lord, and a sign of the Cross;

love
    19   with the peculiar love in negroes of uniting industry
    83   never to have for fellow-voyager a man I loved,
    184   pure tenderness and love, thought Captain Delano,
    185   Unsophisticated as leopardesses; loving as doves.
    223   which the sight-loving Africans hailed with clapping of hands.
    255   an odd instance of the African love of bright colors
    282   But a sort of love-quarrel, after all, thought Captain Delano

lunatic/lunacy
    27   withdraw the half-lunatic Don Benito from his cloudy languor.
    65   sudden, staring, half-lunatic
    120   innocent lunacy
    121   of coursethe idea of lunacy
    121   But if not a lunatic

mad
    346   sulk as he might, and go mad with it, nature cared not a jot;

Madras
    283   a pagoda turban formed by three or four Madras handkerchiefs

Malacca
    245   two long, sharp-ribbed settees of Malacca cane,
    251   seating him in the Malacca arm-chair,

Malay
    158   And among the Malay pirates, it was no unusual thing

Manilla
    17   a nondescript crew such as Lascars or Manilla men,

Mapenda
    400   Matiluqui, Yan, Lecbe, Mapenda, Yambaio, Akim;

237	"master told me never mind where he was, or how engaged,
237	"It is *now,* master.
237	Will master go into the cuddy?"
239	"Then if master means to talk more to Don Amasa,"
239	"why not let Don Amasa sit by master in the cuddy,
239	and master can talk, and Don Amasa can listen,
242	the timely interruption served to rally his master from the mood
251	made a motion as if waiting his master's good pleasure.
251	by throwing back his master's collar and loosening his cravat.
254	so debonair about his master, in a business so familiar
255	and lavishly tucking it under his master's chin for an apron.
262	"Now, master," he said, readjusting the flag,
262	"now, master," and the steel glanced nigh the throat.
264	"You must not shake so, master.
264	See, Don Amasa, master always shakes when I shave him.
264	And yet master knows I never yet have drawn blood,
264	though it's true, if master will shake so, I may some of these times.
264	Now, master," he continued.
264	master can hear, and, between times,
264	master can answer."
266	"See, master—you shook so—here's Babo's first blood."
269	"But answer Don Amasa, please, master,
270	by getting his master to go on with the conversation,
271	that possibly master and man, for some unknown purpose,
273	evincing the hand of a master;
274	which might have lodged down his master's neck;
274	the servant for a moment surveyed his master,
278	"Ah, when will master get better from his sickness;
278	only by accident, Babo had given master one little scratch;
281	Presently master and man came forth;
294	Upon perceiving their master they withdrew,
296	stood behind, not his master's chair, but Captain Delano's.
296	the black was still true to his master;
306	the servant placing a pillow behind his master.
308	with which at intervals he chafed his master's brow;
308	He only rested his eye on his master's,
333	The servant moved before his master, adjusting a cushion;
334	I fear lest, at bottom, you are a bitter hard master."
357	placing his master's hand on his naked shoulder,
360	the scene might too much unstring his master, the servant
364	with desperate fidelity to befriend his master to the last;
369	at the heart of his master, his countenance lividly vindictive,
400	was the man that waited upon his master, Don Alexandro,

178

193	the mad idea now darted into Captain Delano's mind,
193	had a mind to warn the stranger against;
194	his mind, by a not uncongenial transition,
207	these long calms have a morbid effect on the mind,
215	By way of keeping his mind out of mischief
237	"master told me never mind where he was, or how engaged,
253	
	mind,
253	the inflicted sourness of the morbid or cynical mind,
259	from which, perhaps, the best regulated mind is not always free.
269	
	mind,
329	indefinite association in his mind of Babo with Atufal.
352	his mind, responsive to the portent, swarmed with
370	across the long-benighted mind of Captain Delano,
394	not undisturbed in his mind by recent events,
412	and broken in body and mind; that when finally dismissed
420	but the temper of my mind that morning was more than commonly pleasant,

misfortune

33	but know the particulars of the ship's misfortunes,
405	only serve uselessly to recall past misfortunes and conflicts,
407	speaking to him always of his pretended misfortunes,

missal

245	a thumbed missal on it, and over it a small, meagre crucifix

mistrust/mistrusting/mistrusted

124	that he had at all mistrusted incivility, much less duplicity;
124	for such mistrust would yet be proved illusory,
159	And yet, if there was ground for mistrusting his veracity,

monastery

8	appeared like a white-washed monastery after a thunder-storm,
412	but betake himself to the monastery on Mount Agonia without;
432	looked towards the monastery, on Mount Agonia without;

monk

8	nothing less than a ship-load of monks was before him.
398	attended by the monk Infelez;
412	with the monk Infelez, to the Hospital de Sacerdotes.

moralize
423   But the past is passed; why moralize upon it? Forget it.

Mount Agonia
412   but betake himself to the monastery on Mount Agonia without;
432   looked towards the monastery, on Mount Agonia without;

Mozairi, José
402   young clerks of Aranda, José Mozairi, Lorenzo Bargas,
402   but Don Francisco Masa, José Mozairi, and Lorenzo Bargas,

mulatto
28   some petty underling, either a white, mulatto or black,
283   when the steward—a tall, rajah-looking mulatto,
284   the two captains were preceded by the mulatto,
285   while the complexion of the mulatto was hybrid, his physiognomy
286   that when a mulatto has a regular European face, look out for him;
400   a mulatto, named Francesco, the cabin steward,
409   that the mulatto steward, Francesco, was of the first band

murder/murderer/murderous
205   Who would murder Amasa Delano?
222   going to bring about his murder.
268   Well, well, he looks like a murderer, doesn't he?
364   "this plotting pirate means murder!"
373   "'Tis he, Aranda! my murdered, unburied friend!"
382   their most murderous weapons in a hand-to-hand fight,
402   and the Ashantee Lecbe to go and commit the murder;
402   bidding the murder be completed on the deck before him,
409   beside participating in the murder, before mentioned,
409   he ordered every murder, and was the helm and keel of the revolt;
409   but Atufal, with his own hand, committed no murder;
409   that, in the various acts of murder, they sang songs and danced—
417   you half thought me plotting your murder, at those very times

Muri
400   the first was named Muri, and he was killed

mute/mutely/muteness
3   Everything was mute and calm; everything gray.
21   he mutely turned it up into the Spaniard's,
29   undemonstrative invalid gliding about, apathetic and mute,
87   "How like a mute Atufal moves," murmured the servant.

181

88	stood in unquailing muteness before Don Benito,
179	as they became talkative, he by degrees became mute,
201	and knot in head, Captain Delano stood mute;
305	the hand of his servant, mute as that on the wall,
341	while with mute concern his servant gazed into his face.
353	all was eclipsed in sinister muteness and gloom.
430	sometimes ended in muteness upon topics like the above,

mutinous
| 402 | the negroes were now restless and mutinous, |

Nacta
| 400 | the second, Nacta; the third, Yola, likewise killed; |

Nasca
402	and continued their course by it in the vicinity of Nasca;
402	that eight days after parting from the coast of Nasca,
405	reckoned from the time they sailed from Nasca,

Nat
| 205 | that used to go berrying with cousin Nat and the rest; |

nation
| 217 | But as a nation—continued he in his reveries—these Spaniards |
| 256 | is a little different from what it is with other nations. |

nature/natural/naturally
4	a person of a singularly undistrustful [good nature],
21	not unwilling to let nature make known her own case
25	brought out the less good-natured qualities of the negroes,
25	in nature herself, nothing more relaxes good order than misery.
27	there are peculiar natures on whom prolonged physical suffering
31	it seemed but a natural token of the perverse habit
112	some natural respect for his spirit,
118	as if by a natural sequence, to the two whisperers.
121	But the first idea, though it might naturally have occurred
122	Captain Delano's good-nature regained its meridian.
150	looked up with a good-natured grin,
156	it would have been almost against nature,
162	was now good-naturedly explained away by the thought that,
175	seemed not naturally allied to his face,
184	There's naked nature, now; pure tenderness and love,

182

36	"that parcel of negroes, now not more than a hundred and fifty,
44	"I have to thank those negroes you see,
46	those negroes have always remained upon deck—
90	the colossal form of the negro.
101	that that negro alone, of all the band, has given me
173	the negroes, twitching each other aside,
173	saying a blithe word to the negroes,
175	the tar-pot held for him by a negro,
179	The negroes about the windlass joined in with the old sailor;
193	while below the old negro, and, invisible to him,
193	while praising the negroes;
193	by leaguing in against it with negroes?
201	he saw the chained negro, Atufal, standing quietly there.
201	followed by his subordinate negroes, removed
202	An elderly negro, in a clout like an infant's,
202	The negro concluded by begging the knot,
202	the negro received it, and, turning his back,
216	the trampling of the sailor by the two negroes;
220	when some of the eager negroes accidentally jostled
220	each negro and negress suspended in his or her posture,
221	forced every white and every negro back,
228	your negroes here might help along matters some.
252	There is something in the negro which, in a peculiar way,
252	Most negroes are natural valets and hair-dressers;
252	God had set the whole negro to some pleasant tune.
253	the negroes, Barber and Fletcher.
253	But if there be that in the negro which exempts him
253	Captain Delano took to negroes, not philanthropically,
254	all his old weakness for negroes returned.
259	the negro searched among the razors, as for the sharpest,
259	the contrasting sootiness of the negro's body.
261	which playful remark did not fail somewhat to tickle the negro.
273	that the negro seemed a Nubian sculptor finishing off
274	the negro's warm breath blowing away any stray hair
277	and turning, saw the negro, his hand to his cheek.
277	when the negro's wailing soliloquy enlightened him.
280	He was about to speak in sympathy to the negro,
291	"not to speak of negroes, your planter's remark
296	The negro placed a rug under Don Benito's feet,
308	handed the negro a little cup of aromatic waters,
316	The few sailors and many negroes, all equally pleased,
317	the blithe songs of the inspirited negroes.
353	Was the negro now lying in wait?

364	Meantime, the whole host of negroes, as if inflamed
366	Seeing the negro coming, Captain Delano had flung
367	ground the prostrate negro;
371	saw the negroes, not in misrule, not in tumult,
374	Captain Delano bound the negro, who made no resistance,
374	until the negro should have been first put below
377	for the negroes had already proved themselves
381	the negroes sent their yells.
382	The negroes giving too hot a reception, the whites
382	the negroes desisted, though not before many of them
384	the negroes, at present, were clustering.
384	But to kill or maim the negroes was not the object.
385	the ship became unmanageable to the negroes.
388	the negroes wedging themselves to beat it back;
388	irresistibly driving the negroes toward the stern.
388	Here the negroes faced about, and though scorning peace
389	Nearly a score of the negroes were killed.
389	The surviving negroes were temporarily secured,
396	against the negroes of the ship San Domninick,
398	that the negroes were in part as follows:
400	A smart negro, named Dago, who had been for many years
400	Four old negroes, born in Africa, from sixty to seventy,
400	and six full-grown negroes, aged from thirty to forty-five,
400	a powerful negro named Atufal, who being supposed
400	And a small negro of Senegal, but some years among the Spaniards,
400	which negro's name was Babo;
402	That all the negroes slept upon deck, as is customary
402	the negroes revolted suddenly, wounded dangerously
402	the negroes made themselves masters of the hatchway,
402	where the negro Babo was, being the ringleader,
402	the negro Babo asked him whether there were in those seas
402	any negro countries where they might be carried,
402	that the negro Babo afterwards told him to carry them
402	but that the negro Babo replied to him he must carry them in any way;
402	that the negro Babo agreed to it:
402	that the negroes were now restless and mutinous,
402	the negro Babo having required, with threats,
402	because the negro Babo had intimated to him several times,
402	that the negroes Babo and Atufal held daily conferences,
402	and soon after the negroes had their meeting,
402	the negro Babo came to the place where the deponent was,

402	the negro Babo proposed to the deponent to call the mate Raneds,
402	for the negro Babo answered him that the thing could not be prevented,
402	and immediately the negro Babo commanded the Ashantee Martinqui
402	but the negro Babo stopped them, bidding the murder be completed
402	and at the sight of the negroes with their bloody hatchets
402	the negro Babo, for purposes hereafter to appear,
402	the negro Babo ordered to be thrown alive into the sea,
402	frequently asked the negro Babo where they were,
402	that the negro Babo answered nothing till the fourth day,
402	the negro Babo showed him a skeleton, which had been substituted
402	that the negro Babo asked him whose skeleton that was,
402	the negro Babo, coming close, said words to this effect:
402	that the same morning the negro Babo took by succession each Spaniard
402	that then to each the negro Babo repeated the words in the first place
402	the negro Babo harangued them, saying that he had now done all;
402	(as navigator for the negroes)
402	speak or plot anything against them (the negroes)—
402	but finally the negro Babo spared his life,
402	spoke to the negroes peace and tranquillity,
402	as also by the negro Babo, for himself and all the blacks,
402	the negro Babo commanded all the boats to be destroyed
404	the negroes became irritable, and for a chance gesture,
405	and the negroes became uneasy, as soon as at distance
405	that the negro Babo pacified them, assuring them that no fear
405	that for a time the negro Babo
405	and the negro Atufal conferred;
405	that the negro Atufal was for sailing away,
405	but the negro Babo would not,
405	that the negro Babo warned him
405	that the negro Babo then announced the plan
405	that, conscious that many of the negroes would be turbulent,
405	the negro Babo appointed
405	the four aged negroes, who were calkers,
405	with three hundred negroes,
405	in a subsequent fever, many negroes had died;
407	because the negro Babo, performing the office of an officious servant

186

407	for the negro Babo understands well the Spanish;
407	by a secret sign the negro Babo drew him
407	the negro Babo proposed to him to gain from Amasa Delano
407	that the negro Babo answered he might conceive;
407	to induce the negro Babo to give up this new design;
407	that the negro Babo showed the point of his dagger;
407	the negro Babo again drew him aside, telling him that
408	*and a partial renumeration of the negroes,*
409	all the negroes, though not in the first place knowing
409	That the negro, José, eighteen years old,
409	was the one who communicated the information to the negro Babo,
409	and had secret conversations with the negro Babo,
409	that this same negro José was the one who,
409	without being commanded to do so by the negro Babo,
409	the creature and tool of the negro Babo;
409	proposed, to the negro Babo, poisoning a dish
409	because the negroes have said it;
409	that the negro Babo, having another design, forbade Francesco;
409	when, by the negro Babo's orders, he was carrying him to throw
409	in a way the negroes afterward told the deponent,
409	this also the negroes told him;
409	that the negro Babo was he who traced the inscription
409	that the negro Babo was the plotter from first to last;
409	nor did the negro Babo;
409	that, had the negroes not restrained them, they would have tortured
409	the Spaniards slain by command of the negro Babo;
409	they sang melancholy songs to the negroes,
409	that all this is believed, because the negroes have said it.
409	that the negroes broke an arm of one of the cabin-boys
411	This the negroes have since said;
411	lest upon their boarding the negroes should kill him;
411	to believe he some way favored the cause of the negroes,
411	the negro Babo commanded the Ashantee Lecbe to take tar
411	was made by the negroes to appear on the bulwarks;
411	one of the clerks disguised by the negro Babo;
411	that, beside the negroes killed in the action,
411	which one of the shackled negroes had on,
411	was aiming it at the negro's throat;
411	with which he was in the act of stabbing a shackled negro,
411	who, the same day, with another negro, had thrown him down
411	the ship was in the hands of the negro Babo,
427	"The negro."

New World
    402   Christopher Colon, the discoverer of the New World;

Newfoundland
    204   had familiarly lain there, as a Newfoundland dog;
    253   just as other men to Newfoundland dogs.

Nile
    216   as if a child should lead a bull of the Nile by the ring in his nose.

noble
    123   ennobled about the chin by the beard.
    123   He was a true off-shoot of a true hidalgo [noble] Cereno.
    185   a noble account
    411   the noble Captain Amasa Delano also wrenched from the hand

Nubian
    273   a Nubian sculptor finishing off a white statue-head.

owner
    44   less of restlessness than even their owner could have thought
          possible
    46   "Yes, their owner was quite right in assuring me
    75   You are part owner of ship and cargo, I presume;
    76   I am owner of all you see," impatiently returned Don Benito,
    300   —since he was strictly accountable to his owners—
    380   and a duty owing to the owners,
    400   his owner set great store by him.
    402   because the owner, his friend Aranda, told him they were all
    405   acting then the part of principal owner, and a free captain

Pacific
    43   When at last they had worked round into the Pacific,

padlock
    113   The slave there carries the padlock,
    114   padlock and key—significant symbols, truly."

pale
    53   Still, relatively to the pale history of the voyage,
    53   and his own pale face,
    63   To which the pale Don Benito dully muttered,

188

121   But the Spaniard was a pale invalid.
125   Presently, his pale face twitching and overcast,
273   indeed, he sat so pale and rigid now,
311   fluttered against his pale cheek,
388   But the pale sailors' teeth were set;

panic
61   he could not but smile at his late fidgety panic.
173   in the absence of Don Benito, with less of panic than before.
222   he could not but marvel at the panic by which himself had been

Paraguay
36   Paraguay tea and the like—

pardon
83   "Pardon me," said Captain Delano, lowly,
93   "Atufal, will you ask my pardon now?"
96   "say but the one word, *pardon*, and your chains shall be off."
103   But I told him he must ask my pardon.
113   "proud Atufal must first ask master's pardon.
301   "Don Benito, pardon me, but there is an interference
334   "Ah now, pardon me, but that is treating the poor fellow

passion
279   this slavery breeds ugly passions in man.—Poor fellow!

pelican
193   His skin was shrunk up with wrinkles like a pelican's empty
       pouch;

Peru
390   for Conception, in Chili, and thence for Lima, in Peru;
402   and lately appointed to a civil office in Peru,
411   when he should have landed in Peru, his last destination,

phantom
187   and a chance phantom cats-paw
355   Once again he smiled at the phantoms which had mocked him,

physical
171   Soon his physical distress became so great,
315   But this time the start was, perhaps, purely physical.

189

physiognomy
285   his physiognomy was European—classically so.

piety
411   as well as owing to the generosity and piety of Amasa Delano

pilot
29   like pages or pilot-fish within easy call continually hovering
226   would remain on board ready to play the pilot, come the wind
317   Turning, he saw Babo, now for the time acting, under the pilot,
324   the pilot went forward to the forecastle, to see how matters

Pisco
402   that the deponent did not go to Pisco, which was near,

pity/pitiable
25   but surprise was lost in pity, both for the Spaniards and blacks,
370   With infinite pity he withdrew his hold from Don Benito.
421   not only an innocent man, but the most pitiable of all men.

Plaza
5   one sinister eye peering across the Plaza from the Indian loop-hole
433   the head, that hive of subtlety, fixed on a pole in the Plaza,

plebeian
53   not so generally adopted the plain coat and once plebeian
      pantaloons;

Ponce
402   with his Spanish servant Ponce,
402   with Ponce the servant, beside the boatswain,

Portuguese
368   while a Portuguese oarsman shouted to him to give heed
369   with husky words, incoherent to all but the Portuguese.

pray
100   "but this scene surprises me; what means it, pray?"
112   "What, pray, was Atufal's offense, Don Benito?"
346   since, whose fault was it, pray?
402   prayed and conjured, but all was useless; for the negro Babo

preservation/preserved/preserve
48   I owe not only my own preservation, but likewise to him,

religion/religious
    391   many religious institutions
    419   rejoined the Spaniard, courteous even to the point of religion,

republican
    223   He complied, with a republican impartiality
    223   as to this republican element, which always seeks one level,

revelation
    370   a flash of revelation swept, illuminating,
    394   bearing out the revelations of their captain

Rimac
    432   and across the Rimac bridge looked towards the monastery,

Robles, Juan
    402   who were the boatswain, Juan Robles, and the carpenter,
    402   beside the boatswain, Juan Robles, the boatswain's mates,
    402   that the boatswain, Juan Robles, who knew how to swim,

Rover
    204   that boat, Rover by name, which, though now in strange seas,
    207   there's Rover; good dog; a white bone in her mouth.
    210   Meantime, one moment turning to mark "Rover" fighting the tide-rip,
    217   At last "Rover" has come.

Rozas, Juan Martinez de
    389   His Honor Doctor Juan Martinez de Rozas, Councilor

rude
    21   in whose rude face, as occasionally, like a shepherd's dog,
    245   furnished with a rude barber's crotch at the back,

San Dominick
    13   in stately capitals, once gilt, the ship's name, "SAN DOMINICK,"
    31   in a well-appointed vessel, such as the San Dominick might have been
    32   the San Dominick's suffering host repeatedly challenged his eye.
    32   The San Dominick was in the condition of a transatlantic emigrant ship,
    32   What the San Dominick wanted was, what the emigrant ship has,
    43   the San Dominick had been battle-dored about by contrary winds,

402   Babo afterwards told him to carry them to Senegal,
402   if they were not, at all events, carried to Senegal,
402   what was necessary for their design of returning to Senegal,
402   "Keep faith with the blacks from here to Senegal,
402   the deponent obliged himself to carry them to Senegal,

Senor

41   "But be patient, Senor," again turning to Captain Delano,
65   "Doubtless, doubtless, Senor."
126   "Senor, may I ask how long you have lain at this isle?"
130   "And there, Senor, you exchanged your sealskins for teas
135   May I ask how many men have you, Senor?"
138   "And at present, Senor, all on board, I suppose?"
140   "And will be to-night, Senor?"
143   "And—and will be to-night, Senor?"
145   go more or less armed, I believe, Senor?"
150   "Yes, Senor, I have trust in Babo."
229   "They were stove in the gales, Senor."
241   "Be it so, Senor."
248   "Yes, Senor, since we got into mild weather."
250   "Yes, Senor; events have not been favorable to much order
287   "He has, Senor."
291   "Doubtless, doubtless, Senor, but"—glancing at Babo—
298   "You say true, Senor."
379   "What! have you saved my life, Senor, and are you now
425   they but waft me to my tomb, Senor,"

servant

25   his private servant apprehensively followed him.
25   the repute of making the most pleasing body-servant in the world;
25   less a servant than a devoted companion.
29   their delivery was delegated to his body-servant,
35   no one being near but the servant.
37   His servant sustained him, and drawing a cordial from his pocket
41   plaintively sighed the servant;
44   painfully turning in the half embrace of his servant,
52   The servant wore nothing but wide trowsers, apparently,
57   whispered the servant, taking his arm, and with soothing words
77   his servant supported him.
87   "How like a mute Atufal moves," murmured the servant.
91   "See, he waits your question, master," said the servant.
95   "Again, master," murmured the servant,
102   but meeting his servant's kindly glance seemed reassured,

110	"Yes," said the servant, entering a word,
113	here murmured the servant to himself,
114	At once, from the servant's muttered syllables,
117	assisted by his servant[,] somewhat discourteously crossed over
117	while the menial familiarity of the servant lost its original charm
141	presenting an unworthy contrast to his servant,
150	Upon this, the servant looked up with a good-natured grin,
162	under the good nursing of his servant,
167	but the servant was more alert, who, with one hand
167	that if the servant were to blame, it might be more the master's fault
168	congratulating his host upon possessing such a servant,
171	the servant gently conducted his master below.
206	and there was met by Don Benito's servant,
219	Don Benito, with his servant, now appeared;
222	recovering itself from reclining in the servant's arms,
227	the servant, as it happened, having just spied a spot
237	"Master," said the servant, discontinuing his work on the coat
239	said the servant, "why not let Don Amasa sit by master
242	that the servant's anxious fidelity had something to do
251	Here the servant, napkin on arm, made a motion as if waiting
251	the servant commenced operations by throwing back
254	and seeing the colored servant, napkin on arm,
266	or a momentary unsteadiness of the servant's hand,
269	the servant had taken the napkin from his arm,
270	the servant, at convenient times, using his razor,
271	some reciprocal hollowiness in the servant's dusky comment of silence,
272	The shaving over, the servant bestirred himself
274	the servant for a moment surveyed his master,
281	Don Benito leaning on his servant as if nothing had happened.
299	For nothing was to be seen but the hand of his servant
300	was desirous that the servant should withdraw;
302	as in some way a reflection upon his servant.
305	the hand of his servant, mute as that on the wall,
306	the servant placing a pillow behind his master.
308	Meantime his servant knelt before him,
326	while the servant was engaged upon deck.
327	Marking the servant still above, Captain Delano,
327	The servant was likewise advancing.
333	the servant moved before his master, adjusting a cushion;
341	while with mute concern his servant gazed into his face.
351	now supported by his servant, rose to his feet,
357	the servant, placing his master's hand on his naked shoulder,

195

360 the servant seemed anxious to terminate it.
364 the servant, a dagger in his hand, was seen on the rail overhead,
366 so promptly grappled the servant in his descent,
369 the freed hand of the servant aiming with a second dagger—
402 with his Spanish servant Ponce, and the three young clerks
402 with Ponce the servant, beside the boatswain, Juan Robles,
407 performing the office of an officious servant

shadow/foreshadowing/shadowy
3 Shadows present,
3 foreshadowing
3 deeper shadows to come.
17 but a shadowy tableau just emerged from the deep,
89 a resentful shadow swept over his face;
153 The same instant there was a sparkle in the shadowy hatchway,
353 Atufal, the pretended rebel, but punctual shadow,
386 and casting a gigantic ribbed shadow upon the water.
426 what has cast such a shadow upon you?"

shame/ashamed
176 a dark eye, averted as in trouble and shame,
213 Though ashamed of the relapse, he could not altogether subdue it;
321 He proved the same man who had behaved with so shame-faced
an air

sheep/sheepish
71 have you appointed them shepherds to your flock of black sheep?"
179 should simper and cast sheep's eyes.
179 this ursine air was somehow mixed with his sheepish one.
322 "well, no more sheep's-eyes now;—

shepherd
21 like a shepherd's dog, he mutely turned it up into the Spaniard's,
71 appointed them shepherds to your flock of black sheep?"

shrine
411 meant for the shrine of our Lady of Mercy in Lima;

Sidonia, Alonzo
402 that Don Alonzo Sidonia, an old man, long resident

silver
51 with silver buckles at the knee and instep;

196

51   a slender sword, silver mounted, hung from a knot in his sash—
134   "Yes; some silver; not a very great deal, though."
380   including some gold and silver, were worth more
430   And that silver-mounted sword, apparent symbol of despotic

sign
148   as if silent signs, of some Freemason sort,
154   a secret sign I saw passing between this suspicious fellow
221   Thinking that at the signal of the Spaniard he was about
398   and a sign of the Cross;
407   by a secret sign the negro Babo drew him (the deponent) aside,

skeleton
25   and now with nervous suffering was almost worn to a skeleton.
227   warped as a camel's skeleton in the desert,
372   death for the figure-head, in a human skeleton;
386   its skeleton gleaming in the horizontal moonlight,
402

substituted
402   that the negro Babo asked him whose skeleton that was,
402   and asked him whose skeleton that was, and whether,
409   willingly prepared the skeleton of Don Alexandro,
409   riveted the skeleton to the bow;

slave/slavery
9   carrying negro slaves, amongst other valuable freight,
29   alert Spanish boys or slave boys, like pages or pilot-fish
50   slave I cannot call him."
75   but none of the slaves, perhaps?"
110   but poor Babo here, in his own land, was only a poor slave;
110   a black man's slave was Babo, who now is the white's."
116   the entrenched will of the slave.
170   with the strange vanity of a faithful [slave appreciated] by
216   Spanish lad assailed with a knife by the slave boy;
279   Ah[,] this slavery breeds ugly passions in man.—Poor fellow!
302   (whose original office, it now appeared, had been captain of
      the slaves)
317   his original part of captain of the slaves.
333   The slave appears where you saw him,
407   with all the appearance of submission of the humble slave,
411   which being overheard and understood by a slave-boy

somnambulist
12   a strange fowl, so called from its lethargic, somnambulistic

197

character,
34   Don Benito faltered; then, like some somnambulist suddenly

sophisticated
19   had the raw aspect of unsophisticated Africans.
185   Unsophisticated as leopardesses; loving as doves.

soul
36   but then numbering over three hundred souls.
141   for the soul of him Captain Delano could not but look
159   then every soul on board, down to the youngest negress,
209   its course finished, soul gone, defunct.
369   expressing the centred purpose of his soul;
402   charged this deponent to cause mass to be said for his soul
402   soul and body, go the way of Don Alexandro

South America
43   the southernmost civilized port of Chili and South America;
51   South American gentleman's dress to this hour.
53   among South Americans of his class.
121   in every great trading town of South America.

spectre
84   Then, with horrified gestures, as directed against some spectre,

spirit/spiritless/inspirited
21   at one moment casting a dreary, spiritless look upon his excited people,
25   This distempered spirit was lodged, as before hinted,
83   Assured of the welfare of his spirit, its departure
108   he has a royal spirit in him, this fellow."
112   as well as in some natural respect for his spirit, remit him his penalty."
121   what more likely scheme for a young knave of talent and spirit?
308   a little to refresh his spirit by the silent sight of fidelity.
317   the blithe songs of the inspirited negroes.
377   as coming from one whose spirit had been crushed by misery,
402   or you shall in spirit, as now in body, follow your leader,"'

St. Francis
52   made him look something like a begging frair of St. Francis.

St. Maria
1   in the harbor of St. Maria—a small, desert, uninhabited island

198

265   two months and more getting from Cape Horn to St. Maria,

270   it came to pass that the passage from Cape Horn to St. Maria

392   down to the time of her touching at the island of St. Maria.

402   the best way would be to go to the island of Santa Maria,

402   that having determined to go to the island of Santa Maria,

405   they at last arrived at the island of Santa Maria,

St. Nicholas

402   or to the neighboring islands of St. Nicholas;

steward

223   handed a number of jars and cups by one of the steward's aids,

283   when the steward—a tall, rajah-looking mulatto,

284   as if not unconscious of inferiority, eyed askance the graceful steward.

286   But see, your steward here has features more regular

288   while with a final genuflexion the steward disappeared into the cabin;

340   My old steward will give you as fine a cup as ever any sultan

strange/strangely/strangest

2   informing him that a strange sail was coming into the bay.

5   in company with the strange ship entering the harbor—

12   a white noddy, a strange fowl, so called from its lethargic,

17   from that produced by first entering a strange house

17   with strange inmates

17   in a strange land.

17   these strange costumes, gestures and faces, but a shadowy tableau

53   and however strangely surviving in the midst of all his afflictions,

83   not thus strangely would the mention of his name affect you."

121   That strange ceremoniousness, too, at other times evinced,

125   and a strange sort of intriguing intonation in his husky whisper,

155   his mind revolved the strange questions put to him concerning his ship.

161   and laugh at the strange ship for, in its aspect,

170   with the strange vanity of a faithful [slave appreciated] by his master,

179   which sat strangely enough on his weather-beaten visage,

180   feeling a little strange at first, he could hardly tell why,

204   that boat, Rover by name, which, though now in strange seas,

211   upon the strange crowd before and below him,

214   Yes, this is a strange craft;

214   a strange history, too,

214   and strange folks on board. But—nothing more.

242   the American could not but think it another strange instance

272   causing the muscles of his face to twitch rather strangely.

290   For it were strange, indeed, and not very creditable

394   the revelations of their captain in several of the strangest particulars,

stranger

4   the stranger, viewed through the glass, showed no colors;

5   whatever misgivings might have obtruded on first seeing the stranger,

5   This seemed to prove her a stranger, indeed,

6   the longer the stranger was watched the more singular

7   Presuming that the stranger might have been long off soundings,

10   the peculiar pipe-clayed aspect of the stranger was seen

15   negro transportation-ship as the stranger in port was.

21   and rather young man to a stranger's eye,

24   Captain Delano sought, with good hopes, to cheer up the strangers,

121   had not hitherto been wholly a stranger to Captain Delano's mind,

121   he began to regard the stranger's conduct

156   as in ominous comment on the white stranger's thoughts.

170   scorning to hear so paltry a valuation put upon him by a stranger.

173   followed the white stranger up.

193   had a mind to warn the stranger against;

202   for of course the stranger would not care to be troubled with it.

346   as if impatient that a stranger's presence should interfere

356   at thinking of the kindly offices he had that day discharged for a stranger.

stupid/stupidity/stupidly

61   still stupidly intent on their work, unmindful of everything beside,

193   speak well of that stupidity which was blind to his depravity,

193   But they were too stupid.

subordinate/subordination

32   to the absence of those subordinate deck-officers to whom,

62   one of those instances of insubordination previously alluded to.

201   followed by his subordinate negroes, removed to the forward part

320   At each pulley-end stood a subordinate black,

Succor, Lady of

402   to cause mass to be said for his soul to our Lady of Succor:

tongue

   16   was thus made the mark of all eager tongues,

   24   converse with some freedom in their native tongue.

  388   Their red tongues lolled, wolf-like, from their black mouths.

trades

  424   "But these mild trades that now fan your cheek,

  424   Warm friends, steadfast friends are the trades."

tranced/trance

   85   terrifies the Spaniard into this trance

  209   sweeping her further and further towards the tranced waters
       beyond.

trust/trustful (see also: undistrustful, distrust, mistrust)

  149   "Ha, Don Benito, your black here seems high in your trust;

  150   "Yes, Senor, I have trust in Babo."

  204   the sight of that household boat evoked a thousand trustful
       associations,

  322   Good hand, I trust?

true/truth/truly

    9   and the true character of the vessel was plain—

   60   it was, therefore, to tell the truth, not without some lurking
       reluctance,

   64   "Pretty serious sport, truly," rejoined Captain Delano.

  114   "So, Don Benito—padlock and key—significant symbols, truly."

  123   He was a true off-shoot

  123   of a true hidalgo Cereno.

  144   rallying himself into fearless truth,

  159   But, if that story was not true,

  159   what was the truth?

  217   though it's true he rather exceeds any other.

  219   Don Benito, with the true jealousy of weakness,

  264   though it's true, if master will shake so, I may

  265   True, you had calms, and long ones,

  296   the black was still true to his master;

  298   "You say true, Senor."

  392   reveal the true port of departure

  392   and true history of the San Dominick's voyage,

  398   under which he promised to tell the truth of whatever he

  405   that he then, the better to disguise the truth, devised many

white/whites

8	appeared like a white-washed monastery after a thunder-storm,
12	a white noddy, a strange fowl, so called from its lethargic,
15	the visitor was at once surrounded by a clamorous throng of whites and blacks,
26	as well as what seemed the sullen inefficiency of the whites,
28	either a white, mulatto or black,
43	carrying off numbers of the whites and blacks.
51	the black upholding the white,
51	white small-clothes and stockings, with silver buckles
62	enraged at a word dropped by one of his white companions,
89	as with the sudden memory of bootless rage, his white lips glued together.
110	a black man's slave was Babo, who now is the white's."
156	as in ominous comment on the white stranger's thoughts.
159	wailing ejaculations of the indiscriminate multitude, white and black,
173	followed the white stranger up.
173	and his eye curiously surveying the white faces,
173	like stray white pawns venturously involved in the ranks
193	The whites, too, by nature, were the shrewder race.
193	But if the whites had dark secrets concerning Don Benito,
193	Besides, who ever heard of a white so far a renegade
207	there's Rover; good dog, a white bone in her mouth.
221	forced every white and every negro back, at the same moment,
221	whites and blacks singing at the tackle.
223	serving the oldest white no better than the youngest black;
224	Captain Delano would have given the whites alone,
224	mouthfuls all around were given alike to whites and blacks;
236	a messenger-boy, a white, hurried by,
253	almost to the exclusion of the entire white race,
259	and in the white a man at the block.
260	a blood red field diagonal with a lion rampant in a white.
273	seemed a Nubian sculptor finishing off a white statue-head.
290	and not very creditable to us white-skins, if a little of our blood
299	should have committed such wholesale havoc upon the whites,
364	the three white sailors were trying to clamber into the hampered bow.
375	one moment with taunting cries towards the whites,
377	nothing but a total massacre of the whites could be looked for.
382	the whites kept a more respectful distance.
386	One extended arm of the ghost seemed beckoning the whites

to avenge it

388 the whites came to the surface, irresistibly driving the negroes

402 for they threatened to kill all the whites if they were not,

402 that he would kill all the whites the very moment

402 and whether, from its whiteness, he should

402 not think it a white's;

402 and whether, from its whiteness,

402 he should not think it a white's;

402 not to omit any means to preserve the lives of the remaining whites,

411 a dagger, secreted at the time of the massacre of the whites,

432 met, unabashed, the gaze of the whites;

wickedness/wicked

120 two suppositions—innocent lunacy, or wicked imposture.

177 If, indeed, there be any wickedness on board this ship,

411 piety of Amasa Delano incapable of sounding such wickedness;

wolf

288 Their red tongues lolled, wolf-like, from their black mouths.

Yambaio

400 Ashantees—Matiluqui, Yan, Lecbe, Mapenda, Yambaio, Akim;

Yan

400 Ashantees—Matiluqui, Yan, Lecbe, Mapenda, Yambaio, Akim;

409 but this Lecbe and Yan survived;

409 that Yan was bad as Lecbe;

409

prepared

409 that Yan and Lecbe were the two who, in a calm by night,

Yola

400 the third, Yola, likewise killed;

Endnotes

Preface

1. For a thoughtful discussion of Melville's view as to whether the poet or the philosopher was the better teacher, see Thomas J. Scorza, *In the Time Before Steamships: Billy Budd, the Limits of Politics, and Modernity* (DeKalb, Illinois: Northern Illinois University Press, 1978), pp. xxxii–xxxvi.

2. The relationship between "delighting" and "teaching" is treated at some length in Sir Philip Sidney, *An Apology for Poetry*, ed. Forrest G. Robinson (New York: Bobbs-Merrill, 1970), pp. 18–38.

3. Melville expresses his concern about the punctuation in a letter to Dix & Edwards of 24 March 1856. *The Letters of Herman Melville*, ed. Merrell R. Davis and W. Gilman (New Haven: Yale University Press, 1960), p. 180.

Annotated Text of "Benito Cereno"

1. What lies within this "mantled . . . hull" is never fully revealed, for neither Captain Delano nor the reader go below the decks of the San Dominick. Some of the unsettling secrets of that place—especially the cannibalism which implicitly occurred there—are described only haltingly and partially in Benito Cereno's deposition (pars. 395–412). The narrator pointedly stresses the importance of this deposition in paragraph 413, where he remarks that it may serve as "the key" which causes "the San Dominick's hull (to lie) open today."

2. In the tale's concluding paragraph, the head of Babo, the slave-leader, is impaled on a pole and his eyes peer across the Plaza of Lima.

3. The "saya-y-manta" was a robe which concealed a woman so fully that only one eye and a very small portion of the face were revealed to observers.

4. In treating some aspects of the relationships among Catholicism, Spain, Charles V, and Benito Cereno, Melville may have drawn upon portions of William Stirling's "The Cloister-Life of Emperor Charles V," *Fraser's Magazine* XLIII (April and May 1851):367–80, 528–45. (The immediate significance of the reference to the Pyrenees is that Charles V retired to a Benedictine monastery in those mountains.) For a discussion of this relationship, see p. 82 of the interpretive essay and H. Bruce Franklin's *The Wake of the Gods: Melville's Mythology* (Stanford, California: Stanford University Press, 1963), pp. 136–52. For a contention that Stirling's article may not have been drawn upon by Melville, see Hershel Parker's "'Benito Cereno' and *Cloister-Life*: A Re-Scrutiny of a 'Source'," *Studies in Short Fiction* 9 (Summer 1972):221–32.

5. The Dominicans, members of a Roman Catholic religious order founded by St. Dominic in 1216, were originally called "Black Friars" because of their white tunics with black cowls. There are numerous allusions to both this order (e.g., the Spanish ship is named the San Dominick) and its activities (one of the most notable of which was its involvement in the Inquisitions) throughout "Benito Cereno." For the history of this order, see Henry C. Lea, *A History of the Inquisition of the Middle Ages* (New York: Harbor Press, 1955) and William A. Hinnebusch, *The History of the Dominican Order*, 2 vols. (New York: Alba House, 1966).

6. Cf. Ezekiel 37:1–28, where Ezekiel comes upon a valley of dry bones, some of which the Lord later causes to be joined together and, with the addition of sinews, flesh, and breath, formed into a mighty army of men. It is interesting that while the Bible depicts the Lord as being responsible for the restoration of Israel, Melville implicitly depicts His latter day representative, the Church, as being responsible for the destruction of Spain's greatness: the supposedly cannibalized Aranda, his flesh and sinews removed so as to leave nothing but dry bones, is riveted to the prow of St. Dominic's namesake, the San Dominick. (See paragraphs 13, 372, and 402 of the text as well as p. 82 of the interpretive essay.)

7. Jean Froissart (c. 1337–c. 1405) was a 14th-century chronicler and priest who is best known for *Chronicles of England, France, Spain, and the Adjoining Countries*, trans. Thomas Johnes, 2 vols. (New York: P. F. Collier & Son, 1901). Froissart concentrated on wars in general and the activities of warring nobles in particular. G. G. Coulton provides a brief but useful history of Froissart, his works, and his times in *The Chronicler of European Chivalry* (London: Folcroft Library Editions, 1976). For an indication of Melville's familiarity with some of Froissart's work, see Merton M. Sealts, Jr., *Melville's Reading: A Check-List of Books Owned and Borrowed* (Madison: The University of Wisconsin Press, 1966), p. 53, n. 158.

8. Melville's use of Venice and Lima to represent the corruption and enervation attending Church-state alliances is not confined to "Benito Cereno." For instance, in Chapter 54 of *Moby Dick* one character remarks, "'Corrupt as

Lima? So, too, Venice; I have been there; the holy city of the blessed evangelist, St. Mark!—St. Dominic, purge it!" *Moby Dick: An Authoritative Text; Reviews and Letters by Melville; Analogues and Sources; Criticism*, ed. Harrison Hanford and Hershel Parker (New York: W. W. Norton & Co., 1967), p. 215.

9. This passage contains numerous references—"ancient turret," "high-raised quarter-galleries," "unoccupied state-cabin," "arms of Castile and Leon"—that appear to refer to the reign of Charles V that united the kingdoms of Castile and Leon with that of Aragon. See William Stirling, "The Cloister-Life of Emperor Charles V" (n. 4).

10. In Matthew 16:24, Jesus signifies the costs of discipleship by stating, "If any man will come after me, let him deny himself, and take up his cross, and follow me."

11. The significance of the name "San Dominick" is discussed in p. 72 and n. 42 of the interpretive essay.

12. Cf. Genesis 11:1–9 and Acts 2.

13. Oakum was ". . . loose fibre . . . obtained by untwisting and picking old rope . . . ." It was "used in caulking ships' seams, in stopping up leaks, and sometimes in dressing wounds" (*Oxford English Dictionary*).

14. This figure of 190 days should be compared with both the 89-day period specified in the deposition (pars. 398 and 405)and the 62-day period recounted by the actual Amasa Delano. See pp. 72–73 of the interpretive essay for a discussion of the significance of Melville's alteration of this time period.

15. In paragraph 398, it is revealed that the ship had a crew of 36 men "beside(s) the . . . passengers;" that it sailed from Valparaiso bound to Callao; and that it had 160 blacks.

16. As in the case with portions of the deposition, the narrator is selective in what he presents to the reader. Some of the implications of this selectivity are addressed in the interpretive essay, pp. 84–85 and n. 23.

17. This sword, "apparent symbol of despotic command," is later revealed to have an "artificially stiffened" scabbard (par. 430).

18. There are a number of interesting similarities between "Benito Cereno" and the history of St. Francis (1182–1226) and his Franciscans. For instance, it was in the restored chapel of Santa Maria that Francis heard the call to go forth and, in accordance with Matthew 10:7–10, to possess nothing while ministering to the "lost sheep of . . . Israel." Also, on his initial voyage to America, Christopher Columbus was accompanied by Franciscans who established the first New World missions in Santo Domingo. The principal setting of "Benito Cereno" is in the harbor of St. Maria, where it is eventually discovered that Christopher Columbus, the figurehead of the decrepit San Dominick, has been replaced by a skeleton. For an interesting account of the Franciscans, see Omer Englebert, *St. Francis of Assisi*, trans. and ed. Edward Hutton (New York: Longmans, Green & Co., 1950).

19. The reference is to the prominent international family of bankers estab-

lished by Mayer Amschel Rothschild in 18th-century Germany.

20. "Hidalgo" means "noble."

21. In Numbers 15:37–39, the Lord instructs Moses to bid the children of Israel to ". . . make them fringes in the borders of their garments throughout their generations, and that they put upon the fringe of the borders a [ribbon] of blue:

And it shall be unto you for a fringe, that ye may look upon it, and remember all the commandments of the Lord, and do them . . . ."

22. The secretive Order of Freemasons accepted as its most basic tenets the principles of religious toleration and the general equality of all men. The former principle led the Roman Catholic Church vigorously to oppose the Order. Melville frequently refers to "Masonic Signs." See, for example, *Moby Dick*, p. 317, and his letter to Hawthorne of 16 April 1851, *The Letters of Herman Melville*, ed. Merrell R. Davis and William H. Gilman (New Haven: Yale Univ. Press, 1960), p. 125.

23. The doubloon, a Spanish gold coin, was originally worth approximately 33 to 36 English shillings. With the shilling equivalent to approximately 1/26th of a pound sterling, Delano was offering roughly 70 pounds sterling for Babo.

24. "Caffre" means "infidel" and was applied by the Arabs to all non-Mohammedans. It was also used in reference to a race of blacks residing near Cape Colony in South Africa (*Oxford English Dictionary*).

25. Compare these statements with those made in paragraphs 25, 27, 30, 31, 53, 54, 85, 121, and 159. Delano is struggling to discern which character traits are attributable to convention and which to nature.

26. "Old Jack" is a familiar appellation for a sailor (*Oxford English Dictionary*).

27. Barcelona was a powerful trade and banking center located in Northeast Spain on the Mediterranean.

28. "Whiskerando," used here to describe a heavily whiskered man, was also the name of a character in Richard Sheridan's play, *The Critic*. That Melville was familiar with Sheridan's works is suggested by Sealts in *Melville's Reading*, p. 94, n. 471.

29. These passages are replete with suggestions of a duality in nature to which Delano is all but oblivious. For a discussion of the significance of this duality, see pp. 79–81 of the interpretive essay.

30. John Ledyard (1750–1788) was an American adventurer who, among other things, explored the Pacific with Captain Cook. Ledyard died shortly after the commencement of an effort to explore the Niger River. Some of his comments on African women are found in *Proceedings of the Association for Promoting the Discovery of the Interior Parts of Africa* (London: W. Bulmer & Co., 1810), Vol. I, pp. 44–45. A biographical account of his exploits is presented in Jared Sparks, *The Life of John Ledyard, the American Traveller* (Boston: Little, Brown & Co., 1864). In the 1855 *Putnam's Monthly Magazine* version of "Benito

Cereno," Melville attributes the views to Mungo Park (1771–1806), a Scottish physician-explorer who drowned during an 1806 expedition down the Niger River. Park's observations on African women are found in his *Travels In the Interior Districts of Africa; With an Account of a Subsequent Mission to that Country in 1805* (Bristol: P. Rose, 1824), pp. 263–64.

31. The previous references to the "pale," "cadaverous" appearing Don Benito (pars. 53 and 60), coupled with the present description of the San Dominick's quarter-galleries, should be contrasted with the scenes forward of the main-mast. The quarters of the whites are resplendent with the imagery of death while those of the blacks convey a picture of vibrant health (pars. 182–86). This point also seems to have significance for the duality of nature discussed in pp. 79–81 of the interpretive essay.

32. "Parterres" literally means "on or over [the surface of] the ground" (*Oxford English Dictionary*).

33. The Gordian knot has long been used to represent matters of extreme difficulty. An interesting discussion of it in relation to "Benito Cereno" is found in M. L. D'Avanzo, "'Undo it, cut it, quick': The Gordian Knot in 'Benito Cereno,'" *Studies in Short Fiction* 15 (Spring 1979): 192–94. Ammon was an ancient Egyptian deity who was often represented as a ram or as a man with a ram's head.

34. The significance of *Rover* for Delano is discussed in pp. 75–77 of the interpretive essay.

35. The infamous "Gunpowder Plot," which entailed the attempted blowing up of Parliament and King James I on November 5, 1605 in order to further an uprising of English Catholics, was foiled, and Guy Fawks, a conspirator, was arrested as he entered the basement of the House of Lords and later executed. See Cyril Northcote Parkinson, *Gunpowder, Treason, and Plot* (New York: St. Martin's Press, 1977).

36. For a discussion of the partiality of republican Delano in distributing the supplies, see pp. 77 and 79 of the interpretive essay.

37. This scene is resplendent with reminders of the Inquisitions' horrors. See p. 91 and n. 42 of the interpretive essay for a brief treatment of this paragraph's significance.

38. Of the six places mentioned, at least two might be called private, three are associated with warfare — particularly naval warfare — and one clearly concerns religion.

39. The references are to the English author Samuel Johnson (1709–1784) and poet George Byron (1788–1824). It is known that Melville had access to Johnson's *The History of Rasselas, Prince of Abyssinia* and to the complete works of Byron. (See Merton M. Sealts, Jr., *Melville's Reading*, pp. 45–46 and 71–72.) Whether or not they were hypochondriacs, both Byron and Johnson were uncommonly sickly. Byron had a club foot, suffered from a bad leg, and had frequent bouts of disillusionment and depression. (See Leslie A. Marchand,

Byron: A Portrait [New York: Knopf, 1970], pp. 462, 106, and 98.) Johnson suffered from a disease that "disfigured his countenance," impaired his hearing, and blinded him in one eye. While in college, he supposedly was overwhelmed by hypochondria and believed himself insane. (See Robert Anderson, *The Life of Samuel Johnson, LL.D. 1815* [New York: Garland, 1974], pp. 14–15, 26.) Both men did have exceedingly loyal slaves. Byron's Fletcher, while an inveterate complainer when enduring hardships, was the one in whom Byron entrusted his last wishes. (See Marchand, p. 459.) Johnson's Barber was given five years of schooling and the task of carrying out Johnson's desire to have his manuscripts burned. (See Anderson, pp. 179 and 464.)

40. James I (1566–1625) reigned as king of England from 1603 until 1625, during which period his policies towards English Catholics led to considerable discontent among Catholics and Protestants alike. Though Guy Fawks attempted to assassinate him in the previously mentioned Gunpowder Plot, James, son of Catholic Mary Queen of Scots, was suspected of favoring the Catholics.

41. A "harlequin" was a mute character in English pantomime who wore multicolored costumes. Its usage here refers to the multicolored Spanish flag.

42. Nubia was an ancient and once powerful kingdom in N.E. Africa which was converted to Christianity in the 6th century but succumbed to Moslem attacks in the 14th century.

43. A Madras handkerchief, commonly worn as a head-dress by blacks of the West Indies, was made of brightly colored silk and cotton (*Oxford English Dictionary*).

44. Philip D. Chesterfield (1694–1773), an English statesman, is perhaps best remembered as the author of the *Letters to His Son*, a compilation of practical words of advice to his natural son. See *The Letters of Philip Dormer Stanhope, Earl of Chesterfield, with the Characters*, ed. John Bradshaw, 2 vols. (London: George Allen & Unwin Ltd., 1926).

45. This phrase may have reference to the golden scepter held forth by the biblical king to signify safe conduct to and acceptance of those coming into his inner court. (Cf. Esther 4:11).

46. The reference is probably to George III (1738–1820).

47. In the real Amasa Delano's *Narrative*, one of the characters was named "Francisco." Melville alters the spelling to "Francesco" in the narrative portions of both the 1855 and 1856 texts, but occasionally resorts to the original "Francisco" in the deposition sections of both versions.

48. A light, sweet wine from the Canary Isles.

49. In Daniel 5:5–31, the fingers of a man's hand are seen to write on the wall of King Belshazzar's palace. Daniel's interpretation of the writing was that the end of Belshazzar's rule was at hand as a consequence of his opposition to the Lord.

50. Contraction of "studding-sail," which is a sail "set between the leeches

of any of the principal sails during a fair wind" (*Oxford English Dictionary*).

51. See p. 84 of the interpretive essay for a brief discussion of Babo as a captain or commander.

52. The significance of the helmsman's being admonished about his "sheep's eyes" seems to bear on the previously suggested duality-of-nature issue. See pp. 79–81 of the interpretive essay.

53. "With every mast standing and fully rigged; with all sails set" (*Oxford English Dictionary*).

54. Delano's view of nature is discussed in the interpretive essay, pp. 76–81.

55. The hour the ship's bell is striking is three o'clock in the afternoon. (In paragraph 309, the bell is ringing two o'clock in the afternoon.) The scene contains several allusions to the interrelationship between Christianity and the San Dominick which can only be mentioned here. For instance, the intersection of the two passageways with the main cabin appears to form a rough cross. Thus, this cross—the symbol of Christianity—serves as the foundation of the cuddy, that room which is so richly furnished with reminders of the Inquisitions. And it is while "on" this cross that Delano believes he is about to be murdered. In essence, there appears to be a parody of Christ's death on the cross which is distinguished by the fact that Delano, the representative of modern civilization, does not die.

56. Cf. Matthew 26:14–25.

57. A tocsin is an alarm signal usually associated with the ringing of bells.

58. Compare the postures of the three main characters with those of the figures on the ship's shield-piece (par. 12). Also see p. 93 of the interpretive essay.

59. Derived from the Persian "darvish" (beggar), dervish refers to a class of Mohammedan devotees who, in the performance of their ceremonial rituals, were capable of working themselves into frenzies.

60. One thousand doubloons would have been roughly equivalent to 1385 pounds sterling.

61. The two whites who were deliberately killed by Delano's crew were Don Joaquin, Marques de Aramboalaza, and Hermenegildo Gandix (pars. 385, 411). The names of these characters are not found in Delano's *Narrative*; they are wholly the creations of Melville.

62. The recurring references to revenge in this tale (e.g., in paragraph 369 it is described as the "centred purpose" of Babo's soul) lend support to an argument that it is the ineradicable remembrance of past injustices—and the consequent desire to avenge them—that explains the relations between whites and blacks, masters and slaves in "Benito Cereno" and, implicitly, in the world. John H. McElroy makes an interesting case for this view in "Cannibalism in Melville's 'Benito Cereno'," *Essays in Literature* 1 (Fall 1974):206–18. See also pp. 92–93 of the interpretive essay.

63. The mate's cry is a parody of the crucial phrase scrawled beneath the skeleton on the prow of the San Dominick (par. 13). The irony in the words,

213

uttered just after the narrator has described the skeleton as seeming to beckon "the whites to avenge it," involves the problem of Church-state relationships. (See pp. 82–83 of the interpretive essay as well as pars. 372, 387, 402, and 432 of the text.)

64. Literally, the whips of those who drive horse-drawn carts.

65. In 1745, English forces led by Sir John Cope were routed by the Highland-supported Jacobites in the battle of Prestopans in East Lothian, Scotland.

66. The one thing that would most incline the tribunal to suspect that Benito raved would be the matter of Aranda's corpse. In paragraph 409, Benito claims that "he, so long as reason is left him, can never divulge" the way in which Aranda's skeleton was prepared. Since the implicit cannibalizing of the corpse had completely broken Benito's will to resist the blacks, why does he not give an account of it, particularly since the court commanded him to produce "the data whereon to found the criminal sentences to be pronounced" (par. 408)? It is possible that Benito did tell of it but that the narrator has omitted it along "with other things" (par. 406) that he revealed. (See McElroy, pp. 211–12.)

67. In Amasa Delano's *Narrative*, the name of the Spanish ship is the Tryal. For a discussion of the significance of Melville's change of that name to the San Dominick, see p. 72 and n. 42 of the interpretive essay.

68. No such name is mentioned in Delano's *Narrative*.

69. In Delano's *Narrative*, the Spanish captain is named "Bonito Sereno," which can be translated several ways. The most accepted one is "Blessed (or Pleasing) Serenity." There is, of course, irony in this translation, for the real-life Sereno was hardly characterized by "pleasing serenity." Another, more colloquial translation is "Handsome, Shameless Fellow." (See Thomas E. Connolly, "A Note on Name Symbolism in Melville," *American Literature* 25 [January 1954]:490.) Considering the Spaniard's occupation and his treachery towards Delano—whom he tried to cheat out of the salvage rights to the Spanish ship (see *Narrative*, pp. 103–105)—this translation seems to befit Sereno's character better. A third, more obscure meaning is "Pleasing Watchman." There is irony here too, for, according to the *Narrative*, this ineffectual watchman slept through the initial stages of the mutiny (p. 107).

It cannot be known, of course, whether Melville understood all or even any of these meanings of the Spaniard's name. What is known is that he deliberately changed the spelling of the name from "Bonito Sereno" to "Benito Cereno." By so doing, attention is directed both to the meaning of the original name and, more importantly, to that of the new one, which is generally translated as "Pallid Benedictine." However, in the province of Aragon, "cereno" means "strong," "tough," and "durable." If one accepts "Tough Benedictine" as the intended meaning, a little more irony is added to that which is already present in such things as the shaving and "communion meal" scenes aboard the San Dominick. (See J. V. Hagopian, *Insight I: Analyses of American Literature* [Frankfurt am Main: Hirschgraben-Verlag, 1964], p. 154.)

70. There is no such name as "Infelez" ("Unhappy") in Delano's *Narrative*.

71. The name "Francisco" is found in Delano's *Narrative*.

72. No such name is mentioned in Delano's *Narrative*.

73. No such name is mentioned in Delano's *Narrative*.

74. No such name is mentioned in Delano's *Narrative*.

75. No such name is mentioned in Delano's *Narrative*.

76. No such name is mentioned in Delano's *Narrative*.

77. No such name is mentioned in Delano's *Narrative*.

78. "Juan Bautista Gayete" ("John the Baptist Gayete") replaces "Juan Balltista Gayete" in Delano's *Narrative*.

79. No such place is mentioned in Delano's *Narrative*.

80. No such name is mentioned in Delano's *Narrative*.

81. No such name is mentioned in Delano's *Narrative*.

82. No such name or title is mentioned in Delano's *Narrative*.

83. No such name is mentioned in Delano's *Narrative*.

84. No such name is mentioned in Delano's *Narrative*.

85. No such name is mentioned in Delano's *Narrative*. He may be named after the sainted son of a 6th century Gothic king whose feast day is celebrated on April 13th.

86. The name "Manuel Viseaya" appears in Delano's *Narrative*.

87. No such name is mentioned in Delano's *Narrative*. Roderigo's surname is derived from the Spanish verb "hurta," which means to steal by stealth.

88.   No such name is mentioned in Delano's *Narrative*. For a discussion of the significance of "Christopher Colon," see p. 83 of the interpretive essay.

89. The name of the American ship in Delano's *Narrative* is the Perseverance. The Bachelor is one of the two ships hailed by the Pequod in Chapter 115 of *Moby Dick*. Also see p. 72 of the interpretive essay.

90. No such name is mentioned in Delano's *Narrative*.

91. No such place is mentioned in Delano's *Narrative*.

92. No such name is mentioned in Delano's *Narrative*. Martinez Gola means "Warlike Throat," a fitting name for one who was about to slit a helpless black's throat.

93. No such name is mentioned in Delano's *Narrative*. The surname "Barlo" may well be, as Charles E. Nnolm suggests, a corruption of "barlow," which means "a one-bladed jack knife" or dagger. (See *Melville's 'Benito Cereno': A Study in Meaning of Name Symbolism* [New York: New Voices Publishing Co., 1974], p. 50) This meaning would befit the vindictive character of Barlo, for he is one of two Spanish sailors Delano stops in acts of attacking the now shackled blacks.

94. No such place as "Mount Agony" is mentioned in Delano's *Narrative*.

95. No such place is mentioned in Delano's *Narrative*.

96. No such place is mentioned in Delano's *Narrative*.

215

Interpretive Essay

1. A thoughtful discussion of some related themes in *Billy Budd* may be found in Thomas J. Scorza, "Technology, Philosophy, and Political Virtue: The Case of Billy Budd, Sailor," *Interpretation: A Journal of Political Philosophy* 5, No. 1 (Summer 1975):91–107. Also see Scorza, *In the Time Before Steamships: Billy Budd, the Limits of Politics, and Modernity* (DeKalb, Ill.: Northern Illinois University Press, 1979).

2. For example, see Rosalie Feltenstein, "Melville's 'Benito Cereno'," *American Literature* 19 (1947):245 ff.; F. O. Matthiessen, *American Renaissance: Art and Expression in the Age of Emerson and Whitman* (New York: Oxford University Press, 1941), p. 508; and especially Hugh W. Hetherington, *Melville's Reviewers: British and American, 1846–1891* (Chapel Hill: University of North Carolina Press, 1961), pp. 248–55.

3. "Benito Cereno" originally appeared in the October, November, and December 1855 issues of *Putnam's Monthly Magazine*. Shortly thereafter, Melville incorporated it into a collection of his shorter stories entitled *The Piazza Tales*. A strong suggestion of Melville's estimate of the merit of "Benito Cereno" is found in the fact that he originally intended to call his collection *"Benito Cereno" and Other Sketches*. See *The Letters of Herman Melville*, ed. Merrell R. Davis and William H. Gilman (New Haven: Yale University Press, 1960), pp. 178–79; hereafter cited as *Letters*.

4. For a discussion of this controversy, see Harry V. Jaffa, *Crisis of the House Divided: An Interpretation of the Issues in the Lincoln-Douglas Debates* (Seattle: University of Washington Press, 1973), especially pp. 41–62.

5. See Chapter XVIII of Amasa Delano, *A Narrative of Voyages and Travels, in the Northern and Southern Hemispheres: Comprising Three Voyages Round the World, Together with a Voyage of Survey and Discovery in the Pacific Ocean and Oriental Islands* (Boston: E. G. House, 1817). This chapter is reproduced as the next section of this book.

6. In the "Agatha Letter" to Hawthorne, Melville discusses the advantages of having "a skeleton of actual reality to build about with fullness and veins and beauty." (Melville to Hawthorne, August 13, 1852, in *Letters*, p. 157.)

7. Constitution of the United States of America, Article I, Section 9.

8. "Bachelor's Delight" also may have reference to more erotic matters. In one of his collections, Melville groups together two of his shorter stories, "The Tartarus of Maids" and "The Paradise of Bachelors." The former is resplendent with sexual innuendoes, while the latter concerns the opposite, namely, an implied denial of certain desires in favor of attention to things of the mind. In a sense, these two stories portray the two extremes of bachelorhood: dissipation through over-indulgence in bodily pleasures and, conversely, a subjugation of the desires to the rule of reason in pursuit of some higher end.

9. Herbert Aptheker, *American Negro Slave Revolts* (New York: Interna-

tional Publishers, 1943), p. 96 ff.

10. The author of an article crudely entitled "About Niggers" blatantly parodies the uprising on Santo Domingo in order to expose the ridiculousness of the white masters' reactions to that revolt. (See *Putnam's Monthly Magazine*, December 1855, p. 609.) The fact that this author could parody the uprisings suggests that he believed his readers would readily understand that the island of Santo Domingo was the subject. That knowledge of Santo Domingo was common-place among literate Americans of the 1850s also can be inferred from the fact that in *Uncle Tom's Cabin*, the widely popular anti-slavery novel written in 1851, the island is briefly mentioned almost casually in the course of a discussion about how slaves should be treated. (See Harriet Beecher Stowe, *Uncle Tom's Cabin* [New York: Airmount Publishing Co., Inc., 1967], p. 252.)

11. Later on, in one of the few departures from the prevailing lack of color, the reader sees Babo using the predominately red and white ensign of Spain as a barber's bib for Benito. Shortly thereafter, the ensign's redness is matched by Benito's blood (pars. 260, 266).

12. Delano speaks 59 times; Benito, 54; and Babo, 16. Comparatively, the knotmaker speaks only three times and the mate once.

13. J. Hagopian, *Insight I: Analyses of American Literature* (Frankfurt am Main: Hirschgraben-Verlag, 1964), p. 152.

14. "Benito Cereno," par. 17. Similar references to the "aura" of enchantment aboard the San Dominick are found in pars. 157, 187, 189, 190, 355, and 420.

15. In essence, Delano is a man forced from the Cave. (Cf. Plato, *Republic* 514a–517c.)

16. "Benito Cereno," pars. 193, 203–4, 207, 210, and 217.

17. "Benito Cereno," par. 424. That these "friends" of Delano's may have been less than "warm" and "steadfast"—that they may even have been uncaring and unfeeling—is suggested by the previous statement that "nature cared not a jot" about men's troubles (par. 346).

18. Consider the discussion of both the piloting art and the comparison of "knowledge itself" with a "particular kind of knowledge" in *Republic* 341c and 438d, respectively.

19. The blacks' ignorance of these useful sciences is also depicted in the killing of the mate, Raneds, when he was in the act of taking a navigational fix (par. 404). That murder, inspired by superstitious ignorance, had the effect of assuring the preservation of Benito Cereno, for he was "the only remaining navigator on board . . ." (par. 404).

20. In Delano's eyes, Babo is certainly an inferior, for his conventional label of "slave" brands him as such. Benito, the ineffectual invalid, is treated with respect by Delano, but it is his office to which the respect is given; Delano's manner towards Benito himself is tinged with pity.

21. See William Braswell, *Melville's Religious Thought: An Essay in Interpre-*

tation (Durham, North Carolina: Duke University Press, 1943).

22. 2 Samuel 20:9–12.

23. "Benito Cereno," par. 193. The narrator's deft mingling of what may be his own views with those of Delano presents the reader with some difficult problems. First, who is the narrator? He is never identified. Is he Melville speaking his own mind? Among other reasons, the contradictions between some of the narrator's views and the teaching of the tale strongly argue against such a simplistic identification. The narrator's views about blacks (e.g., pars. 193, 252–53) are not that unusual; one might reasonably expect them to be uttered by a typical American of the 1850s. From this perspective, it might be more plausible to see the narrator as an intelligent representative type of that era. Secondly, both the narrator's deceptiveness in mingling his views with Delano's and the similarity of his views with those of the American suggest the possibility that the treatment of Delano may be open to question. If the narrator is being less than candid about Delano, if he is withholding or altering information about the American, the reader will be hampered in his quest for Delano's "true character." It may be, of course, that one of the reasons for the narrator's substitution of his own views for Delano's is to illustrate the pitfalls of tales that are retold. The reteller (in this case, the narrator) may well filter the "facts" through the medium of his own opinions before presenting them to his audience.

24. "Benito Cereno," pars. 182–85 (emphasis added). These passages are strongly reminiscent of portions of Rousseau's *Second Discourse*. Cf. Jean Jacques Rousseau, *The First and Second Discourses*, ed. Roger D. Masters, trans. Roger D. and Judith R. Masters (New York: St. Martin's Press, 1964), especially pp. 117 and 137.

25. Appropriately, the phrase "there's naked nature" contains the work's central reference to "nature."

26. The savage side of the negresses is revealed by Benito in his deposition. He claims that they "used their utmost influence to have [him] made away with; that, in the various acts of murder, they sang songs and danced—not gaily, but solemnly; and before the engagement with the boats, as well as during the action, they sang melancholy songs to the negroes, and that this melancholy tone was more inflaming than a different one would have been, and was so intended . . ." (par. 409).

27. Cf. Amasa Delano in Gross, p. 80.

28. See Hagopian, p. 151.

29. In his deposition, Benito describes how his boatswain, "who knew how to swim, kept the longest above water, making acts of contrition, and, in the last words he uttered, charged this deponent to cause mass to be said for his soul to our Lady of Succour" (par. 402). In the narrative, we read of the blacks having worshipped the beckoning, open sea (par. 375).

30. See William Stirling, "The Cloister-Life of Emperor Charles V," *Fraser's*

Magazine (April and May 1851):367–80 and 528–45. A discussion of Stirling's work as a source for "Benito Cereno" is found in H. Bruce Franklin, *The Wake of the Gods: Melville's Mythology* (Stanford, California: Stanford University Press, 1963), pp. 136–52. However, Hershel Parker, in "'Benito Cereno' and Cloister-Life: A Re-Scrutiny of a 'Source'," *Studies in Short Fiction* 9 (1972):221–32, argues that Melville may not have drawn upon Stirling's article as a source.

31. Almost from its inception, Charles' reign as the Holy Roman Emperor was beset by strife between his own Roman Catholic Church and the emerging Protestant sect led by Luther. Tormented by gout and his failures to achieve reconciliation between the Protestants and the Catholics by political or military means, Charles abdicated after renouncing his claims to the crowns of various nations during 1555–56. See *The New Encyclopaedia Britannica*, 1974 ed.

32. Stirling, p. 370.

33. Stirling, p. 543.

34. Melville's references to "New-Found-Land" dogs may be a play on an aspect of this: it is the man from the New Found Land, Delano, who saves those from the Old Land.

35. In his deposition, Benito Cereno notes that the blacks, "as is *customary in this navigation*" slept on deck (par. 402, emphasis added). He also states that because Aranda "told him that they were all tractable . . . none wore fetters." If Aranda believed this, he obviously would not bring fetters with him. However, after the uprising, the blacks were shackled (pars. 389, 411). Delano, captain of a sealer, probably would not have had such items on the Bachelor's Delight; conceivably, the chains were secured from the San Dominick, which had them on board from previous voyages.

36. "Benito Cereno," par. 66. The irony is heightened when it is later revealed that Benito does, indeed, hold his office by a paper grant—the result of a written agreement with Babo (par. 402).

37. This view is similar to that advanced by Abraham Lincoln in the Lyceum Speech of January 27, 1838. See *The Collected Works of Abraham Lincoln*, ed. Roy Basler (Rutgers, New Jersey: Rutgers University Press, 1953), I, pp. 108–15.

38. Feltenstein, p. 252.

39. Stanley T. Williams, "'Follow Your Leader': Melville's 'Benito Cereno'," *The Virginia Quarterly Review* 23 (1947):73.

40. Cf. Delano in Gross, pp. 83–89.

41. Williams, p. 75.

42. One of the most remarkable ironies in Melville's tale is the way in which the pagan Babo, on board the namesake of the Dominicans' patron saint, plays the part of Satan to its fullest, inflicting inhuman tortures on the Spanish Catholics in a manner reminiscent of the Dominicans' tortures of pagans and heretics. This irony reaches its height when Babo "tortures" Benito Cereno in the cuddy, which is furnished with reminders of the Inquisitions (par. 245). The

Inquisitions, although later expanded to include trials of political as well as religious heretics, originally were directed against followers of the various Manichaean sects. These sects were composed of believers in a fundamental duality of good and evil in the world. For them, Satan was a co-ruler of men with Christ.

43. I owe recognition of the similarities between Babo and Iago to Arthur L. Vogelbeck, "Shakespeare and Melville's 'Benito Cereno'," *Modern Language Notes* 67 (1952): 113–16.

44. Cf. "Benito Cereno," par. 431, and William Shakespeare, *Othello,* ed. Alvin Kernan (New York: New American Library, 1963), V, ii, 300.

45. Allan Bloom, "Cosmopolitan Man and the Political Community: *Othello,*" in Allan Bloom with Harry V. Jaffa, *Shakespeare's Politics* (New York: Basic Books, 1964), p. 39. Portions of the following discussion owe much to Bloom's treatment of Iago.

46. For a discussion of the connection between a recognition of likeness and the extension of rights, see Joseph Cropsey, "The Right of Foreign Aid," in his *Political Philosophy and the Issues of Politics* (Chicago: University of Chicago Press, 1977), pp. 191–94.

47. Consider the equation of Babo with a shepherd's dog and Delano's naive perception of blacks as relatively care-free (and, hence, thought-free), happy-go-lucky individuals. "Benito Cereno," pars. 21 and 252–53, respectively.

48. We are not told of any inhumane actions inflicted by the whites on the blacks prior to the revolt. However, judging by the whites' actions once they are again the masters, the reader is left with no doubts as to the whites' ability to act brutishly. "Benito Cereno," par. 411.

49. In a sense, Babo's muteness in the face of the white man's injustice is a confirmation of his unfitness for civil society. Aristotle states that "speech is designed to indicate the advantageous and the harmful, and therefore also the right and the wrong; for it is the special property of man in distinction from the other animals that he alone has perception of good and bad and right and wrong and the other moral qualities." *Politics* 1253a 12–18.

There is another possible explanation of Babo's muteness. Montaigne, an author with whom Melville was reasonably familiar, wrote an interesting essay entitled "Of Cannibals" which bears on the civilization-barbarism issue. (See Michel Eyquem de Montaigne, *Complete Works: Essays, Travel Journal, Letters,* trans. Donald M. Frame [Stanford, Calif.: Stanford University Press, 1957], pp. 150–59. For Melville's familiarity with Montaigne, see Merton M. Sealts, Jr., *Melville's Reading* [Madison, Wisconsin: The University of Wisconsin Press, 1966], p. 80.) Montaigne describes how certain South American savages, when captured, would refuse to acknowledge defeat or to give evidence of fear. Babo's muteness might be construed as such defiance. Additionally, Montaigne relates that the conquerors eventually would cannibalize their captives in order to exhibit the utmost contempt for them. The cannibalization of Aranda by the black savages certainly might be perceived as an instance of such contempt.

It is appropriate to note that Melville's first novel, *Typee*, treats the civilization-barbarism issue within the context of a white sailor living among cannibals. For a thoughtful interpretation of this work, see Thomas J. Scorza, "Tragedy in the State of Nature: Melville's *Typee*," *Interpretation: A Journal of Political Philosophy* 8, No. 1 (January 1979): 103–20.

50. Compare with Socrates' enforced detention by Polemarchus' slave (*Republic* 327b).

51. See pp. 85–86.

52. Herman Melville, *Moby Dick: An Authoritative Text; Reviews and Letters by Melville; Analogues and Sources; Criticism,* ed. Harrison Hanford and Hershel Parker (New York: W. W. Norton & Co., 1967), p. 251.

53. The narrator describes Atufal as Babo's "countryman" (par. 95). It is also carefully stated that Babo is a native of Senegal (par. 400).

54. Again, there is abundant irony in Delano's good-humored references to the sight-loving Africans; it is Delano who is easily seduced by sights (pars. 223, 261).

55. Herman Melville, *Mardi and a Voyage Thither*, ed. Harrison Hayford, Hershel Parker, and G. Thomas Tanselle (Evanston, Ill.: Northwestern University Press and The Newberry Library, 1970), p. 533.

56. "Benito Cereno," par. 360. In the context, the implication seems to be that the two captains are being "braced-up" by the black. Taken a step further, one could see the black's supporting role as symbolic of the crucial part slaves played in the development of the Spanish-American and American regimes.

57. "Benito Cereno," pars. 402, 409, and 411. The actions of the freed blacks and whites toward each other perhaps should be seen in the light of Delano's earlier reflection that there "are peculiar natures on whom prolonged physical suffering seems to cancel every social instinct of kindness" (par. 27). Two questions immediately suggest themselves: What are those peculiar natures? And, would Delano's responses to the blacks (and to the whites) have been different had he been a newly-freed slave?

58. "[U]ppermost and central of which [stern-piece] was a dark satyr in a mask, holding his foot on the prostrate neck of a writhing figure, likewise masked." "Benito Cereno," par. 12.

Bibliography

Adler, Joyce Sparer. "Melville's 'Benito Cereno': Slavery and Violence in the Americas." *Science and Society* 38 (Spring 1974): 19–48.

Altschuler, Glenn C. "Whose Foot on Whose Throat? A Re-examination of Melville's 'Benito Cereno.'" *CLA Journal* 18 (March 1975):383–92.

Avanzo, M. L. "Undo it, Cut it, Quick: The Gordian Knot in 'Benito Cereno.'" *Studies in Short Fiction* 15 (Spring 1978):192–94.

Bernstein, John. "'Benito Cereno' and the Spanish Inquisition." *Nineteenth Century Fiction* 16 (March 1962):345–50.

Bernstein, John. *Pacifism and Rebellion in the Writings of Herman Melville*. The Hague: Mouton, 1964.

Berthoff, Warner. *The Example of Melville*. Princeton: Princeton University Press, 1962.

Blackmur, Richard P. "The Craft of Herman Melville." *Virginia Quarterly Review* 14 (Spring 1938):266–72.

Bone, Robert A. *The Negro Novel in America*. New Haven: Yale University Press, 1958.

Booth, Wayne C. *The Rhetoric of Fiction*. Chicago: University of Chicago Press, 1961.

Bowen, Merlin. *The Long Encounter: Self and Experience in the Writings of Herman Melville*. Chicago: University of Chicago Press, 1960.

Braswell, William. *Melville's Religious Thought: An Essay in Interpretation*. Durham, North Carolina: Duke University Press, 1943.

Bredahl, Axel Carl, Jr. *Melville's Angles of Vision*. Gainesville: University of Florida Press, 1972.

Brophy, Robert J. "Benito Cereno, Oakum, and Hatchets." *American Transcendental Quarterly* 2 (1969):89–90.

Brown, Sterling A. *The Negro in American Fiction*. Port Washington, New York: Kennikat Press, 1968.

Browne, Ray B. *Melville's Drive to Humanism*. Lafayette, Indiana: Purdue University Studies, 1971.

Bryant, John. "The Comic Debate in 'Benito Cereno'." *Extracts, An Occasional Newsletter* 33 (Feburary 1978):2–3.

Bucho, Luella M. "Melville and Captain Delano's Narrative of Voyages: The Appeal of the Preface." *American Notes and Queries* 16 (June 1978):157–60.

Butler, John F. *Exercises in Literary Understanding*. Chicago: Scott, Fonsman, 1956.

Canaday, Nicholas, Jr. "A New Reading of Melville's 'Benito Cereno.'" Edited by Waldo McNeir and Leo B. Levy. *Studies in American Literature*. Baton Rouge: Louisiana State University Press, 1960.

Cardwell, Guy A. "Melville's Gray Story: Symbols and Meaning in 'Benito Cereno'." *Bucknell Review* 8 (May 1959):154–67.

Carlisle, E. Fred. "Captain Amasa Delano: Melville's American Fool." *Criticism* 7 (Fall 1965):349–62.

Chase, Richard V., ed. *Melville: A Collection of Critical Essays*. Englewood Cliffs, New Jersey: Prentice-Hall, Inc., 1962.

Chase, Richard V. "The Classic Literature: Art and Idea." *Paths of American Thought*. Edited by Arthur M. Schlesinger, Jr. and Morton White. Boston: Houghton, Mifflin, 1963.

Chase, Richard V. *Herman Melville: A Critical Study*. New York: Macmillan Co., 1949.

Cochran, Robert. "Babo's Name in 'Benito Cereno': An Unnecessary Controversy?" *American Literature* 48 (May 1976):217–19.

Connolly, Thomas E. "A Note on Name-Symbolism in Melville." *American Literature* 25 (January 1954):489–90.

224

Cook, Richard M. "Evolving the Inscrutable: The Grotesque in Melville's Fiction." *American Literature* 49 (January 1978):544–59.

Davis, Merrell R., and William H. Gilman, eds. *The Letters of Herman Melville*. New Haven, Connecticut: Yale University Press, 1960.

Davis, O. B. *Introduction to the Novel*. Rev. 2nd ed. Rochelle Park, New Jersey: Hayden Book Co., 1976.

D'Azevedo, Warren L. "Revolt on the 'San Dominick.'" *Phylon,* 17 (June 1956): 129–40.

Donaldson, Scott. "The Dark Truth of *The Piazza Tales*." *PMLA*, 85 (October 1970):1082–86.

Dryden, Edgar A. *Melville's Thematics of Form: The Great Art of Telling the Truth*. Baltimore: Johns Hopkins Press, 1968.

Ekner, Reidar. "*The Encantadas* and *Benito Cereno*—On Sources and Imagination in Melville." *Moderna Sprak* 60 (1966):258–73.

Eroslen, Klans. "Melville's *Benito Cereno.*" *Kleine Bertrage* 21 (1961):27–33.

Evans, David. "Singing-stammerer Motif in Black Tradition." *Western Folklore* 35 (April 1976):157–60.

Farnsworth, Robert M. "Slavery and Innocence in 'Benito Cereno.'" *ESQ* 44 (1966):94–96.

Feltenstein, Rosalie. "Melville's 'Benito Cereno.'" *American Literature* 19 (November 1947):245–55.

Fiedler, Leslie A. *Love and Death in the American Novel*. New York: Stein and Day, 1975.

Fiedler, Leslie A. "The Blackness of Darkness: The Negro and the Development of American Gothic." *Images of the Negro in American Literature*. Edited by Seymour L. Gross and Edward Hardy. Chicago: University of Chicago Press, 1966.

Fisher, Marvin. *Going Under: Melville's Short Fiction and the American 1850s*. Baton Rouge: Louisiana State University Press, 1977.

Fogle, Richard Harter. "Benito Cereno." *Melville: A Collection of Critical Essays*. Edited by Richard V. Chase. Englewood Cliffs, New Jersey: Prentice-Hall, 1962.

Fogle, Richard Harter. *Melville's Shorter Tales*. Norman, Oklahoma: University of Oklahoma Press, 1960.

Fogle, Richard Harter. "The Monk and the Bachelor: Melville's 'Benito Cereno.'" *Tulane Studies in English* 3 (1953):155–78.

Forrey, Robert. "Herman Melville and the Negro Question." *Mainstream* 15 (February 1962):23–32.

Franklin, Howard Bruce. *The Wake of the Gods: Melville's Mythology.* Stanford, California: Stanford University Press, 1963.

Franklin, Howard Bruce. "Apparent Symbol of Despotic Command: Melville's 'Benito Cereno.'" *New England Quarterly* 34 (December 1961):462–77.

Freeman, John. *Herman Melville.* New York: Haskell House Publishers, 1974.

Gaillard, Theodore L., Jr. "Melville's Riddle for Our Time: 'Benito Cereno.'" *English Journal* 61 (April 1962):479–87.

Galloway, David D. "Herman Melville's 'Benito Cereno': An Anatomy." *Texas Studies in Language and Literature* 9 (Summer 1967):239–52.

Geist, Stanley. *Herman Melville: the Tragic Vision and the Heroic Ideal.* Cambridge, Massachusetts: Harvard University Press, 1939.

Gibson, William M. "Herman Melville's 'Bartleby The Scrivener' and 'Benito Cereno.'" *The History of an Era: Essays and Interpretations.* Edited by George Hendrick. Frankfurt: Diesterweg, 1961.

Glicksberg, Charles Irving. "Melville and the Negro Problem." *Phylon* 11, No. 3 (1950):207–15.

Green, Jesse D. "Diabolism, Pessimism, and Democracy: Notes on Melville and Conrad." *Modern Fiction Studies* 8 (Autumn 1962):287–305.

Grejda, Edward S. *The Common Continent of Men: Racial Equality in the Writings of Herman Melville.* Port Washington, New York: Kennikat Press, 1974.

Gross, Seymour L. "Hawthorne versus Melville." *Bucknell Review* 14 (December 1966):89–109.

Gross, Seymour L., ed. *A "Benito Cereno" Handbook.* Belmont, California: Wadsworth Publishing Co., Inc., 1965.

Gross, Seymour L. "Mungo Park and Ledyard in Melville's *Benito Cereno*." *English Language Notes* 3 (December 1965):122–23.

Gross, Seymour L., and John E. Hardy, eds. *Images of the Negro in American Literature.* Chicago: University of Chicago Press, 1966.

Guttmann, Allen. "The Enduring Innocence of Captain Amasa Delano." *Boston University Studies in English* 5 (Spring 1961):35–45.

Haber, Tom Burns. "A Note on Melville's 'Benito Cereno.'" *Nineteenth Century*

226

Fiction 6 (September 1951):146–47.

Hagopian, John V., and Martin Dolch. *Insight I: Analyses of American Literature*. Frankfurt Am Main: Hirschgraben-Verlag, 1962.

Hagopian, John V. "Melville's l'homme révolté." *English Studies* 46 (October 1965): 390–402.

Hakntani, Yoshinobu. "Hawthorne and Melville's *Benito Cereno*." *Hiroshima Studies in English Language and Literature* 10 (1963):58–64.

Hawthorne, Nathaniel. *Mosses From an Old Manse*. 2 vols. Boston: Houghton, Mifflin, and Co., 1886.

Hays, Peter. "Slavery and 'Benito Cereno': An Aristotelian View." *Etudes Anglaises* 23 (January-March 1970):38–46.

Hetherington, Hugh W. *Melville's Reviewers, British and American, 1846–1891*. Chapel Hill, North Carolina: University of North Carolina Press, 1961.

Hoeltje, Hubert H. "Hawthorne, Melville, and Blackness." *American Literature* 37 (March 1965):41–51.

Howard, Leon. "Herman Melville." *Six American Novelists of the Nineteenth Century: An Introduction*. Edited by Richard J. Foster. Minneapolis: Minnesota University Press, 1968.

Howard, Leon. *Herman Melville: A Biography*. Berkeley: University of California Press, 1951.

Hurtgen, James. "Herman Melville's Political Thought: An Examination of *Billy Budd, Sailor (An Inside Narrative)*." Dissertation, State University of New York at Buffalo, 1974.

Ilson, Robert. "Benito Cereno from Melville to Lowell." *Salmagnmli* 1, IV (Winter 1966–67):78–86.

Jackson, Margaret Y. "Melville's Use of a Real Slave Mutiny in 'Benito Cereno.'" *College Language Association Journal*. 4 (December 1960):79–93.

Johnson, P. D. "American Innocence and Guilt: Black-White Destiny in 'Benito Cereno.'" *Phylon* 36 (December 1975):426–34.

Justman, Stewart. "Repression and Self in 'Benito Cereno.'" *Studies in Short Fiction* 15 (Summer 1978):301–06.

Kaplan, Sidney. "Herman Melville and the American National Sin: The Meaning of 'Benito Cereno.'" *Journal of Negro History* 41, (October 1956):311–38; 42 (January 1957):11–37.

Karcher, Carolyn L. "Melville and Racial Prejudice: a Re-evaluation." *Southern*

Review 12 (April 1976):287–310.

Karcher, Carolyn L. "Melville's 'The Gees': A Forgotten Satire on Scientific Racism." *American Quarterly* 27 (October 1975):421–42.

Karcher, Carolyn L. *Shadow Over the Promised Land: Slavery, Race, and Violence in Melville's America*. Baton Rouge: Louisiana State University Press, 1980.

Kaul, A. N. "Herman Melville: The New World Voyageur." *The American Vision: Actual and Ideal Society in Nineteenth Century Fiction*. Edited by A. N. Kaul. New Haven: Yale University Press, 1963.

Kazin, Alfred. "On Melville as Scripture." *The Inmost Leaf: A Selection of Essays*. New York: Harcourt, Brace, 1955.

Keeler, Clinton C. "Melville's Delano: Our Cheerful Axiologist." *College Language Association Journal* 10 (September 1966):49–55.

Kellner, Robert Scott. "Melville's 'Benito Cereno': The Captain as Coward." *North Dakota Quarterly* 45 (1977):61–75.

Keppler, Carl F. *The Literature of the Second Self*. Tucson, Arizona: University of Arizona Press, 1972.

Knox, George. "Lost Command: 'Benito Cereno' Reconsidered." *The Personalist* 40 (Summer 1959):280–91.

Knauf, David. "Notes on Mystery, Suspense, and Complicity: Lowell's Theatricalization of Melville's 'Benito Cereno.'" *Educational Theater Journal* 27 (March 1975):40–55.

Lannon, Diedre. "A Note on Melville's 'Benito Cereno.'" *Massachusetts Studies in English* 2 (Spring 1970):68–70.

Lawson, John Howard. *The Hidden Heritage: A Rediscovery of the Ideas and Forces that Link the Thought of Our Time with the Culture of the Past*. New York: Citadel Press, 1950.

Lebowitz, Alan. *Progress Into Silence: A Study of Melville's Heroes*. Bloomington: Indiana University Press, 1970.

Levin, Harry. *The Power of Blackness: Hawthorne, Poe, Melville*. New York: Alfred A. Knopf, Inc., 1958.

Leyda, Jay, ed. *The Complete Stories of Herman Melville*. New York: Random House, 1949.

Leyda, Jay, ed. *The Melville Log: A Documentary Life of Herman Melville, 1819–1891*. 2 vols. New York: Gordian Press, 1969.

Lonoff, Sue. "Perplexed Navigation: Teaching 'Benito Cereno.'" *Extracts: An Occasional Newsletter* 33 (February 1978):3.

Lowell, Robert. *The Old Glory.* Rev. ed. New York: Farrar, Straus & Giroux, 1968.

Lowrance, Mason I., Jr. "Veils and Illusion in 'Benito Cereno.'" *Arizona Quarterly* 26 (Summer 1970):113–26.

Magowan, Robin. "Masque and Symbol in Melville's 'Benito Cereno.'" *College English* 23 (February 1962):346–51.

Mandel, Ruth B. "The Two Mystery Stories in 'Benito Cereno.'" *Texas Studies in Literature and Language* 14 (Winter 1973):631–42.

Mandell, Marvin. "Martyrs or Murderers? A Defense of Innocence." *Midwest Quarterly* 18 (January 1977):131–43.

Margolies, Edward. "Melville and Blacks." *CLA Journal* 18 (March 1975):364–73.

Matlack, James. "Attica and Melville's 'Benito Cereno.'" *American Transcendental Quarterly* 26 (Spring 1975):18–23.

Matthiessen, Francis Otto. *American Renaissance: Art and Expression in the Age of Emerson and Whitman.* New York: Oxford University Press, 1941.

McCarthy, Paul. "Elements of Anatomy in Melville's Fiction." *Studies in the Novel* 6 (Spring 1974):38–61.

McElroy, John Harmon. "Cannibalism in Melville's 'Benito Cereno.'" *Essays in Literature* 1 (Fall 1974):206–18.

Melville, Herman. *Battle-Pieces and Aspects of the War.* Gainesville, Florida: Scholars' Facsimiles & Reprints, 1960.

Metzger, Charles R. "Melville's Saints: Allusion in 'Benito Cereno.'" *ESQ* 58 (1970):88–90.

Miller, James E. *A Reader's Guide to Herman Melville.* New York: Farrar, Straus and Cudahy, 1962.

Mitchell, Charles. "Melville and the Spurious Truth of Legalism." *The Centennial Review* 12 (1968):110–26.

Montaigne, Michel Eyquem de. *Complete Works: Essays, Travel Journal, Letters.* Stanford, California: Stanford University Press, 1957.

Monteiro, G. "On the Author of the Greatest Sea-Book Known: Commentary on Herman Melville at the Turn of the Century." *Biographical Society of America Papers* 73 (January 1979):115–20.

Mumford, Lewis. *Herman Melville: A Study of His Life and Vision*. Rev. ed. New York: Harcourt, Brace & World, 1962.

Neider, Charles, ed. *Short Novels of the Masters*. New York: Rinehart, 1948.

Nicol, Charles. "The Iconography of Evil and Ideal in 'Benito Cereno.'" *American Transcendental Quarterly* 7 (Summer 1970):25–31.

Nnolim, Charles E. *Melville's "Benito Cereno": A Study in Meaning of Name Symbolism*. New York: New Voices Publishing Co., 1974.

O'Brien, Edward J. "The Fifteen Finest Short Stories." *Forum* 79 (June 1928): 908–14.

Oliviero, Toni H. "'See Yon Bright Sun': Melville's Metaphysics of Joy and Despair in 'Benito Cereno.'" *Extracts: An Occasional Newsletter* 33 (February 1978):3.

Pafford, Ward and Floyd C. Watkins. "'Benito Cereno': A Note in Rebuttal." *Nineteenth Century Fiction* 7 (June 1952):68–71.

Parker, Hershel. "'Benito Cereno' and *Cloister-Life*: A Re-Scrutiny of a 'Source.'" *Studies in Short Fiction* 9 (Summer 1972):221–32.

Patterson, Frank M. "The *San Dominick's* Anchor." *American Notes and Queries* 3 (October 1964):19–20.

Perkham, Morse. "Hawthorne and Melville as European Authors." *Melville and Hawthorne In the Berkshires: A Symposium*. Edited by Howard P. Vincent. Kent, Ohio: Kent State University Press, 1968.

Phelps, Leland. "The Reaction to 'Benito Cereno' and *Billy Budd* in Germany." *Symposium* 13 (Fall 1959):294–99.

Phillips, Barry. "'The Good Captain': A Reading of 'Benito Cereno.'" *Texas Studies in Literature and Language* 4 (Summer 1962):188–97.

Pilkington, William T. "'Benito Cereno' and the 'Valor-Ruined Man' of *Moby-Dick*." *Texas Studies in Literature and Language* 7 (1965–66):201–07.

Pilkington, William T. "Melville's 'Benito Cereno': Source and Technique." *Studies in Short Fiction* 2 (Spring 1965):247–55.

Pilkington, William T. "'Benito Cereno' and the American National Character." *Discourse* 8 (Winter 1965):49–63.

Pommer, H. F. "Melville as Critic of Christianity." *Friend's Intelligencer* 102 (1945): 121–23.

Pullin, Faith, ed. *New Perspectives on Melville*. Kent, Ohio: Kent State University Press, 1978.

Putzel, Max. "The Source and the Symbols of Melville's 'Benito Cereno.'" *American Literature* 34 (May 1962):191–206.

Ramakrishna, P. "Moral Ambiguity in Melville's 'Benito Cereno.'" *Criticism and Research* (1966):136–45.

Ray, Richard E. "'Benito Cereno': Babo as Leader." *American Transcendental Quarterly* 7 (Summer 1970):31–37.

Ridge, George Ross and Davy S. "A Bird and a Motto: Source for 'Benito Cereno.'" *Mississippi Quarterly* 7 (Winter 1959–1960):22–29.

Rohrberger, Mary. "Point of View in 'Benito Cereno': Machinations and Deceptions." *College English* 27 (April 1966):541–46.

Roundy, Nancy. "Present Shadows: Epistemology in Melville's 'Benito Cereno.'" *Arizona Quarterly* 34 (Winter 1978):344–50.

Runden, John P., ed. *Melville's "Benito Cereno": A Text for Guided Research.* Lexington, Mass.: D.C. Heath, 1965.

Schiffman, Joseph. "Critical Problems in Melville's 'Benito Cereno.'" *Modern Language Quarterly* 11 (September 1950):317–24.

Scorza, Thomas J. "Technology, Philosophy, and Political Virtue: The Case of *Billy Budd, Sailor.*" *Interpretation: A Journal of Political Philosophy* 5, No. 1 (Summer 1975):91–107.

Scudder, Harold H. "Melville's 'Benito Cereno' and Captain Delano's *Voyages.*" *PMLA* 43 (June 1928):502–32.

Sealts, Merton M., Jr. *Herman Melville's Reading in Ancient Philosophy.* Dissertation, Yale University, 1942.

Sealts, Merton M., Jr. *Melville's Reading: A Check-List of Books Owned and Borrowed.* Madison, Wisconsin: University of Wisconsin Press, 1966.

Short, Raymond W. "Melville as Symbolist." *University of Kansas City Review* 15 (1949):38–49.

Simbuli, David. "*Benito Cereno* as Pedagogy." *CLA Journal* 9 (December 1965):159–64.

Simpson, E. E. "Melville and the Negro: from *Typee* to 'Benito Cereno.'" *American Literature* 41 (March 1969):19–38.

Stein, William Bysshe. "The Moral Axis of 'Benito Cereno.'" *Accent* 15 (Summer 1955):221–33.

Stern, Milton. *The Fine Hammered Steel of Herman Melville*. Urbana: University of Illinois Press, 1957.

Stirling, William. "The Cloister-Life of the Emperor Charles V." *Fraser's Magazine* XLIII (April and May, 1851):367–80 and 528–45.

Stone, Geoffrey. *Melville*. New York: Sheed and Ward, 1949.

Stowe, Harriet Beecher. *Uncle Tom's Cabin*. New York: Airmont Publishing Co., Inc., 1967.

Swanson, Donald R. "The Exercise of Irony in 'Benito Cereno.'" *American Transcendental Quarterly* 7 (Summer 1970):23–25.

Thompson, Lawrence R. *Melville's Quarrel with God*. Princeton, New Jersey: Princeton University Press, 1952.

Valenti, Peter L. "Images of Authority in 'Benito Cereno.'" *CLA Journal* 21 (March 1978):367–79.

Van Doren, Carl. "A Note of Confession." *Nation* 127 (December 5, 1928):622.

Vanderbilt, Kermit. "'Benito Cereno': Melville's Fable of Black Complicity." *Southern Review* 12 (April 1976):311–22.

Vanderhaar, M. M. "Re-examination of 'Benito Cereno.'" *American Literature* 40 (May 1968):179–91.

Vogelback, Arthur L. "Shakespeare and Melville's 'Benito Cereno.'" *Modern Language Notes* 67 (February 1952):113–16.

von Abele, Rudolph. "Melville and the Problem of Evil." *American Mercury* 65 (November 1947):592–98.

Watters, Reginald E. "Melville's 'Sociality.'" *American Literature* 17 (March 1945): 33–49.

Welsh, Howard. "Politics of Race in 'Benito Cereno.'" *American Literature* 46 (January 1975):556–66.

Widmer, Kingsley. *The Ways of Nihilism: A Study of Herman Melville's Short Novels*. Los Angeles, California: California State Colleges, 1970.

Widmer, Kingsley. "The Perplexity of Melville: 'Benito Cereno.'" *Studies in Short Fiction* 5 (Spring 1968):225–38.

Williams, Stanley T. "'Follow Your Leader': Melville's 'Benito Cereno.'" *Virginia Quarterly Review* 23 (Winter 1947):61–76.

Winters, Ivor. "Herman Melville and the Problems of Moral Navigation." *Maule's Curse: Seven Studies in the History of American Obscurantism*. Con-

232

necticut: New Directions Press, 1938.

Wright, Nathalia. *Melville's Use of the Bible*. Durham, North Carolina: Duke University Press, 1949.

Wright, Nathalia. "Biblical Allusions in Melville's Prose." *American Literature* 12 (May 1940): 185–99.

Yamaya, Saburo. "Poe, Hawthorne, and Melville's 'Benito Cereno.'" *Studies in English Literature* 4 (March 1961): 21–32.

Yellin, Jean F. "Black Masks: Melville's 'Benito Cereno.'" *American Quarterly* 22 (Fall 1970): 678–89.

Zaller, Robert. "Melville and the Myth of Revolution." *Studies in Romanticism* 15 (Fall 1976): 607–22.

Zirker, Priscilla A. "Evidence of the Slavery Dilemma in *White-Jacket*." *American Quarterly* 18 (Fall 1966): 477–92.

Zlatic, Thomas D. "'Benito Cereno': Melville's 'Back-Handed-Well-Knot.'" *Arizona Quarterly* 34 (Winter 1978): 327–43.

DATE DUE